Venezuela's *Movimiento al Socialismo*

Venezuela's *Movimiento al Socialismo*

From Guerrilla Defeat to Innovative Politics   Steve Ellner

Duke University Press   *Durham and London 1988*

© 1988 Duke University Press
All rights reserved
Printed in the United States of America
on acid-free paper ∞
Library of Congress Cataloging-in-Publication
Data on last page of this book

To my wife,
Celenia,
and my children,
Michelle María and
Michael Eduardo

Contents

Foreword

At first glance, the 1970s appear gloomy in Latin America. Military regimes stepped up repression, squeezed the working classes, and stifled political activity. The 1973 overthrow of Salvador Allende and his replacement by General Pinochet in Chile seemed to set the tone for the decade.

Yet a closer look reveals a great deal of political innovation in the past two decades (including Allende's socialist experiment). Steve Ellner's book provides striking evidence that politics were alive and well in Venezuela during the 1970s and early 1980s. The Movement toward Socialism (MAS) that he carefully depicts and analyzes was a new phenomenon, yet one that drew on historical roots and experiences in other nations. Ellner's book stands as a major contribution to comparative politics and to Venezuelan studies.

Ellner, who lived and taught in Venezuela for the time covered by this study, has become a leading analyst of Venezuela's leftist politics. His research draws on scores of interviews, a close reading of mainstream as well as partisan newspapers, analysis of party congresses and documents, statistical sources, and a broad familiarity with leftist parties in other countries. He also takes excursions into labor and student politics when they impinge upon his research. He skillfully traces the labyrinthine paths of ideological debate across party and national lines. In short, this is comparative political history at its best.

As political parties go in Latin America, MAS is a mere teenager. Formed in the winter of 1970–71 out of a split in the Venezuelan Communist Party (PCV), MAS has weathered only three presidential elections, and it has yet to win more than 6 percent of the national vote. Strongly committed to socialism, MAS has not yet been admitted as a regular member of the Socialist International because another

Venezuelan party, the Democratic Action (AD), prevented it. None of MAS's leaders have achieved much identification outside of Venezuela. Finally, the party has drawn most of its support from the urban middle class and has not been successful in appealing to working-class voters. So, one might ask, why such a detailed examination?

The answer has two parts. First, MAS conducted politics in ways never before tried in Venezuela, as suggested in a key party document, *The New Mode of Being Socialist* (1974). This allowed it to exercise influence beyond what simple voter turnouts would suggest. Its early attention-getting successes made it the pacesetter of other leftist parties. Second, MAS is not alone in seeking a different road to socialism: it is one of dozens of "new left" parties that have arisen in the Western world in the past few decades. As Ellner emphasizes, MAS operates in harmony with Eurocommunist parties, after which it was partly modeled.

In its first decade and a half, MAS underwent a remarkable peregrination on the political spectrum. For about four years it stood to the left of its parent PCV, which it criticized for orthodoxy and subservience to Moscow. When oil prices skyrocketed in 1973–74 and brought great prosperity to Venezuela, however, MAS leaders decided that they would have to give their party an upbeat, reformist, forward-looking image. Thus began their shift to the right until they nearly joined the big two, AD and COPEI, near the mainstream. They deemphasized socialism as a goal and focused on democracy, both internally and in the polity as a whole. The peak of procedural liberalization came with the adoption of Document 80 at its 1980 convention. MAS embraced immediate reforms (not always socialist) in society and economy in order to improve everyone's standard of living. Its leaders advocated an independent foreign policy and stressed the positive by pointing to socialist advances in Spain, France, and Greece. Meanwhile, they stopped Yankee-baiting and even praised democratic practices in the United States. They continued to eschew alliances with other leftist parties but swapped their broad movement strategy for a more traditional partisan one. By posing as the responsible left, they hoped to break out of the narrow confines of what they called the "leftist ghetto," where ideological parties never attracted the voting majority.

What was more, MAS leaders, many of whom had been guerrilleros in the 1960s, turned to elections as the true Venezuelan road to socialism. They made votes the principal measure of success and set out to reap them with modern forms of politics, including festive campaigns, primaries, publicity, opinion surveys, and the like. Although they never achieved sufficient votes to claim major party status, they did manage to expand their following beyond their original stronghold in Caracas. And ironically, AD and COPEI encouraged MAS as a loyal opposition because it was easier to work with than the more doctrinaire left.

By the early 1980s electoral failure dogged the MAS leadership. Spurred by a fall in oil prices and official austerity measures, MAS shifted back toward the left, criticizing the government and holding up socialism as the best solution. This return to basics, signaled by the 1985 accession of Freddy Muñoz to party leadership, will undoubtedly continue through the 1988 elections.

The story of MAS has great intrinsic interest as a case study, tracing as it does the trajectory of postguerrilla politics in a world where bipolarism has broken down. MAS leaders showed remarkable ideological flexibility, political pragmatism, and old-fashioned skill. They might even be said to have adopted a populist strategy for gaining power, except they did not adopt charismatic leadership. Moreover, their open, participatory style embarrassed other parties into democratizing their procedures. And finally, they demystified the United States as the bugaboo of the left, taking a more mature approach to international affairs.

MAS has even greater interest for students of comparative politics. Ellner suggests many parallels with socialist and communist experiences elsewhere, but the opportunities for continued analysis are rich. Political scientists and historians of Latin America and Europe should pay attention to MAS, for out of its failures might emerge the lessons for a successful road to socialism.

Historians are loath to predict the future, and Ellner wisely refrains from projections. He points out, however, that some two-thirds of the Venezuelans polled by John Martz preferred socialism over capitalism. That suggests that the potential for a broad-based socialist party is great, if only the leaders can get their appeal to the voter. One thing is certain: those who wish to accompany Venezuelan politics into the 1990s had better pay close attention to Ellner's excellent study.

Michael L. Conniff
University of New Mexico
September 1987

Preface

The Movimiento al Socialismo (MAS) attracts a certain type of political activist whose motivations and relationship to the organization are distinct from those of other leftist parties. Most important, rank-and-file MASistas are prone to examine thoroughly and debate among themselves party directives and, in cases of differences of opinion, to offer alternatives. This participative zeal naturally has its pitfalls, as excessive internal debate impedes organizational activity. However, it is a welcome corrective to the tendency—which is marked in other parties in Venezuela, particularly outside of the central region—to accept uncritically party orders and policies and to dissent only when the established leadership is challenged at the highest levels and the party is on the verge of a schism. It is my opinion that this readiness to put forward personal viewpoints, unencumbered by fears of the vertical line of command, is MAS's most attractive characteristic, and perhaps its outstanding feature.

The eagerness of party members to discuss political issues openly facilitated the task of gathering information for this study. MASistas are generally not suspicious of the motives of those who inquire about their party's internal life, unlike other leftists, who, for understandable reasons, are guarded in conversations with North Americans. Furthermore, the dichotomy between information that is designed for public consumption and information that is disseminated exclusively within the party is barely evident in MAS. Because printed materials prepared for party members are not branded "confidential," it was relatively easy for me to gain access to internal documents that, though not made public, are nevertheless not restricted to MASistas.

The extent of my indebtedness to individual MAS members for their collaboration cannot be easily measured or conveyed. The list of names of those—especially in the rank and file of the party—who were generous with their time and unsparing in their efforts to assist me is indeed long. I will cite just a few of those who were the most helpful: Juan Pereira, Arturo Tremont, Freddy Muñoz, Juan Rodríguez, Lenin Hernández, and Fernando ("Guerrita") Aranguere.

Special thanks must be extended to Susan Berglund and Dick Parker (of the Central University of Venezuela) and Kathy Waldron (of Citibank in New York)—all three historians—who read over the manuscript at various stages and whose suggestions regarding style and content were extremely valuable. Finally, the moral encouragement of my wife, Celenia, and the inspiration provided by her and our two children, Michelle María and Michael Eduardo (who was born while the work was in progress), were essential ingredients in the overall effort that went into this study.

Acronyms

AD	Acción Democrática (Democratic Action)
ANAPO	Alianza Nacional Popular (National Popular Alliance)
APRA	Alianza Popular Revolucionaria Americana (American Popular Revolutionary Alliance)
ATISS	Asociación de Trabajadores de la Industria Siderúrgica (Association of Workers of the Steel Industry)
COPEI	Comité de Organización Política Electoral Independiente (Committee of Independent Political Electoral Organization)
CTV	Confederación de Trabajadores de Venezuela (Confederation of Venezuelan Workers)
CUTV	Central Unitaria de Trabajadores de Venezuela (United Center of Workers of Venezuela)
FCU	Federación de Centros Universitarios (Federation of University Centers)
FDP	Fuerza Democrática Popular (Popular Democratic Force)
MAS	Movimiento al Socialismo (Movement toward Socialism)
MEP	Movimiento Electoral del Pueblo (People's Electoral Movement)
MIR	Movimiento de la Izquierda Revolucionaria (Movement of the Revolutionary Left)
PCE	Partido Comunista de España (Communist Party of Spain)
PCF	Communist Party of France
PCI	Communist Party of Italy
PCM	Partido Comunista de Mexico (Communist Party of Mexico)
PCV	Partido Comunista de Venezuela (Communist Party of Venezuela)

PRIN   Partido Revolucionario de Integración Nacionalista
       (Revolutionary Party of Nationalist Integration)
PRP(C) Partido Revolucionario del Proletariado (Comunista)
       (Revolutionary Party of the Proletariat—Communist)
SIDOR Siderúrgica del Orinoco (Orinoco Steel Works)
SUTISS Sindicato Unico de Trabajadores de la Industria Siderúrgica
       (Single Union of Workers of the Steel Industry)
UCV   Universidad Central de Venezuela (Central University of
       Venezuela)
URD   Unión Republicana Democrática (Democratic Republican Union)
UTIT   Unión de Trabajadores de la Industria Textil (Union of Workers
       of the Textile Industry)

Introduction
MAS's Originality and the Venezuelan
Road to Socialism

The Communist dissidents who participated in the founding convention of the Movement toward Socialism (MAS) in January 1971 were imbued with a sense of commitment, enthusiasm, and optimism, which led them to believe that the socialist cause would triumph in Venezuela in the not-too-distant future. The early MASistas were convinced that their revisions of orthodox Marxist thinking and practice were original for a leftist organization in the nation and even throughout the world. During MAS's first fifteen years the zeal and confidence of MASistas abated, as was to be expected given the party's performance in national elections, which was far below expectations, and its truncated growth on all fronts. Nevertheless, by the mid-1980s, in spite of MAS's ideological evolution, the MASistas continued to consider themselves a unique organization, though for different reasons from those offered at the outset.

An important objective of this study is to ascertain the extent to which MAS's claim to uniqueness is grounded in fact. At the time of its founding some political commentators claimed that the party was a replica of the Eurocommunist parties, with their emphasis on democracy and independence from Moscow, and their defense of individual roads to socialism for each nation. MAS leaders have denied that their party is based on the Eurocommunist model or any other, for that matter. Chapter 1 examines the Eurocommunist movement in order to specify areas of similarity and differences. It is my contention that the overlap in policy between Eurocommunism and MAS is substantial, but that the two diverge in fundamental ways in their ideologies and philosophical outlooks.

Chapter 2 briefly reviews the history of the Venezuelan left since the opening of the modern democratic period in 1936 in order to place MAS's emergence in an historical context. The MASistas maintain that their ideological positions were relevant to Venezuelan society only in recent years and that MAS's political formulas were inapplicable before the late 1960s when the founding of MAS was first considered. The MASistas have not closely identified themselves with any political movement before that time, nor have they made an effort to systematically examine modern Venezuelan history in order to determine the appropriateness of their theories to specific historical situations. Thus the MASistas have never made clear whether they side with the positions of the Communist Party (PCV) in the 1940s and 1950s or those of its populist rivals who were grouped in Acción Democrática (AD). Undoubtedly, this ahistorical attitude was compatible with MAS's claim that it was a unique party whose political formulas were original. The overview of the Venezuelan left in this chapter will explore the antecedents, dating back to 1936, to the issues raised by the MASistas.

MAS's ahistorical outlook bears the mark of New Left thinking. The New Left was an outgrowth of the student movement of the 1960s throughout the Western world that culminated in the events of May 1968 in France. The New Leftists generally viewed themselves as the product of postindustrial capitalism and thus confronting novel problems that were unrelated to the past struggles of the traditional left. The early MASistas also came of political age as students in the 1960s and assimilated the ahistorical attitude and claim to uniqueness of the New Left. Chapter 3 explores the political baptism of the to-be-MASistas in the guerrilla movement of the early and mid-1960s and the student upheavals in Venezuela, which were influenced in large part by events in Paris in 1968. Emphasis will be placed on the strong generational attachment and identification of the majority of the founding MASistas.

Study of the founding of MAS and its subsequent transformation is interesting for what it says about the evolution in New Left thinking following the 1960s. The New Left is commonly viewed as a phenomenon of the 1960s that came and went in the course of the decade. Nevertheless, its influence has been far from transient. New Leftists and those who, like the MASistas, were indebted to New Left thinking went on to play leading roles in political, cultural, and intellectual movements in the 1970s (the Green Party in West Germany, to name but one). The study of MAS is interesting since it points to the alternative approaches that were likely choices for those whose political formations were shaped by the New Left.

In dealing with Eurocommunism, the history of the Venezuelan left and the New Left, chapters 1 through 3 trace the historical and international strands that contributed to MAS's ideological makeup. The chapters that follow, and particularly the concluding section, attempt to provide an idea of the degree to which MAS retained its basic original formulations in spite of the party's reversals on various key issues in the course of its history.

Chapter 4 discusses MAS's ideological and programmatic positions. A number of important policies upheld by MAS diverge from those defended by the traditional left in Venezuela and elsewhere, thus lending credence to the party's claim to originality. MAS's conscious rejection of intransigent postures, such as hardened opposition to the government and to U.S. foreign policy, is uncommon if not unique for a Latin American party that is firmly committed to socialism. Indeed, MAS has questioned the traditional leftist assumption that the U.S. government will automatically strike against any third world government that attempts to implant socialism, even when such a regime maintains a truly neutral foreign policy. Other examples of departure from traditional leftist positions are MAS's avid praise for the democratic commitment of the Venezuelan armed forces and support for its incorporation into the institutional life of the nation; and the party's replacement of the slogan "nationalization," which was considered an example of a traditional left banner that had lost its revolutionary implications, with the allegedly more far-reaching catchword "socialization."

Chapter 5 discusses MAS's changing attitude toward interparty electoral unity. During its early years MAS upheld a hardened position of spurning alliances with parties that did not adhere to socialism, and thus refused to form part of the broadly based leftist alliance known as the New Force in the 1973 presidential elections. MAS's subse- quent move to the right was accompanied by a modification in its attitude toward leftist unity. MAS now refused to enter into interparty agreements, not so much because they took in the nonsocialist left, but on account of their inclusion of the PCV and other parties whose commitment to democracy was open to question. MAS's position both before and after 1973 had in common an emphasis on ideological objectives—that is, socialism and democracy—at the expense of the short-term demands that the policy of alliances was designed to achieve.

MAS's position on interparty relations will be compared with the strategies that have been followed by leftist parties in other historical and national contexts. The Popular Front formations of the 1930s, whose most outstanding success in Latin America was the leftist coalition that came to power in Chile in 1938, are contrasted with the electoral unity of more recent years, whose most notable example was the Popular Unity government of Salvador Allende. The Chilean case is particularly significant because Allende's election coincided with the founding of MAS and naturally exerted an influence on the Venezuelan left at the time.

The main difference between the Popular Front in Chile and elsewhere in the 1930s and the Popular Unity (Unidad Popular, or UP) of Allende was that in the former case, unlike the latter, the nonsocialist left was in a dominant position. Allende and his supporters, on the other hand, as well as the Venezuelan leftists who attempted to achieve unity in the 1973 elections and thereafter, refused to submerge socialist objectives for the sake of unity with parties to their right. Thus the unity strategy of the 1930s diverged significantly from that of more recent years. Popular frontism (in which major concessions are made to the nonsocialist left) has become a veritable anachronism in Venezuela and elsewhere. It is this author's contention that MAS's arguments in opposition to unity on the basis that popular frontism was not a viable strategy were misleading since that approach was not, in fact, being considered by the rest of the Venezuelan left at the time.

The discussion of interparty leftist unity is particularly relevant since it has become a major challenge to the left over the last several decades. Where the left has knocked on the doors of power in Latin America, it has done so on the basis of formal unity among diverse parties or movements committed to socialism: the Popular Unity in Chile, the Sandinistas in Nicaragua, the Farabundo Martí Front in El Salvador, and Peru's United Left in the elections of 1985. The days in which one leftist party, specifically the Communist Party, could seriously consider arrogating to itself the title of vanguard on the basis of a monolithic set of positions have definitely passed, as a result of the proliferation of parties and ideological currents on the Latin American left.

MAS's participation and performance in the national elections of 1973, 1978, and 1983 as well as the municipal contests of 1979 and 1984 are traced in chapters 6, 7, and 8. Throughout this period the social democratic AD and the social Christian COPEI (Comité de Organización Política Electoral Independiente) virtually monopolized Venezuelan electoral politics, as their combined vote varied between 75 and 92 percent. This situation was referred to in Venezuela as "bipolarization," which meant, in effect, that many sympathizers of the smaller parties, including those of the left, were moved in the heat of the campaign to vote for AD or COPEI, which were the only parties with a realistic possibility of winning. This voting behavior con-

March for the 1978
presidential campaign.

Some of the twenty-one members of the PCV that left the party to found MAS in 1971. *Bottom row from left to right:* Carlos Arturo Pardo, Rafael Guerra Ramos, Hector Rodríguez Bauza, Freddy Muñoz, Pompeyo Márquez, Eloy Torres, Germán Lairet, José Antonio Urbina, and Teodoro Petkoff. *Top row from left to right:* Jesús Valedón, Francisco Mieres, Claudio Cedeño, Rafael Martínez, Hector Marcano Coello, Alexis Adam, and Juvencio Pulgar.

Pompeyo Márquez in center
talking to the press at the
time of the founding of MAS
in 1971.

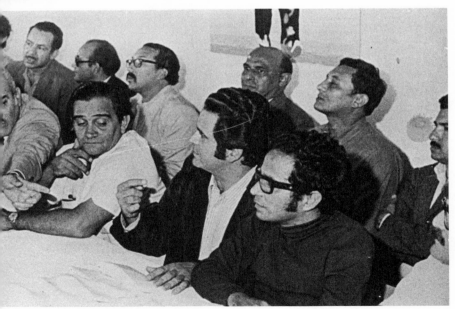

Teodoro Petkoff. Courtesy
of Teodoro Petkoff.

José Vicente Rangel

demned the left to a reduced portion of the electorate, which in the presidential contests did not exceed 9 percent.

The four main parties on the left consisted of MAS (by far the largest), the Movimiento de la Izquierda Revolucionaria (MIR, which had broken off from AD in 1960 and later, under the influence of the Cuban revolution, participated in the guerrilla struggle), the Movimiento Electoral del Pueblo (MEP, which split off from AD in 1967 and then moved progressively to the left), and the PCV. None of the smaller leftist parties, generally identified with the ultra-left, received more than 1 percent of the vote.

By tracing MAS's electoral strategy in the national elections of 1973, 1978, and 1983, chapters 6 through 8 highlight the evolution of MAS's positions. MAS has moved considerably to the right in such areas as foreign affairs and economics. In addition, MAS's decision to run party leader Teodoro Petkoff in the 1983 presidential race after having put up the independent leftist José Vicente Rangel in the previous two opportunities was significant for what it said about MAS's changing priorities. Shortly after its founding MAS emphasized the need to create a broad-based movement (referred to as the "movement of movements") that would not be controlled by any political party. The selection of Rangel, an independent, to represent the party in the presidential elections was compatible with this broad-based approach. In later years, however, MAS attempted to pattern itself, in certain ways, after AD, especially in its efforts at building a powerful cohesive political organization. As part of the strategy of projecting MAS as a party rather than a movement, the MASistas decided to choose a MASista instead of an independent as presidential candidate.

A number of decisions made by MAS in the labor and student movements, as discussed in chapter 9, demonstrated the party's willingness to take risks and carry out bold policies that diverged from what was generally expected of a socialist party. In organized labor the most important move in this regard was MAS's withdrawal from small and ineffective leftist-controlled labor organizations and its incorporation in the AD-controlled Confederación de Trabajadores de Venezuela (CTV), which other leftist parties had abandoned in the previous decade. An equally far-reaching decision was MAS's announcement, shortly after its birth in 1971, that it would participate in university elections at the Universidad Central de Venezuela (UCV), which was under military occupation, in spite of the boycott that other leftist parties had called for to protest government intervention on campus. In both instances MAS's audacity paid off, and specifically in the case of the UCV, MAS established itself as the largest party on campus.

6

These successes boosted morale in the fledgling organization. Although other sectors of the left sharply criticized MAS at the time, they soon copied its lead. In organized labor, for instance, MIR and other leftist parties attacked MAS for having joined labor organizations that served the interests of the class enemy but soon thereafter decided to work within the CTV and its affiliates where, after all, the vast majority of organized workers were located.

MAS's strength throughout its history has been concentrated on university campuses and especially in the student movement, in which it established itself as the dominant party shortly after its founding. Almost all the Communist youth leaders who controlled the student movement at the UCV and elsewhere in the 1960s passed over to MAS at the party's birth in 1971. MAS's success on this front was also a reflection of the weakness of AD—by far the largest and best-organized party in the nation—which was never able to regain its influence among students after the defection of its youth contingent with the founding of MIR in 1960. In the labor movement, on the other hand, MAS not only failed to draw top PCV leaders to its ranks, but throughout its history it has been unable to challenge AD, which remains firmly in control of the CTV.

In many ways MAS was a pacesetter on the Venezuelan left. The reforms and policies it initiated were first criticized and then copied by other leftist parties, particularly MIR. Most important was MAS's praise of the nation's democracy and its commitment to work to perfect democratic institutions rather than to undermine or destroy them in accordance with the traditional mentality of the left. In addition, the same leftists in MIR and other parties who harshly attacked MAS's abandonment of the Marxist-Leninist camp and of such concepts as the "dictatorship of the proletariat" would several years later follow in its footsteps.

MAS's originality—both on a national and international scale—was most evident in the restructuring and statutory reforms it carried out beginning in the late 1970s. These modifications, discussed in chapter 10, took in a wide range of activities and lent credence to the party's claim that it was in the vanguard in the effort to achieve internal democracy. For example, MAS broadened participation in the party's national leadership by divesting the position of secretary general of its all-encompassing powers. In addition, MASistas strove to create a federalist structure whereby lower levels of leadership were to enjoy semiautonomous status in the organization.

The most far-reaching internal reform was the "legalization" or free play of factions and their proportional representation in the party's leadership. Under this system groups of MASistas were free to organize support within the party and to participate in the decision-making process even though they lacked majority backing. The arrangement was designed to democratize the party by providing each member with the liberty to promote his or her ideas within the party. In addition, under this system minority factions could form their own slate and thus appeal directly to the party's rank and file in internal elections, rather than having to work at conventions through uncommitted delegates, who could easily be manipulated and won over by the party's "machine."

Chapter 11 deals with the factional struggle in MAS throughout its history. MAS was born with an "orthodox" grouping led by Pompeyo Márquez, which favored unity of the left, and a "renovation" wing headed by Teodoro Petkoff, which was accused of being "sectarian" because of its hostility toward other sectors of the left. Petkoff's group (the *teodoristas*) split in the late 1970s between the followers of Luis Bayardo Sardi, who called for building on the innovations of previous years, and the more orthodox Freddy Muñoz, who felt that the party had gone too far in its renovation impulse. The free play of factions and the problems it has created merit a detailed discussion since perhaps no other party throughout the world has gone so far in implementing such a novel arrangement. Undoubtedly, in spite of certain pitfalls, the system points the way to workable solutions to the obstruction of internal democracy inherent in traditional structures.

In spite of MAS's reforms designed to facilitate democracy and participation, new leaders have not been incorporated into the party's top national leadership. MAS's main founding heads were Communist leaders who have retained control of the organization ever since. With just a few exceptions, they belonged to the generations that came of political age in the struggle against dictator Marcos Pérez Jiménez in the 1950s and the guerrilla movement of the 1960s. The most prominent founding MASistas were among the most prestigious and active members of the Venezuelan Communist movement; theirs were impeccable records of personal sacrifice and dedication.

Márquez, who grew up in the working-class district of San Juan in Caracas, first became involved in politics through the student movement. At the time of the Hitler-Stalin pact and the Soviet invasion of Finland in 1939, both of which he defended, Márquez decided to join the PCV. Within ten years he became a member of the party's Political Bureau. Márquez assumed the position of provisional secretary general, in place of Jesús Faría, who was jailed in 1950, until the overthrow of Pérez Jiménez in 1958. During this period he went by the pseudonym Santos Yorme. In the following decade, because of the jailing and exile of Faría and other older PCVistas, Márquez (alias

8

Carlos Valencia and Octavio Rojas) continued at the helm of the PCV. Márquez himself was captured in 1964, and three years later, along with fellow PCVistas Guillermo García Ponce and Teodoro Petkoff, he managed to flee from the military prison San Carlos. The escape, which was made possible by a 200-foot tunnel built from a neighboring grocery store by two leftists, received international publicity. (One of the two was later killed by agents of the military intelligence service—according to some, in reprisal for his participation in the escape.)[1]

Teodoro Petkoff Malec was born in the port town of La Guaira near Caracas in 1928, the son of Bulgarian immigrants who were professionals of Jewish descent.[2] Petkoff joined the Communist Party as a high school student in Caracas in 1949. He participated in the struggle against the Pérez Jiménez dictatorship along with two younger brothers, one of whom, Mirko, was killed in 1956 at the hands of the police. Petkoff was elected national deputy in the 1958 elections and then graduated from the Universidad Central in 1960 in economics. In early 1962 he participated, along with fellow PCVista Douglas Bravo, in the founding of one of the first guerrilla fronts in the state of Falcón. Petkoff escaped from his military captors in 1963, when he slid down a nylon string from the seventh floor of a hospital under military surveillance and again in 1967 when he fled from San Carlos. Shortly after receiving amnesty from President Rafael Caldera in 1969, he published a critique of the Soviet invasion of Czechoslovakia that set off intense debate in the PCV, leading to the division in the party the following year.[3]

Other leading MASistas also played active roles in the turbulent events of the 1960s. Freddy Muñoz and Juvencio Pulgar, both of whom were to head internal factions, were elected to the prestigious position of president of the Federación de Centros Universitarios (FCU) at the UCV. Another founding MAS member, Alexis Adam, had also been FCU president at the UCV when in 1969 he was seriously wounded by gunshots in a campus confrontation with Copeyano students. MAS's representative before the Supreme Electoral Council (CSE), Antonio Jose Urbina, had been the head of the Communist Youth during the 1960s. Other important founding MASistas had played active roles in the guerrilla movement. Alfredo Maneiro, who would leave MAS shortly after its founding, had helped form an embryonic guerrilla band in the state of Mérida even before the PCV officially committed itself to the armed struggle, and later he became a commander in the eastern part of the country. Along with future MAS leaders Germán Lairet and Tirso Pinto, Maneiro initially sided with Douglas Bravo in his rejection of the PCV's decision to scale down the guerrilla struggle, but at the last moment he decided to stay in the party rather than join Bravo's splinter group.[4] Other important MASistas included scholars such as sociologist José Agustín Silva Michelena and economists Francisco Mieres and Armando Cordova, as well as painter Jacobo Borges and scriptwriter José Ignacio Cabrujas, to name but a few of the most prominent.

Given the caliber of the founding MASistas and the great expectations the party generated, it was natural that interest in MAS's birth and early development would go beyond the borders of Venezuela. Shortly after the founding of MAS, Leonid Brezhnev attacked Petkoff in a speech delivered at the Twenty-fourth Congress of the Soviet Communist Party. Brezhnev stated that the examples of Petkoff in Venezuela, Roger Garaudy in France, and others "could multiply, and demonstrate that the struggle against revisionism and nationalism continues to be a task of paramount importance" (see Appendix 1). Dissident Communists in other countries hoped that the division in the Venezuelan Communist Party would be reproduced in parties throughout the world and would signal the development of a new International based on heterodox notions. Such world-renowned figures as novelist Gabriel García Márquez in Colombia and the Greek composer Mikis Theodorakis (himself a member of the dissident Greek Communist organization known as the Communist Party of the Interior) publicly identified themselves with the MASistas. García Márquez handed over the 100,000 bolivares (worth nearly $25,000) that were the proceeds of the "Rómulo Gallegos International Novel Award" to the fledgling MAS in Caracas and stated that, had he been Venezuelan, he would have joined the party. Theodorakis composed the music for MAS's official anthem entitled "Indeed We Can! Socialism Indeed is Coming!" The anthem was frequently sung at rallies during the 1973 electoral campaign.

The MASistas have produced an impressive body of political literature. Their writings in party publications and elsewhere reflect the rich discussions that have always characterized the internal life of the party. Whereas in AD, COPEI, and the rest of the left a few leaders have been responsible for the theoretical formulations of their respective parties, MAS's entire leadership has actively participated in theoretical debate. As a consequence, to do justice to MAS it is necessary to focus on the ideas that emanated from the party. In addition, this study addresses, though in more cursory form, MAS's role in the Venezuelan political party system, internal party dynamics, and the relationship between MAS's evolution and the socioeconomic and political conditions in the nation.

MAS's performance has fallen far short of the expectations of most of its members and sympathizers. This disappointing record may be attributed in large part to the party's failure to firmly establish a worker base, an objective that MAS, with its rejection of traditional Marxist class analysis, never set as a priority. The history of the left is replete with examples of parties that quickly emerged from the middle sectors, only to fade thereafter because of their inability to attract large numbers of workers.

Nevertheless, MAS has played an important role in the Venezuelan political party system. Although MAS is dwarfed by AD and COPEI, it has maintained its rank as the third-largest party in the nation. The possibility of an alliance of MAS and either AD or COPEI when that party is out of power, which would channel discontent and galvanize public opinion, has always loomed as a threat to the government. Fear of such a pact has led the governing party to make concessions to the opposition by taking its viewpoints and interests into account. Furthermore, the willingness of a leftist party like MAS to act as a loyal opposition and to accept and even praise the rules of the political game does much to legitimize the democratic system. Equally significant, MAS's example of electoral participation and respect for legal norms has been copied by other parties on the left.

Just as it would be a mistake to dismiss MAS as a relatively insignificant organization because of its meager electoral showing, it would be unfair to relegate it to the same category as so many other nonruling Latin American leftist parties that have rejected imported ideological models—the Intransigent Party of Argentina, the Movement of the Revolutionary Left of Bolivia, and the Movement of United Popular Action (MAPU) in Chile, to name but three. What makes MAS outstanding and worthy of detailed study is its rich internal discussions and its willingness to consider and put into practice novel approaches. MAS has few equivalents on this score in Latin America or elsewhere. Not only are its reforms interesting in the abstract, but some of them may well prove viable in the long run.

1 The International Setting

When MAS was founded in January 1971, the party closely identified itself with the international Communist movement from which it had emerged, to the extent that it baptized itself the "New Communist Force." MAS, however, quickly discarded the Communist label and thereafter disclaimed systematic adherence to Leninism and even Marxism. This rejection of *isms* is consistent with the party's claim to uniqueness, specifically, that its policies are new and its message original. In addition, MASistas have raised the banner of "the Venezuelan road to socialism" and have vigorously denied that they have been influenced by other Communist parties, particularly those of Europe.

MASistas often maintain that the view of MAS as an outgrowth of imported models (such as Eurocommunism) is an example of the erroneous tendency to deny originality of thinking to Latin Americans, and to attribute political and cultural developments throughout the continent to influences from abroad.[1] In claiming to be uniquely Venezuelan, MAS has been reluctant to develop exclusive ties with political parties of similar ideological orientations in other nations, or to regularly attend conferences of international political movements.

Just as MAS has not made a consistent effort to insert itself in an international setting, it has also been uninterested in claiming for itself a place in the historical-political context of Venezuela. Unlike other cultural, political, and religious movements of all times, MAS has not systematically analyzed its nation's recent history in order to closely identify itself with a particular political tradition. Having rejected Communism, with its relatively important presence in Venezuela over the last half-century, MAS has been cut off from the past. MAS historians have even written off the socioeconomic and political conditions in Venezuela preceding MAS's emergence as irrelevant to the party's basic concern of achieving democratic socialism and incompatible with the party's main strategy, which is seen as applicable only in recent times.[2] In short, MAS's ahistorical attitude and its rejection of imported models creates the impression that the party lacks international and historical links, or that any effort to establish such ties is a difficult, if not futile, task.

The MASistas have overstated their case; their party hardly emerged in a vacuum. Trends on the international left and particularly in European Communist parties exerted a certain influence on MAS in its formative stages, as has the social democratic movement in more recent years. In addition, MAS has to be seen in the context of Venezuelan history, since key issues that the party raised were part of ongoing polemics that began long before 1971.

The first two chapters attempt to ascertain the extent to which MAS grew out of these national and international developments. This chapter summarizes the phenomenon known as Eurocommunism in order to explore areas of convergence and dissimilarities; chapter 2 reviews the history of the Venezuelan left. This examination is designed to draw connections between MAS and political movements outside of the context of contemporary Venezuelan politics, a method that is employed in subsequent chapters as well.

The comparative approach is valuable in that studies of this type—as one Latin Americanist has noted in connection with national studies—"are always better understood when seen in comparative perspective."[3] Moreover, comparisons with the European Communist movement indicate the extent to which Eurocommunism played a role in Venezuela. Although direct influence is difficult to prove, especially because the MASistas themselves deny there was any, similarities between the two movements on a wide range of positions would imply that influence was felt. Otherwise, it would be impossible to explain the overlap of policies among parties in nations with such widely differing socioeconomic, political, and cultural conditions. Furthermore, MAS's use of slogans coined by the Eurocommunists would suggest conscious emulation. Examining both similarities and dissimilarities provides a basis for measuring the degree to which influence was exerted.

The Emergence and Consolidation of Eurocommunism

The move away from rigid Marxist dogma by European Communists in the 1960s and 1970s was denominated by political pundits as a new *ism,* called Eurocommunism.[4] In certain respects the doctrines embraced by the Eurocommunist parties represented a thorough break with Communist orthodoxy. Independence from the center of the world Communist movement in Moscow, maintenance of cordial relations with nonleftist parties and willingness to enter into alliance with them, and support for diverse forms of democratic participation both before and after the socialist revolution were increasingly stressed. Left-wing opponents of Eurocommunism claimed that these developments represented an irreversible trend whose product would be social democracy with its renunciation of class struggle and revolution. Events, however, did not bear out this presumably pessimistic prophecy. On the one hand, the French Communist Party (PCF), after flirting with Eurocommunism for several years, by the late 1970s reverted to its former orthodox line. On the other, the Italian Communist Party (PCI), rather than drift away from Marxism, held firmly to its positions, which, although heterodoxical for a Communist party, were not so thoroughly transformed as to threaten its standing in the world Communist movement.

The emergence of Eurocommunism provides an interesting contrast to other disjunctions in Marxism and other movements throughout history. In cases in which the ideology in dispute is deeply rooted and requires an all-encompassing commitment, the split usually produces violent conflict and mutual animosities. In these situations the breakaway is spearheaded by lower-level leaders or the breakaway group claims that the movement has strayed from its original aims and dogma. The Protestant Reformation, for instance, was characterized by both developments. Luther, Calvin, and other religious rebels occupied low places in the church hierarchy and invoked biblical teaching to strike against the Christian establishment and its practices. Likewise, the leaders of the innumerable divisions in the Communist movement over the last hundred years, such as Trotskyism and Maoism, have claimed that Marxism in its pure and original form had been betrayed.

Eurocommunism, on the other hand, did not give rise to internecine conflict, nor were its leaders young rebels who were determined to take on the older members of an establishment. The movement was led by top veteran Communist leaders who, influenced partly by the student upheavals of the late 1960s, wanted the party to strike out in new directions in response to changing conditions and times. They reflected upon their own and their party's past errors of dogmatism while urging their more intransigent comrades to relinquish outdated formulas. Largely absent from these criticisms and self-criticisms were diatribes, sharp personal accusations, and sweeping condemnations.

The Eurocommunists had no intention of severing ties with either the world Communist movement or their own Communist past. Santiago Carrillo, whose Communist Party of Spain (PCE) had most distanced itself from Marxist orthodoxy, acknowledged that maintaining the Communist label was convenient in that its alternative, social democratic thinking, had assumed nonrevolutionary connotations. In addition, the PCE had earned a reputation of heroism during the Civil War and the subsequent repression, which a complete rupture with the past would sacrifice.

Eurocommunist moderation in criticizing orthodoxy was thus dictated by the perceived need to retain membership, however peripheral, in the world Communist movement. In basing their political calculations on the avoidance of a complete rupture with the Soviet Union and its most loyal Communist allies, the Eurocommunists displayed a keen pragmatism, which has been the movement's outstanding characteristic. This skill is further demonstrated by the ability of the Italian Communists to play a significant role in propping up their nation's delicate political edifice and avoiding democracy's total collapse, while at the same time adhering to a philosophy of revolutionary change and representing militant sectors of the nation's working class.

Pragmatism and realism were also attributes of the two outstanding precursors of Eurocommunism, Antonio Gramsci and Palmiro Togliatti, whose contributions we will now turn to. In the years just before the triumph of Mussolini, Gramsci expressed his reservations regarding the Comintern's early sectarian policies only to a close circle of friends, so as not to risk a showdown with the international Communist movement.[5] Gramsci's discretion was typical of other original Marxist thinkers such as José Carlos Mariátegui, Georg Lukács, and the Eurocommunists, who were committed to working within the Communist movement in spite of serious criticisms of its positions.

The legacy that Gramsci left to Eurocommunism, however, was not that of a practical politician but, rather, that of a theoretician. During his extended stay in prison, Gramsci elaborated a strategy for revolution that rejected the facile and automatic application of revolutionary models that had proved successful in Russia in 1917. Gramsci maintained that in European countries with ample democratic experience, Communists had to win "a war of positions" by becoming a dominant force within the nation's institutional structures and winning over large numbers of people to the idea of socialism. This approach was meant to substitute for the Bolshevik model of an "assault on power" when revolutionary conditions were ripe. Russia's backward political state and weak civil institutions in 1917, Gramsci felt, had left the Bolsheviks with no alternative but to establish hegemony through a sudden and forceful seizure of power.

In devising an alternative strategy for European Communists, Gramsci prefigured Eurocommunism in two important respects. First, his postulation that individual characteristics, such as the democratic tradition of the country, bear heavily on the political approach to be followed anticipated the PCI's call for the "Italian Road to Socialism." Second, Gramsci spurned mechanical Marxism, which would have had Communists wait around and prepare themselves for the moment when objective conditions opened possibilities for the seizure of power. Instead, Gramsci embraced a voluntaristic position, which emphasized the initiatives of the Communist Party and its ability to win over large numbers of people to the socialist banner in order to penetrate the power structure in a nonrevolutionary period.

Although Gramsci did not achieve international renown until several decades after his death in 1937, his theories did exert a strong influence on Togliatti, who conducted PCI affairs until his own death in 1964. Toward the end of World War II and in its immediate aftermath, Togliatti displayed a degree of independence from official Communist policy emanating from the Soviet Union. During these years the PCI leadership emphasized alliances with other democratic parties, particularly the Socialists and Christian Democrats, in opposition to fascism, which threatened the nation's fledgling democracy. This policy forced the PCI to tone down its rhetoric and modify other concepts and practices generally associated with the Communist movement. The PCI heads rejected immediate social revolution, which many lower-level party leaders, emboldened by the popular armed resistance to fascism, had supported. Instead, the PCI called for a "democracy of a new type," which would create conditions conducive to socialism at a later date.

Khrushchev's denunciation of Stalin at the Twentieth Congress of the Soviet Communist Party in 1956, the Sino-Soviet dispute, and the student protest movements of the late 1960s all helped undermine the monolithism of the international Communist movement and its claim to being the dominant force on the left throughout the world. Khrushchev's revelations about Stalin and the subsequent liberalization in the USSR had complex and unforeseen repercussions, as shown, for instance, in Hungary, where the situation completely escaped Soviet control, resulting in the invasion of 1956. In the case of Western Europe, those Communists who had long favored greater autonomy for their party vis-à-vis the Soviet Union and particularly intellectuals who had shared misgivings regarding Stalin were given impetus and encouragement.

Communist leaders such as Togliatti and Carrillo also came out in support of change but were particularly cautious lest their parties be overtaken by events, as in Hungary. These leaders had long been closely identified with the Soviet leadership, whose maximum authority, of course, had been Stalin. They feared that talk of the cult of the personality and its natural antidote of collective leadership would spill over to their own parties. Furthermore, Togliatti warned that the denunciation of Stalin could be used by the right-wing enemy to discredit Communism.[6] At the same time he attempted to take advantage of the introspection and internal debate in the PCI set off by the Khrushchev speech in order to advance his own positions, such as the importance of forming alliances with other progressive forces and the uniqueness of the Italian road to socialism. In addition, he called for "polycentrism" in the international Communist movement in response to the steady ascendance of the Soviet Union as a world power, which meant that its survival no longer depended on a subservient bloc of supporters to defend it. The Communists who most contributed to making polycentrism a reality were not "anti-Stalinists" who gained the upper hand in 1956, but rather party leaders like Togliatti and Carrillo, whose loyalty to the Soviet Union up until that point had been unquestionable. Some of those who began to challenge Soviet dominance in the world Communist movement, especially the Chinese, felt betrayed by Khrushchev who, without consulting them, had destroyed an idol of the movement and thus undermined the legitimacy of their own leadership.

Much of the Chinese criticism of the Soviet Union and its allies was initially directed at the PCI, which, more than any other member of that camp, adhered to positions that were contrary to those assumed by Peking. While the Chinese upheld a dogmatic brand of Marxism and assumed a particularly aggressive posture toward the capitalist enemy, the PCI leaders became the foremost defenders of peaceful coexistence and the electoral road to power. According to the Chinese, the PCI was following in the footsteps of Yugoslavia, which had been justifiably expelled from the world Communist movement (specifically, the Cominform) in 1948 and which now, at the prompting of Khrushchev, was being asked to return.

Despite these differences, at least one important Chinese stand was favorably received by PCI leaders. The Chinese insisted that each Communist party, regardless of size, be treated as an equal within the Communist movement, and not be subjected to high-handed treatment by the more powerful parties, or by the Soviet Union in particular. In calling for recognition of the rights of individual parties, the Chinese insisted that criticisms within the movement remain unpublicized and that differences be resolved through consultation and unanimous consent.[7] The PCI leaders sympathized—perhaps even empathized—with China's condition as an outcast because they, too, upheld important differences with the world Communist movement that could later lead to their banishment as well. In light of their similar predicaments, the PCI was much less strident in its criticisms of the Chinese Communist Party than were other Communist parties (including that of France, which was second in size only to the PCI in Western Europe). By the 1970s the PCI and other Eurocommunist parties refused to attend international conferences called by Moscow for the purpose of condemning China.[8]

The PCI, like the Chinese, assigned great importance to the third world as a locus of political struggle, while tending to minimize the role of Soviet bloc nations in the struggle for socialism. The PCI criticized Soviet leaders for exaggerating the significance of the Soviet economy as a showcase to the world and an example of the viability of the socialist system. The enthusiastic support of the Italians for "third worldism" was different, at least in degree, from the position of the Soviets, who were more critical of the shortcomings of movements that were militantly anti-imperialist but not heavily committed to socialism.[9]

The student upheavals throughout Europe, beginning in France in May 1968, were initially directed not only against the establishment but, to a certain extent, the traditional left as well, and thus represented a generational challenge to the Communist parties. Although some Communists reacted to these events with uneasiness and suspicion and spoke disparagingly of their spontaneous nature, others viewed them as basically constructive. In subsequent years the PCI, among other parties, examined the significance of the student protests and criticized its own failure to spearhead the movement from the outset.[10] As a result of this introspection and of the affiliation with the PCI and other Communist parties of a large number of students who had participated in the struggles of the 1960s, much of the content and style of the youth movement rubbed off on European Communism. In particular, such New Left ideas as rejection of bureaucracy, grass-roots participation, and pluralism were incorporated into party thinking. In addition, student rebelliousness influenced some Communists to modify orthodox theory and practice that had subordinated all struggles to those of industrial workers. Some Eurocommunist leaders viewed students as forming part of either a "new working class" or else a broadly based historical bloc that was the driving force in the movement against capitalism. These theories led Communists to embark on a new strategy designed to open the party up to diverse strata of the population, including some relatively privileged sectors.

In the 1970s Eurocommunism as a movement came into its own as unorthodox ideas became accepted even by parties such as the PCF, which had previously hewed strictly to the Soviet-endorsed line. These modifications in doctrine and practice were so multifaceted as to justify the application of the *ism* label. Perhaps the most far-reaching change was the way in which Communist parties viewed their relationship with other parties, institutions, and sectors of the population, both before and after the revolution. The previously accepted dogmatic concept had grown out of the Soviet experience in 1917 in which Bolsheviks viewed their party as *the* party of the working class, which imposed its will on other political groups and social classes.

Eurocommunism substituted this vanguard concept with a pluralistic vision that recognized the rights of nonsocialist parties to openly compete for power in a democratic socialist society. The PCI departed from orthodox tradition by calling the Italian Socialist Party, like itself, a party of the working class. These statements were even formulated in closed Communist Party meetings, thus demonstrating that they went beyond mere party rhetoric.[11] The modifications reflected a new strategy of the PCI, which emphasized alliances with parties to its right. Previously, orthodox Communists had constantly formulated proposals for interparty agreements but limited them to short-term objectives. Adherence to pluralism was also reflected in the Eurocommunist insistence that labor unions and other mass organizations maintain their institutional autonomy and not be dominated by any one political party intent on promoting its own interests.

While the Eurocommunists called for unity of all progressive forces, the Socialist International, which since its reestablishment in 1951 had been closely identified with the U.S. camp in the Cold War, moved in a similar direction. François Mitterrand pioneered in the implementation of this policy in the mid-1960s, for which he was criticized at the time by the German Social Democrats. The staunchest defenders of unity in both Communist and Socialist parties tried to overcome the mutual suspicion that dated back to the immediate aftermath of the Russian Revolution. Indeed, each was disposed to meet the other side halfway in accepting part of the blame for the long-standing hostility between the two movements. While the left-wing Socialists recognized their movement's legacy of support for colonialism and anticommunism, the Eurocommunists were self-critical of their past record of dogmatism.[12]

In the view of political scientist Maurice Duverger in his *Open Letter to Socialists*, the biggest stumbling block to unity was the highly centralized internal structure of the Communist parties, which was based on the Leninist model. Duverger and other left-wing socialists pointed out that the Socialist parties, with their internal democracy and emphasis on electoral politics, were more susceptible to splits than were the Communist parties, which were highly disciplined and oriented toward mass political work rather than elections.[13] They argued that upon uniting with Communists, the Socialists would run the risk of facing an internal division and would be exposed to accusations of having sacrificed democratic principles. For these reasons, Socialist parties in France, Spain, and elsewhere have insisted on the democratization of the Communist parties as a sine qua non for unity. Duverger expressed hope that Communist-Socialist convergence would transform both movements and eliminate the objectionable policies and practices of each one.[14]

In the 1960s the Communist parties of various Asian countries broke away from the Soviet camp. The Japanese Communist Party, after sympathizing with the Chinese position in the early part of the decade, began to model itself after Eurocommunism and—unlike the less influential Australian Communist Party, which also maintained an independent line—retained its membership in the world Communist movement.[15] In Latin America, a short-lived faction of intellectuals within the Brazilian Communist Party called for policies similar to those advocated by Togliatti following the denunciation of Stalin in 1956.[16] Of the two political parties in the continent most influenced by Eurocommunism after 1970, MAS and the Mexican Communist Party (PCM), the latter is a closer replica of that movement. Unlike MAS, the PCM remained a part of the world Communist movement and, as in the case of Eurocommunism, did not veer in the direction of non-Marxist positions. Like European Communist parties, the PCM criticized Chinese policies in the 1960s but in the following decade refused to condemn China in deference to the principle of polycentrism. The PCM's pro-unity stand has been innovative and far-reaching. Not only has the party allied itself with Trotskyists in trade union and university elections and called them a "constructive force," but in 1982 it coalesced with five smaller parties to form the Partido Socialista Unificado de Mexico. The Communist Party's commitment to unity and its firm opposition to the Mexican government has allowed it to eclipse the Partido Popular Socialista, previously the largest party on the Mexican left, which has offered the government practically unconditional support.[17]

Before we turn to Eurocommunism's influence on MAS, two general remarks are in order. First, the label of *rightist* or *leftist* does not neatly apply to Eurocommunism. It is true that the Eurocommunists embrace a gradualist notion of social change that is to the right of the orthodox concept of revolution. Nevertheless, neither the term *leftist* nor *rightist* is appropriate for the concept of polycentrism and the recognition that the particular conditions in each nation determine the different roads to socialism. Thus both the "leftist" Chinese leadership and the PCI formulated the concept of the autonomous status of each Communist Party, in spite of their diametrically opposed positions on other issues. In addition, the Eurocommunist stand in favor of unity was neither inherently leftist nor rightist. Although the PCI tried to develop harmonious relations with parties to its right, the same nonsectarian approach was also applicable to organizations to the left of the Communist Party. This has already been noted in the case of the Mexican Communist Party, as well as those Eurocommunists like Carrillo who were impressed by the student upheavals of the late 1960s and called for greater Communist efforts to open up to student radicals.

The second observation concerns Moscow's reaction to Eurocommunism. Obviously, the Soviet leadership has modified its behavior since the days of the Comintern, when political strategy and policy were handed down to each Communist Party.[18] During that period unconditional support for the Soviet Union was expected of each party. Frequently, factions and splinter groups that were pro-Soviet but diverged slightly from the official line were either denounced by Moscow or simply did not receive endorsement. The emergence of Eurocommunism has compelled the USSR to be more flexible in its dealings with Communist parties. This change is due in part to the fact that the PCI, the largest and perhaps most prestigious Communist party outside of the socialist bloc, is in the vanguard of the movement. In addition, Soviet strength on economic, military, and diplomatic fronts has altered the mentality of the nation's leaders and encouraged them to think less in terms of a world polarized between faithful allies and inveterate enemies. The alignment of a host of African governments, which were committed to socialism but not led by Communist parties, with the Soviet camp has also influenced Moscow to be more accepting of diversity. As a result, Soviet leaders have generally held back from unleashing sharp public attacks against Eurocommunism despite their obvious disapproval of the thrust of the movement. When Moscow has engaged in polemics over the theoretical positions upheld by the Eurocommunists, it has been mainly interested in discrediting the criticisms of the Soviet Union that European Communist parties, especially the PCE, have formulated.[19]

The Influence of Eurocommunism on MAS

In public statements and even more in informal conversations, leading MASistas have emphatically denied that their party was ever modeled after Eurocommunism or that they have been systematically influenced by it. The absence of formal ties or even regular interchanges between MAS and Communist parties of other nations lends credence to this claim. Communist parties such as those of Italy, Spain, and Mexico, despite their leaders' sympathies for many of MAS's positions, at least in its early years, form part of and pay allegiance to the international Communist movement. Their membership precludes open support for MAS, which is a rival of an established Communist party. Furthermore, MAS has assumed certain positions that are quite different from and, in some cases, diametrically opposed to those of the Eurocommunists.

Nevertheless, influence is not entirely lacking. The Venezuelan Communist Party maintained particularly close ties with the PCI in the 1960s, during which time the Italians furnished material support for the armed struggle in Venezuela.[20] In spite of the PCI's advocacy of the peaceful road to socialism, the party favored the Chinese position of elevating the importance of, and providing greater support for, third-world struggles. This position may have explained the PCI's willingness to come to the aid of the insurgent Venezuelan left, especially in light of Moscow's lukewarm attitude toward Latin American guerrilla movements. Future MASistas, who were then young PCVistas committed to the guerrilla struggle, engaged in lengthy conversations with their Italian comrades, particularly during their exile in Europe in the late 1960s. The Venezuelans were encouraged by the fact that innovative ideas were emerging from within international communism and articulated by veteran leaders whose loyalty to the movement was beyond question. The similarity between MAS upon its founding in 1971 and Eurocommunism on a wide range of theories, policies, and slogans was further evidence that influence was exerted.

The areas of agreement and similarity between MAS and the Eurocommunist parties are indeed extensive. Both have replaced the orthodox Communist notion of a sudden seizure of power with a gradualist vision of expansion of democratic liberties and institutional opportunities for mass participation preceding the achievement of socialism. This process includes the circumscription of executive power and the broadening of the authority of congress, which is seen as receptive to popular interests. Such a democratic vision suggests a peaceful road to socialism, a concept given impetus by Khrushchev in 1956 and later elaborated on and deepened by Togliatti. Some leading MASistas have actually called on their party to rule out the possibility that true socialism, which implies full-fledged democracy, can be achieved through violence.[21] Both MASistas and Eurocommunists attempted to justify their faith in the peaceful achievement of socialism by emphasizing the deep-rootedness of democratic traditions in their respective countries.[22] Sociologists and economists of the Eurocommunist parties, unlike their counterparts in the more orthodox PCF, emphasize the staying power of capitalism and its ability to avoid major economic crises.[23] Likewise, the MASistas spurn the traditional Marxist tendency to dwell on the imminence of one final cataclysm that will spell the doom of capitalism.

The gradual, peaceful road to socialism requires the support of the large majority of the population rather than the militant minority that backed the Bolsheviks in 1917. This strategy has led both MAS and the European Communist parties to emphasize the revolutionary potential of the middle sectors, in contrast to orthodox Marxism, which assigns the central role to the industrial working class. The Eurocommunists and MAS have underscored the progressive character of small- and medium-sized business interests and have tried to drive a wedge between this "traditional" petty bourgeoisie and the larger, mostly monopolistic, capitalist interests. MAS has placed representatives of small- and medium-sized business interests on its slates for Congress; the Eurocommunists have talked about infiltrating petty bourgeois organizations for the purpose of exercising a direct influence over their members.[24] These similarities cover a wide enough area that it can be assumed that Eurocommunism, older than MAS, served as an inspiration to the Venezuelans.

MAS's use of slogans that were first popularized by the Eurocommunists is also evidence that influence was felt. For instance, a favorite MAS slogan, "a new majority," was previously employed by Togliatti to describe the PCI's efforts to reach out to large numbers of people who were not identified with the nation's left.[25] Another MAS slogan, "socialists are fit to govern," which was designed to demonstrate that the party was willing to assume positions of responsibility at the institutional level, was coined by leftist European politicians long before the founding of MAS.[26]

The similarity between MAS and Eurocommunism is especially

striking given the highly marked contrasts between Venezuela and European nations. MAS, for example, argues for the peaceful, democratic road to socialism on the basis that such a strategy is compatible with Venezuela's political culture, which is alleged to resemble that of Western Europe, as against those nations with a tradition of authoritarian governments. This view is based on Gramsci's observation, frequently recalled by the PCI, that the Bolshevik model of a quick, forceful seizure of power is not applicable to Western democracies, where the achievement of socialism need not be accompanied by a violent rupture with the past. That MASistas place Venezuela in the same category as the politically advanced Western European nations is stretching the point somewhat, especially in light of the nation's long history of military rule. Nevertheless, MAS's reliance on this Gramscian concept clearly demonstrates that it has assimilated ideas that are fundamental to Eurocommunism.

Aside from these similarities, MAS's stands, political behavior, and position within the context of Venezuelan politics contrast sharply with the Eurocommunist parties in several important respects. First, MAS has been more persistent in devising new and original ways of projecting its socialist message by stressing such symbols as patriotism and youth, while avoiding standard Marxist rhetoric based on class struggle. This original style is embodied in the slogan "New Mode of Being Socialist," which has been frequently used by MASistas, although it was first coined by Eurocommunists.[27] Second, MAS's professed neutrality in international affairs has been translated in practice into harsh criticism of Soviet policy and reassurances to Washington that a socialist Venezuela would not jeopardize U.S. interests. Eurocommunists, on the other hand, are more critical toward the United States, in part because of their wholehearted support for European economic integration, with its corollary of opposition to U.S. penetration.[28] Third, MAS recruits mainly from the middle sectors and, unlike the PCI and PCE, has never enjoyed a sizable following in organized labor. It may be added, however, that MAS's greatest strength is on campus; it has been heavily influenced by intellectuals, as have the PCE and PCI. (Intellectuals have a significant input in the Eurocommunist current that dominates the PCE and PCI and is often at odds with Communist trade union leaders who belong to their party's orthodox wing.)[29] Fourth, MASistas have freely modified and experimented with party statutes and internal structure in order to promote participative democracy. Ideological groupings within the party have not only been officially recognized but been given the right to be represented at all levels and to carry out certain activities both internally and publicly. Eurocommunists, on the other hand, have largely held to the Leninist model of democratic centralism, with its emphasis on party discipline and unanimous acceptance of the decisions of the majority.

A fifth difference between Eurocommunism and MAS, particularly in its early years, holds important political and even philosophical implications. Upon its founding, MAS proclaimed socialism a realizable goal in the near future and on this basis rejected the strategy of forming alliances with nonsocialist parties, which the PCI and other Eurocommunist parties have long advocated. Some Venezuelan leftists considered MAS's position reckless in that it passed over the antiimperialist stage prior to socialism, which was of paramount importance and merited the cooperation of all progressives, both socialist and nonsocialist.

The MASistas relied on a voluntaristic line of reasoning to support their contention that socialism would be realized quickly. Just how quickly depended on the degree to which revolutionaries dedicated themselves to the task of creating socialist consciousness and the general populace became receptive to it. For that reason, MASistas stressed the importance of socialist propaganda, in part inspired by Gramsci's belief that the ideological struggle struck the capitalist system where it was most vulnerable.

MAS's optimism regarding socialism's short-term possibilities, its stress on ideology, and its rejection of interparty alliances stand in sharp contrast with Eurocommunism. Both the PCI and PCE, rather than harp on the imminence of socialism as MAS did, have designed strategies to face fascist regimes or the danger of their reappearance. In response to this perceived threat the Eurocommunists have opened up to parties to their right. This policy became especially marked in the case of Italy following Berlinguer's "historical compromise" speech announcing Communist intentions of going beyond alliances of progressive parties by reaching an institutional agreement with the Christian Democrats.

The differences between the political party systems of Venezuela and European nations partly explain the different approaches. In Italy, Spain, and other European nations, because the non-Communist Marxist left was of minimal political importance, the Communists' unity strategy implied alliances with parties to their right. The policy of opening up to the right was less risky than pursuing alliances with groups on the far left, which would have undermined the democratic and "responsible" image that the Eurocommunists attempted to project. MAS, on the other hand, has not come close to monopolizing the Venezuelan left, and thus the banner of unity in that nation has come to refer to agreements among socialists. As discussed in chapter 5, after its early years of existence, MAS staunchly turned down proposals for intraleft unity on grounds that other leftist parties favored totalitarian solutions that ran counter to its own democratic commitment.

Another explanation for the dissimilarity in the evolution of MAS and the Eurocommunist parties can be found in the makeup of their leadership. The Eurocommunist movement was led by veteran Communists whose ascendance within their respective parties had been made possible by their well-tested cautiousness and loyalty to the Soviet Union. These attributes were largely lacking in the MAS leadership. The MASistas were younger, and their initiation into politics in the 1960s had coincided with the Venezuelan left's decision to take up the armed struggle, a move not wholeheartedly supported by Moscow. This difference in age and background explains why the MASistas went further than the Eurocommunists in questioning and modifying established Marxist dogma and pursuing innovative and experimental policies.

MAS and the Two-Stage Theory of Revolution

Whereas Eurocommunists attempted to promote interparty unity, the founding MASistas committed themselves to purely socialist positions that would not be diluted for the sake of unity with other parties, especially those to its right. Their stand, which was branded sectarian by other leftists interested in achieving broad unity, was related to MAS's assertion that the next stage in Venezuela's development was socialism that need not be relegated to the distant future. MAS staunchly rejected the concept of "revolution in two stages" in developing countries, which placed democracy and national liberation before socialism on the agenda of revolutionary change. This thesis had dominated leftist thinking for over half a century. Because of its relevance to both the emergence of MAS and the party's subsequent transformation, a brief historical overview of the two-stage theory is appropriate.

The two-stage theory of revolution in underdeveloped countries was devised by the Russian Social Democratic Party at the beginning of the century, in reaction to populism with its faith in the peasantry and belief that feudal Russia could pass directly to socialism without previously undergoing capitalist development. The Social Democrats defended the Marxist view that the proletariat, not the peasantry, would lead the struggle for socialism. Taking into account the reduced size of that class in Russia, the Social Democrats called for the establishment of a revolutionary government whose objectives would include distribution of land to the peasants, democracy, national liberation, and industrialization. This regime would strengthen the hand of the leftists by destroying feudalism and the tsar's bureaucratic machinery, thus paving the way for the implantation of socialism—the second stage. In his *Two Tactics of Social Democracy in the Democratic Revolution* published in 1905, Lenin assigned the leading role in the first stage to the workers supported by the peasants; he maintained that power would be achieved through revolutionary struggle, specifically a political strike. Furthermore, the first stage would "pass into" the second, not through a second, socialist revolution but, rather, by way of a relatively short transitional phase. Although the interests of the liberal bourgeoisie would be well served by the objectives of the first stage, Lenin claimed that that sector would not play a consequential role in favor of national liberation, since it would be alienated by the radical and violent unfolding of events, and the thoroughness of the rupture with the feudal past.

The Bolsheviks' principal Marxist rivals, the Mensheviks, rejected this concept of an "uninterrupted revolution" and instead embraced a more mechanical view of Marx's thinking on socialist revolution. The Mensheviks' main theorist and the founder of Marxism in Russia, Georgi Plekhanov, had made a thorough break with his own populist past by postulating that the working class was without allies in the struggle for socialism. Plekhanov recalled Marx's view that capitalism had to mature and the working class grow before socialist change would be feasible. On this basis, the Mensheviks recognized the prolonged duration of the first stage, during which time industrialization would augment the ranks of the working class and allow it to assume its historical role in the struggle for socialism (that is, the second stage).

The 1917 Russian revolution did not fit neatly into the model of uninterrupted revolution, for the changes of regimes of February and October were in themselves separate revolutions without a transition from one to the other. Nevertheless, the events in 1917 did vindicate Lenin's position that the second stage could come on the heels of the first.

Lenin modified the views he presented in *Two Tactics* after 1920 when the international Communist movement entered its "second period" (which lasted until 1927), which was marked by moderation and the abandonment of the call for immediate socialist revolution. The Third Congress of the Comintern in 1921 not only called for Communists to support anti-imperialist movements led by the national bourgeoisie but recognized that in certain areas the national feudal aristocracy also played a positive role in the struggle.[30]

In subsequent years different versions of the two-stage theory of revolution in underdeveloped countries were formulated both in and out of the world Communist movement. In *El antiimperialismo y el APRA* the Peruvian Victor Raúl Haya de la Torre put forward the argument that the middle class, rather than the workers, would play the hegemonic role in the first stage since it stood to lose the most by imperialist penetration.[31] During his exile from Venezuela in the early 1930s and under the influence of Haya,[32] Rómulo Betancourt also rejected the primacy of the working class in the first stage and instead argued for a multiclass approach. At the same time he called for the formation of a small coterie of professional revolutionaries who (in the tradition of Louis Blanqui) would seize the opportunity presented by the disorder and popular mobilization produced during the first stage in order to take the reins of power and decree socialism. Up until that point, however, the revolutionaries should refrain from publicly pronouncing themselves in favor of socialism in order not to needlessly alarm the oligarchic and imperialist enemies.[33]

In the "left" periods of the world Communist movement (specifically, the "third period" of 1928 to 1934 and the two years following the signing of the Hitler-Stalin pact of 1939), Latin American Communist parties generally upheld Lenin's original formulation regarding the nonrevolutionary role of the bourgeoisie in the first stage. For the most part, however, up until the 1970s Latin American Communists accepted the need to ally with the progressive sector of the bourgeoisie (known as the "national bourgeoisie") and tacitly rejected Lenin's original thesis that the first stage had a socialist content, inasmuch as it would quickly evolve into the second stage. Latin American Communists viewed Getulio Vargas of Brazil and Juan Domingo Perón of Argentina (after his election in 1946) as typical representatives of the "national bourgeoisie" who, as such, merited at least the qualified support of progressive parties.[34]

The Cuban revolution in 1959 and the theory of dependency, which Latin American economists formulated in the 1960s, encouraged Communists and leftists in general to reconsider their adherence to the concept of the revolution of national liberation in which the national bourgeoisie played a major role. The Cuban revolution seemed to confirm Lenin's initial prediction, which Latin American Communists had been loath to accept, that in underdeveloped countries the first, nonsocialist stage of the revolution would not be backed by any sectors of the bourgeoisie and would quickly transform itself into socialism. The leaders of the parties of the middle class and the bourgeoisie vacillated in their support for the Twenty-Six of July Movement during its early years, when it stood for democratic and nationalist goals, and went into open opposition as soon as the revolution became radicalized. After the triumph of the revolution the Cuban Communists (grouped in the Popular Socialist Party) dropped their initial reserves toward the movement and maintained that it was based on "the most radical sector of the petty bourgeoisie" (i.e., the middle class) as against the national bourgeoisie. This analysis implied that the revolution was far-reaching and worthy of Soviet support since its potential for socialism was unfettered by the participation of the bourgeoisie.[35]

In the early 1960s many of Castro's youthful supporters throughout Latin America broke with traditional populist parties to participate in guerrilla struggles. This "Jacobin Left," as Robert Alexander has called it,[36] rejected the two-stage theory, which both pro-Moscow and pro-Chinese parties defended. Jacobin Left theorists generally maintained that a national bourgeoisie independent of and at odds with foreign interests either never existed in Latin America or else succumbed to multinational control at the dawn of the age of imperialism at the turn of the last century.[37]

The Jacobin Left was heavily influenced by the theory of dependency, which postulated that the Latin American economy as a whole, extending from urban to peripheral areas, was fully integrated into world capitalism and that the economic elite including the entire bourgeoisie upheld and defended the system. This theory represented a challenge to the orthodox Communist version of the two-stage concept of revolution by refuting three of its basic premises. First, it argued against the existence of a remnant feudal structure whose destruction, according to the orthodox Communists, was a key objective of the first stage of the revolutionary process. Second, the theory of dependency denied that the absence of stable democracy and the incompleteness of the agrarian reform—both of which were accomplishments of the capitalist revolution in the developed nations—made Latin America any the less capitalist. The established economic system in Latin America was capitalist just as it was in the developed nations, and thus the "bourgeois democratic revolution," which orthodox Communists envisioned for Latin America, was an anachronism. Third, the bourgeoisie in toto, according to the *dependentistas*, was fully integrated into the world capitalist system and its interests were basically harmonious with it. The model of the "national bourgeoisie," which would support third-world revolutionary struggle for economic independence, was thus not viable.

The Latin American Communist movement was not impervious to the influence of dependency theory. After a period of internal debate, the majority of Latin American Communist parties by the 1970s arrived at the conclusion that none of the sectors of their nations' bourgeoisie could be counted on to play a significant role in the struggle against imperialism. This new formulation was not, however, offered in the way of self-criticism of past policy. Unlike most of the Jacobin Left, which viewed the national bourgeoisie as a phenomenon only of the remote past, the Communists asserted that that class had lost its autonomous status only in recent years, as a result of the penetration of foreign capital during the process of import substitution. Thus, previous Communist support for parties and governments that were alleged to represent the national bourgeoisie had not been a mistake.

On the basis of this revision many Latin American Communists called for a "revolution of a new type," which sets out to achieve national liberation but which "looks toward socialism." One orthodox Venezuelan Communist wrote in 1969 that, although the first stage of the revolution would be "anti-imperialist" and not "anti-capitalist," it would nevertheless be "in transit to socialism" and would thus facilitate the rapid implantation of the socialist system.[38] This model, of course, was not at all new in that it approximated what Lenin had proposed in *Two Tactics* as far back as 1905.

The Communists pointed to several other auspicious developments that favored the insertion of socialist goals from the outset of the revolutionary process in underdeveloped countries. Not only had the balance of power at the international level shifted in favor of the socialist bloc, but the working class, the main agent of socialism, had grown considerably in underdeveloped countries.[39] Furthermore, in the early part of the century intra-imperialist rivalry had often encouraged developed nations to give aid to certain third-world revolutions in opposition to rival countries. With intracapitalist friction now greatly reduced, the anti-imperialist movements were no longer closely tied to the metropolis and were thus free to embrace socialist goals.

In addition to these explanations offered by Communists, two other recent developments accounted for the change in their thinking. First, a host of African nations, after throwing off the yoke of colonial rule, declared themselves socialist and aligned themselves with the Soviet bloc. This relatively swift transformation apparently proved that the impetus of the war against colonialism and imperialism could carry over to the achievement of socialism. Second, radical populist parties in Latin America that had allegedly articulated the interests of the national anti-imperialist bourgeoisie moved increasingly to the center, and thus the leftist camp became devoid of a nonsocialist bloc. Latin American leftists, now thoroughly united in their socialist commitment, had no reason to submerge socialism for the sake of unity with the nonsocialist left in the upcoming struggle for revolutionary change.

Communist parties that broke with the traditional two-stage scheme found support from important theorists in the Soviet Union. The revision lessened the gap, at least on the theoretical front, between the Communist movement and the Jacobin Left, whose relations in the 1960s had been conflictive and at times bitter. The elimination of this source of theoretical conflict on the left in turn led to electoral pacts and other unity agreements among socialist parties in a number of third-world nations after 1970.[40]

Diverse positions related to the two-stage theory of revolution are no longer the source of the profound differences that exist on the left in many Latin American countries, including Venezuela. The important Venezuelan leftist parties are in basic agreement that none of the sectors of the bourgeoisie (which, of course, does not include small and medium-sized business interests) can be counted on in the struggle against imperialism. Two distinct theories regarding revolutionary stages are discernible. Some leftists, including PCVistas, maintain that the anti-imperialist stage will incorporate socialist objectives and (as Lenin stated in *Two Tactics*) will evolve into socialism.[41] Other leftists such as the founding MASistas have argued that anti-imperialism and socialism are twin goals that will be achieved simultaneously at the outset of the revolutionary process. The differences in the political implications of these two positions are not particularly great in that both point to the need to exclude parties of the national bourgeoisie from alliances, at least in normal times, and to recognize the socialist content of the revolutionary struggle. This near convergence at the theoretical level contrasts with the divisions that plagued the left in Venezuela and elsewhere prior to the 1970s due to adherences to the Bolshevik and Menshevik interpretations of the two-stage theory, which implied two distinct political strategies.

As will be seen in the following chapters, MAS, from the time of its founding in 1971, turned down proposals for unity of the left on grounds that they were designed to bring about the "national bourgeois revolution," which was no longer historically viable. It could be said, however, that in attacking the orthodox viewpoint based on the Menshevik model, the MASistas were really beating a dead horse, since the left by then was nearly united in its rejection of that position. During those years the PCV had dropped the notion of the "progressive national bourgeoisie" and embraced a model more akin to that proposed by the Bolsheviks, whereby the anti-imperialist stage would pass into socialism. As stated above, the differences between this strategy and that which sees national liberation as concurrent to the achievement of socialism, which MAS embraced, is not that great. The friction that developed between MAS and the rest of the left is not attributable to the theory of revolutionary stages, as the MASistas have claimed, and thus explanations have to be sought elsewhere.

2 The National Setting: An Historical Overview of the Venezuelan Left

Theoretical and practical issues related to interparty relations have generated sharp debate on the left ever since the first modern parties made their appearance in Venezuela in the 1930s. Thus the polemic within the Venezuelan Communist movement in 1970 regarding the PCV's policy toward progressive nonsocialist parties—which did much to define the position of the future MASistas—was not a recent issue of contention but rather one in a long series of disputes spanning the previous forty years. For this reason a brief historical review of the Venezuelan left is in order, for the purpose of placing MAS's rejection of interparty unity and its stands on other important issues in historical perspective.

The Venezuelan Left Since 1936

The year 1936 marked the opening of the modern era in Venezuela when, following the death of long-standing dictator Juan Vicente Gómez, democratic liberties were tolerated and frequent strikes and mass mobilizations were organized by newly founded political and labor organizations. In previous years young leftists, both in Venezuela and in exile, had formed two organizations: the Partido Comunista de Venezuela (PCV) and the Agrupación Revolucionaria de Izquierda (ARDI), led by Rómulo Betancourt, which rejected imported socialist models. Betancourt had harshly criticized the PCV for emphasizing far-reaching radical demands that ordinary Venezuelans could not readily grasp. He hailed the Communist decision to embark on the popular front strategy in which leftist rhetoric was toned down for the purpose of unifying progressive organizations in opposition to fascism.[1] In Venezuela this approach was translated into the organic unification of the two main political groups on the left in 1936, one led by Communists and the other by ex-ARDI members. The resultant Partido Democrático Nacional (PDN), also known as the "Single Party of the Left," did not have a counterpart in other nations during this period since popular frontism elsewhere did not entail the merger of already existing organizations.[2]

By early 1937 the left suffered a series of defeats in short succession, including the denial of legal recognition to the PDN, the back-to-work order ending a forty-three-day oil workers' strike, and finally the exile of forty-seven important leaders of the opposition. The mass response to these blows was negligible. In a little over twelve months the popular movement had come full circle, at first animated by newly granted liberties but in the end burnt out and unable to resist a renewal of government repression.

In the immediate aftermath of 1936, as well as in the more distant future, the leading participants in the events of 1936 sustained different opinions regarding the left's failure to capitalize on the popular upsurge of that year. Betancourt, who became increasingly vocal in his denunciation of Communism, pointed to the left's setback in 1936 as proof that alliances with the Communists were doomed to failure. Juan Bautista Fuenmayor, who was the PCV's secretary general for the next ten years, viewed the left in 1936 as excessively radical, sectarian, and unwilling to appreciate the moderate postures of certain important members of the government. This attitude of flexibility and restraint would evolve into the World War II Communist position of cooperation with a moderate antifascist government, a policy known internationally as "Browderism."[3]

A third point of view was not as systematically articulated as the first two (both Betancourt and Fuenmayor wrote extensively about the period and were thus able to build upon their theories and interpretations) and has been mainly put forward by various leftist historians in recent years. According to this view, the main leftist leaders who directed the popular struggle in 1936 underestimated the movement's strength and thus failed to exploit its potential. One version of this theory states that the Caracas-based political parties trailed behind the most important sector of the mass movement, namely the oil workers of the state of Zulia. Thus, for instance, an indefinite strike that was organized in June to protest repressive legislation was called off by the parties after the fourth day in Caracas but lasted several days more in Zulia.[4] This viewpoint also deplores the fact that labor and political leaders respected the government's back-to-work decree ending the oil workers' strike in January 1937 rather than search for new ways to continue the struggle.[5]

Another version of the same thesis maintains that the leftists in 1936 should have openly questioned the government's right to exist instead of placing their faith in a gradual, peaceful evolution toward full-fledged democracy. The left should have thought in terms of replacing an illegitimate government and, ultimately, of gaining power for itself. This viewpoint is expressed by the Chilean historian Luis Vitale, who wrote: "In 1936 the problem of the seizure of power was considered by the popular movement, but the proletariat and radicalized middle sectors lacked an adequate political direction."[6]

The sudden and unexpected popular upsurge of 1936 was not at all an historical anomaly. Similar movements commonly occur in other societies in transition between traditional and modern structures, in which both emerging and well-established classes suffer dislocations due to internal migration, the penetration of foreign capital into peripheral areas, and the like. Radical *isms* have a special appeal during these trying moments. As English historian Eric Hobsbawm has pointed out, these ideologies may be accepted as much for what they offer in the way of illusions regarding the return to an idyllic past as for the purpose of moving ahead to a new and better society.[7] In spite of the transitional nature of the periods, prolonged upheavals and a revolutionary situation can result, as occurred in Mexico after 1910. In the case of Venezuela, however, the passivity of the Venezuelan peasantry, which still constituted the overwhelming majority of the population despite recent population movements to urban and petroleum areas, made it unlikely that 1936 would have produced a violent rupture with the past. Thus the above-mentioned thesis regarding the left's quest for power in 1936 overestimates the political strength of the discontented, nonprivileged classes, which were abetted by radical members of the emerging middle sectors.

In the years following the repression of early 1937 democratic liberties were gradually restored. Betancourt and his followers, who in 1941 founded Acción Democrática (AD), continued to uphold radical positions while dropping their commitment to socialism. AD—with its ideological vagueness, antiestablishment rhetoric, resentment of the elite, restraint toward mass mobilization, and charismatic leadership in the person of Rómulo Betancourt—fit the mold which historians have generally labeled "populism." Like the interaction between Communists and populists in other Latin American countries, AD-PCV rivalry intensified during these years. Communist parties generally maintained harmonious relations with governments like that in Venezuela, which implemented moderate reforms and extended democratic liberties. That the Communists supported these moderate regimes while clashing with populist parties like AD is attributable to several factors. Most Latin American nations bowed to U.S. pressure to sever diplomatic relations with Axis powers, a decision which the Communists applauded and which stood in contrast with the more ambivalent attitude of the populists toward the Allied cause. In addition, many populists had embraced Marxism in their youth and thus welcomed the opportunity to polemicize with the Communists in order to disassociate themselves from their own past.

Another important source of friction was the competition between Communists and populists who represented overlapping constituencies. Both vied for influence in labor and, in some cases, peasant movements, which the moderate government parties were not particularly interested in organizing or controlling. Specifically in the case of Venezuela, AD took advantage of a temporary government crackdown on Communist trade unions in 1944 by setting up parallel labor organizations. AD justified the move with the slogan "to divide is to locate," which meant that the existence of separate AD and PCV unions would provide workers the opportunity to choose between the ideologies the two parties represented. Betancourt was convinced that if the selection was clear-cut the average Venezuelan worker would decide in favor of AD's nationalist creed over the totalitarian dogma of the PCV. In this sense, AD (like MAS thirty years later) preferred emphasizing its ideological differences with leftist rivals over pursuing a strategy of unity around the struggle for concrete demands.[8]

The differences between the PCV and AD came to a head in October 1945 when the latter party supported a military coup that brought it to power, while Communists took up arms in defense of the moderate regime. The three-year AD populist government, like its counterparts in many other Latin American nations, failed to mobilize large numbers of supporters in the worker, peasant, and student movements in November 1948 in the face of a military coup. AD was victimized by its own anticommunism in that it turned down the PCV's offer to join forces to resist the conspirators. The repressive military regime of Pérez Jiménez (1948–1958) undid many of the radical reforms implemented by its predecessors. Differences in strategy and mutual hostility between AD and the PCV held back their cooperation in the underground until the last two years of the dictatorship, when both parties agreed to form a broad front for the sole purpose of carrying on the struggle for democracy.

Throughout the 1940s and 1950s the PCV's effort to formulate a policy toward AD provoked internal debate and at times factional struggle within the Communist movement. In each of three periods— the moderate government of 1941–1945, the AD administration of 1945–1948, and the military regime of 1948–1958—different obstacles to AD-PCV unity presented themselves and distinct pro- and anti-unity currents emerged in the Communist movement. AD's lukewarm support for the Allies during the first period, the government's discrimination against non-AD labor unions in the second, and AD's pursuance of a putschist strategy in the early part of the third were all major impediments to harmonious relations.

Internal discussion in the PCV regarding these policies, as well as other issues, produced two important schisms. In 1944 about half of the members of the PCV broke off from the party, which they criticized for having abandoned militant struggle, and formed the Partido Communista de Venezuela Unitaria (PCVU). The dissidents' criticisms of official Communist policy actually anticipated those leveled at U.S. Communist chief Earl Browder and ratified by Moscow over a year later.

Although most of the PCVU members reunited with the PCVistas in 1946, a handful of important leaders formed the Partido Revolucionario del Proletariado (Comunista)—the PRP(C)—in spite of the efforts of top international Communist leaders to achieve a reconciliation. The short-lived PRP(C) refused to work within AD-led trade unions, for which it was obliquely censured by international Communist spokesmen. It also diverged from the orthodox position in maintaining that the Venezuelan "progressive bourgeoisie" had virtually ceased to exist (thus rejecting the previously discussed theory of the "national bourgeois revolution"). In 1952 the PRP(C) was dissolved and many of its members returned to the PCV. The two divisions demonstrated that a large number of Venezuelan Communists were sufficiently freethinking as to defy the international line while continuing to identify with the world Communist movement.

The overthrow of Pérez Jiménez in January 1958 initiated the recent democratic period in which the ex-populist-turned-moderate AD has alternated several times in power with the equally moderate social Christian COPEI. The PCV and the pro-Castroite MIR (a breakaway from AD) tried to take advantage of the effervescent popular movement and economic recession after 1958 by engaging in armed struggle, but with disastrous results. In its commitment to armed warfare the PCV went against the general tide of the Latin American Communist movement. Unlike its counterparts elsewhere in the continent, the PCV immersed itself in the armed struggle for several years. In some countries such as Guatemala, Communists also participated in guerrilla warfare, but their party vacillated at the very outset, for which it was bitterly denounced by pro-Castro guerrillas.[9] That Venezuela was a formal democracy made the decision to resort to arms especially bold. The PCV also defied Moscow by maintaining a neutral position in the Sino-Soviet dispute throughout most of the 1960s. Indeed, PCV leaders went to Cuba, the Soviet Union, and China to sustain lengthy conversations with the heads of state of those nations in an abortive effort to bridge the gap between them.[10]

In the second half of the decade the PCV gradually played down the armed struggle and in 1969 was granted legal status by the newly elected Copeyano president Rafael Caldera. The admission of defeat was painful for the Communists and stimulated a process of self-criticism, personal recriminations, and search for new political formulas. The internal debate gave way to the founding of MAS in January 1971.

MAS was inspired by certain European Communist parties in its rejection of the hegemonic role of the Soviet Union in the world Communist movement. In addition, it criticized the PCV for submerging its socialist message in order to line up with more moderate parties in seeking democratic and nationalistic objectives. The formulation of both these criticisms induced some MAS leaders to review the recent history of Venezuela in order to place their positions in historical perspective. This examination was not particularly thorough, but it did represent a dimension of the division that is worth pursuing. On the basis of our brief overview of the Venezuelan left, we will look at two basic issues that were raised.

1. The Relatively Autonomous Behavior of the Venezuelan Communist Party

Although the large majority of the founding members of MAS had belonged to the Communist Youth over the previous decade, a few of the party's important figures were veteran leaders of the Communist movement. Among these older members, the most prominent was MAS's Secretary General Pompeyo Márquez, who had been provisional secretary general of the PCV in the 1950s and secretary of organization during the following decade. Márquez attempted to make a case for the argument that the PCV had always maintained an independent criteria in the international Communist movement and that this tradition was broken by those PCVistas who assumed control of the party following the guerrilla defeat.[11] Márquez discussed the importance he had assigned as a PCV leader to analyzing conditions in Venezuela and the value he had attached to the positive contributions of Venezuelans who were not associated with the Communist movement.[12] In addition, the PCV was alleged to enjoy a greater degree of internal democracy and rank-and-file participation in decision making than was common among other Communist parties at the time.[13]

Márquez critically recalled his attendance at the Twentieth Congress of the Soviet Communist Party in 1956, when foreign delegates were led to believe that the day of Khrushchev's secret report on Stalin was a recess in the proceedings.[14] According to Márquez's thesis, the PCV's independent thinking was manifested in its refusal to join the Communist chorus against Stalin. Future MASista Teodoro Petkoff (at the time a young rank-and-file Communist) published a defense of Stalin and, of greater significance, for several years the PCV was low-keyed in its criticism of the deceased Soviet leader's cult of the personality.[15]

Márquez also pointed to the PCV's decision to broaden the appeal of the struggle against the Pérez Jiménez dictatorship by replacing the call for national liberation with democratic slogans.[16] This emphasis on democracy (as was the case with the strategies designed by the Italian and Spanish Communist parties) diverged, albeit subtly, from the general Communist line, which placed the accent on economic and nationalistic objectives. Márquez and other MASistas viewed the PCV's initiation of the guerrilla struggle in the 1960s as further evidence of the party's independent spirit.[17]

In addition to the stands cited by Márquez, the two previously mentioned divisions in the PCV in the mid-1940s also formed part of the Venezuelan Communist tradition of relative independence. In the case of the PCVU, in which the then young Márquez played an important role, Communist dissidents split the PCV more or less in half and attacked the policies that were closely associated with the prestigious president of the U.S. Communist Party, Earl Browder.

Nevertheless, it is open to question whether these and other examples of independence make the PCV unique or strikingly dissimilar to its counterparts throughout the continent. Indeed, the divergences between Venezuelan Communists and Moscow are significant not so much for their implications with regard to the PCV, but rather for what they say about the world Communist movement. Since the dissolution of the Comintern in 1943, differences among Communist parties have not always been suppressed or even overtly discouraged, as was the case until then. This policy of relative autonomy was explicitly embraced by the international Communist movement after the abolition of the Cominform in 1956, though the Soviet leaders, of course, stopped far short of the "polycentrism" advocated by Togliatti.

During these years Venezuelan Communists began to enjoy a greater radius of liberty vis-à-vis Moscow, as did their counterparts in other Latin American nations. Venezuela was not the only example in Latin America of "dual Communism," as some students have called the coexistence of two Communist parties in the same nation, both recognized by the international Communist movement. In Mexico, for instance, as many as three such parties attempted to win over Moscow to their positions throughout the 1950s. In addition, in the 1960s Soviet leaders refrained from criticizing the Venezuelan Communist decision to resort to armed warfare, in spite of their obvious disapproval. Standard books on Latin American Communism, particularly those by Robert Alexander, Victor Alba, and Rollie Poppino, fail to recognize this post-1943 modification in Moscow's behavior, which, although generally subtle, held important political implications.[18] Furthermore, these works fail to appreciate the diversity within the Latin American Communist movement, in which parties like that of Venezuela sometimes assumed ideological and strategic positions that departed from the general line.[19]

2. *Viewing Socialism as a Realizable Goal in the Present Stage*

The Communists who broke away from the PCV in December 1970 criticized the party leadership for upholding the Menshevik doctrine of revolution in two stages, which relegated socialism to the distant future. According to the dissidents, the PCV had subordinated the socialist message to calls for national liberation and, even worse, abolition of feudalism, even though feudal structures were no longer existent in Venezuela. After the division in the Communist Party the MASistas began to criticize the PCV for its outdated political style and time-worn formulas. This ineffectiveness was connected in the minds of the MASistas with the PCV's virtual abandonment of any hope that the socialist cause would someday triumph. The MASistas, for their part, attempted to propagandize around socialism, which they claimed could be achieved without having to pass through intermediate stages. Unlike the traditional left with its mechanical notions of change based on objective conditions, they felt that historical mission, dedication, and optimism regarding socialism's short-term possibilities in Venezuela acted as independent variables of undeniable importance.[20]

MAS's criticism of the traditional left in Venezuela for having always lacked a "vocation for power" suggested the need for an examination of modern Venezuelan history, which was only superficially offered by the MASistas. Such an historical treatment, had it been systematically presented, probably would have started out in the year 1936 and argued that the left lost an exceptional opportunity by not consciously pursuing a strategy—or at least addressing itself to the possibility—of gaining power. As was previously discussed, several leftist historians have maintained that the leftist parties trailed behind the mass movement in 1936 instead of following a bolder approach.

In October 1945 the attainment of state power by the left again became a possibility with the military conspiracy, which involved top AD leaders. The Communists, who fought against the coup d'etat at the time, have severely criticized AD for its participation in the movement on grounds that it broke the "constitutional thread," with its gradual amplification of democratic structures. MAS leaders such as Teodoro Petkoff, on the other hand, side with AD's view that October 18, 1945 represented for Venezuela a watershed of modernization, or as the coup's most fervent supporters put it, a "second independence."[21] Petkoff's defense of the October coup puts in evidence MAS's attraction to realistic and even pragmatic strategies for the pursuance of state power.

MAS writers assigned principal credit to the PCV, whose clandestine organization was headed by Pompeyo Márquez, for designing the strategy of creating a broad alliance in the struggle against the Pérez Jiménez dictatorship. Although the democratic objective of the movement preempted the more far-reaching traditional Communist goal of national liberation, it did allow the PCV to participate in the establishment of a new government in Venezuela for the first and only time in its history. Manuel Caballero, a prominent MAS historian, points to a report issued by Pompeyo Márquez to the Communist Party's Central Committee in February 1957 in which "for the first time, a Marxist party in Venezuela dealt with the question of power, albeit in a confusing, elusive and elliptic form." Caballero views the document as a bridge between the anti-Pérez Jiménez struggle and the guerrilla movement in the following decade, when the achievement of state power was a central objective.[22]

All political commentators agree that the decision to take up arms in the 1960s led to a disastrous defeat from which the left's recovery was slow and difficult. Nevertheless, the MASistas, who as Communists had generally been the most fervent champions of and participants in the struggle, have not in any way recanted, nor have they accepted moral responsibility for the violence that was unleashed. On the contrary, they maintain, as they did at the time, that government repression pushed them to the fateful decision.

In spite of the disastrous outcome of the guerrilla movement, the MASistas claim that the experience was not entirely negative. They point out that at least the left dared to place the attainment of state power on the agenda of political struggle and that this legacy positively shaped the thinking of leftists—in particular, the MASistas.[23] MAS argues for the feasibility of socialism in the not-too-distant future, a postulate that rival leftist parties have attacked with the slogan "socialism is not around the corner." In short, MASistas who have reflected on recent Venezuelan history attach much importance to the instances when the left thought beyond the implementation of merely piecemeal reforms and in favor of the achievement of power for the sake of such far-reaching goals as the establishment of democracy (in the 1950s), national liberation (in the 1960s), and socialism (following the founding of MAS in 1971).

The Location of the Left in Venezuela's Party System

The emergence of MAS has to be seen in the context of the evolution of Venezuela's political party system, dating back to the 1940s. The experience of the 1945–1948 *trienio* period of AD rule and its violent disruption bore heavily on the thinking of the nation's political leaders and in turn shaped interparty relations in the following decades. The two main parties founded in the beginning of the *trienio,* COPEI and the Unión Republicana Democrática (URD), attacked the AD government relentlessly, and some of their members, at lower leadership levels, actually conspired with military officers. AD, for its part, denounced COPEI and URD as being instruments of the oligarchy, and only in the final weeks of the *trienio* did it make an abortive effort to establish a dialogue with the opposition. Official sectarianism during the period was reflected in the preferential treatment the Ministry of Labor accorded to AD-controlled unions, and in the trials—which lacked legal precedent—of prominent members of previous governments on charges of misuse of public funds. The harshness of relations between AD and the opposition was generally viewed as a major cause for the 1948 coup.

The resistance to the Pérez Jiménez government began to gain impetus only after the nation's four major parties—AD, COPEI, URD, and the PCV—put aside animosities and combined efforts. This spirit of all-encompassing unity was embraced by the four parties in the underground, but not by their counterpart organizations in exile. The decision of leaders of AD, COPEI, and URD abroad to exclude the PCV from interparty agreements at the time of the overthrow of Pérez Jiménez set a long-lasting precedent. On the eve of the 1958 elections the three non-Communist parties agreed to form a coalition government, regardless of the electoral outcome. Following the 1963 elections the coalition was revived under a different set of partners, none of which belonged to the Marxist left. Finally, AD and COPEI reached an agreement in 1970 known as the "institutional pact," in which the presidencies of the most important congressional commissions and the nation's main labor federation as well as other positions were shared among themselves. This pact, with few modifications, has remained in effect ever since.

The system of ruling alliances both reflects and perpetuates "bipolarization," in which AD and COPEI maintain a near monopoly in the nation's political life. As a result, the left has been forced into a marginal role in the Venezuelan political party system. In the months prior to elections, for instance, many leftist sympathizers are swept by the enthusiasm of the campaign, which centers mainly on AD and COPEI candidates, by voting for one of the two parties with a realistic possibility of winning. Furthermore, AD's and COPEI's appropriation of positions in the labor movement, the armed forces, the peasant movement, and the judiciary—in accordance with the institutional pact—has encouraged the ambitious members of those institutions to join one of the two major parties, regardless of ideological convictions.

The example of the alliances of ruling parties after 1958 inspired leftists to follow suit. Moderate leftist and Marxist parties reacted to the institutional pact of 1970 by taking steps to form the New Force, whose principle objective was to put up a common candidate for the presidential elections of 1973. The proponents of the New Force argued that if leftists succeeded in uniting in the face of the institutional pact, the electorate would become polarized between the left, on the one hand, and AD-COPEI, on the other, and in the process the latter would be exposed as ruling-class parties with essentially the same concerns and interests. In addition, these leftists viewed unity as essential in order to avoid being dismissed by the vast majority of voters as marginal, uninfluential, and inordinately fragmented.

The Communist dissidents who became founding members of MAS drew different conclusions from the bipolarization process and the left's isolation, which they saw as evidence of the extraordinary strength of the political system and the dominant bloc. They felt that unity would not produce the desired results as long as the left remained outside of the political mainstream and divorced from the nation's political culture. As a result, the MASistas discarded standard leftist slogans that were not readily grasped by the majority of Venezuelans and attempted to copy the style and some of the policies of AD and COPEI. In future years MAS briefly allied itself with either AD or COPEI in order to drive a wedge between the two parties and debilitate the institutional pact. In short, unlike other leftist parties, which maintained a distance from the political system in order to mount a frontal attack against it, the MASistas have followed a strategy of boring within the system in order to undermine its cohesiveness with the hope of radically changing it at a future date.

3 Division in the Venezuelan Communist Party

Internal Debate over the Armed Struggle

The division in the PCV in 1970 grew out of differences within the party that dated back to the decision to embark on the strategy of guerrilla warfare in 1962 and was especially aggravated by the admission of defeat several years later. The internal conflict had a generational content in that the younger party militants, whose initiation into political activity immediately preceded and followed the overthrow of Pérez Jiménez in 1958, were the most vocal supporters of the armed struggle. At the heart of the polemic between the dissidents and the orthodox PCVistas was the question of when revolutionaries should take up the struggle for state power, an issue that was directly related to the guerrilla experience. It was not surprising, then, that the 1970 schism reflected generational strains. Most of the party's "generation of '58" and almost all of its youth leaders joined MAS, whereas the older Communists, with just a few notable exceptions, remained in the PCV.

On the face of things, Venezuelan Communists were virtually unanimous in their support of armed warfare. Nevertheless, the way the decision was reached provoked resentment that would surface several years later. Following 1958, the PCV and its leftist allies (in the URD and MIR) found themselves at the helm of a convulsive mass movement that was set in motion by the overthrow of Pérez Jiménez and that faced increasing government repression. These rapidly unfolding events swelled the ranks of the PCV's youth group, though many of the newcomers did not thoroughly assimilate party doctrine. The breach between the party's established leaders and the young, recent recruits was evident in the confrontational tactics that the youth members employed in street protests, and that they subsequently called on the party to sanction as faits accomplis. The inevitable result of this escalation in tactics was armed warfare, which was, in effect, stumbled upon rather than arrived at on the basis of an analysis of objective conditions.[1]

With the advantage of hindsight, older party leaders years later would claim that the youth wing imposed the guerrilla strategy on the party. Nevertheless, their own behavior had been far from exemplary. With the exception of just one PCV veteran on the Central Committee (Pedro Ortega Díaz), the old-timers failed to raise their voices in opposition to the armed struggle. Some PCV youth were inspired by the example of party standard-bearer Gustavo Machado who, as far back as 1929, had led an armed expedition against Venezuelan dictator Juan Vicente Gómez.[2] Nevertheless, both Machado and PCV secretary-general Jesús Faría held serious reservations regarding the decision to take up arms, which they failed to express forcefully in the midst of the general enthusiasm for the armed struggle. During these years party youth maintained much greater direct contact and a relationship of closer rapport with Pompeyo Márquez and Guillermo García Ponce (both members of the party's "middle" generation) than with Machado, Faría, and other top party leaders.

The PCV heads, having been pushed into the decision to take up arms by a volatile situation of antigovernment activity that they did not control and by the concomitant repression, failed to properly prepare for the new phase of the struggle. As a result of this awkward transition to guerrilla warfare, the top party leaders were easily rounded up and jailed at the outset. Only six Communists of the eighty-member Central Committee participated directly in the armed struggle.[3] Leadership in the movement for the most part devolved on secondary cadre, thus creating a division in authority between the jailed leaders and guerrilla commanders. This ambiguous situation produced resentment in both groups. On the one hand, jailed PCV leaders disclaimed responsibility for certain guerrilla actions, maintaining, in some cases erroneously, that PCVistas were not involved in the operations.[4] On the other hand, guerrilla chiefs felt that decision making should be theirs by virtue of the greater risks they were assuming and their greater liberty of action. Furthermore, they objected to the vacillating attitude of the older PCVistas toward the armed struggle.

A group of younger Communist guerrillas, including Douglas Bravo and Teodoro Petkoff, pledged themselves to the task of displacing their older comrades in the PCV leadership, whom they considered unfit for the historical tasks facing the party. A showdown occurred in 1965 when a series of defeats on both political and military fronts led top PCV leaders to call for scaling down guerrilla activity in order to facilitate an agreement with the government. This proposition was rejected by Bravo, a guerrilla chief who advocated a strategy of "prolonged popular war" based mainly in rural areas. Bravo's resistance to the party's line led to his expulsion from the PCV in 1966.

Petkoff, who as the youngest member of the Central Committee had performed well as a guerrilla fighter, considered Bravo's defiance of the party inopportune and actually supported his expulsion. Not only did Petkoff view Bravo's call for an intensification of guerrilla activity ill timed in light of the left's weakened position, but he also realized that the overriding majority of the PCVistas were not prepared to side with the young Communist leaders against the old-timers. Petkoff publicly criticized Bravo for engaging in "factionalism" and thus violating "sacred Leninist principles of organization." At the same time he urged those who were closest to him in the PCV to dedicate themselves to the task of "salvaging the party" while "working with diligence to reactivate the armed struggle" at a future date.[5]

One of the facets of the guerrilla experience that engendered the most bitterness—and is still a source of recrimination and controversy on the left—is the way in which the PCV in the mid-1960s and MIR a few years later disengaged from the struggle. Dissidents in both organizations accused their respective leaders of abruptly phasing out the guerrilla struggle, virtually by decree.[6] They charged that the parties' rank and file was not consulted, nor offered cogent explanations regarding the new policy and the errors previously committed. Neither the PCV nor MIR reached an accord regarding cessation of hostilities with the government. Thus, the guerrillas who were still at large were exposed to retaliation, leaving many of them with a feeling of having been betrayed by the parties of the left.

Specifically in the case of the PCV, two documents calling for a cease-fire were simultaneously issued by Communist leaders in San Carlos military prison in 1966. One was signed by future MASistas Márquez, Petkoff, and Freddy Muñoz, while the other bore the names of Gustavo and Eduardo Machado and Guillermo García Ponce, all three of whom were to form part of the orthodox wing of the PCV at the time of the MAS split. Although the differences in the wording of the two communiques were subtle, they nevertheless manifested two distinct positions in the PCV that would play a role in the division of the party in 1970. The Márquez-Petkoff-Muñoz document failed to commit itself explicitly to a permanent withdrawal from the guerrilla struggle.[7] Márquez and company may have been influenced by the necessity of avoiding an abrupt change of strategy in

order to first prepare the party's base for the new phase of the struggle—as Petkoff has subsequently claimed.[8] Nevertheless, a second
explanation for the hesitance to accept a definitive withdrawal is more
plausible. Petkoff and Muñoz represented the younger generation in
the party, which had been more vocal in support of the guerrilla
struggle and more directly involved in it than the party's older leaders.
The sting of defeat was greater for the younger Communists, and
thus it was more difficult for them to come to terms with the new
situation. Rather than renounce guerrilla warfare altogether, Petkoff
envisioned a "tactical retreat" with the option of renewing the armed
struggle at a future date. Indeed, Petkoff, after fleeing the military
prison of San Carlos (along with Márquez and Guillermo García
Ponce) in 1967, wrote that "for us the armed struggle is a fundamental way to power in Venezuela, and any democratic or revolutionary
change must necessarily be associated with [it]."[9]

The two positions regarding the type of retreat to be carried out
were related to different opinions regarding the errors that had been
committed in the guerrilla period. Petkoff and other younger Communists who had been closely involved in the guerrilla movement
rejected the thesis of many of their older comrades that the decision
to take up arms in itself had been a blunder. The future MASistas, who
were considered to be the "left" of the party's leadership because of
their emphasis on the struggle for state power, pointed to tactical
mistakes, including those of a "rightist" deviation. At the time of the
overthrow of Pérez Jiménez in 1958, it was claimed, the PCV should
have taken advantage of the strength of the popular movement and
the prestige of the left by calling for radical socioeconomic changes,
rather than "elections now," which became the slogan of the day.
This "rightist" error, they maintained, led to its opposite, namely, the
"leftist" decision to take up the armed struggle. Although most
PCVistas concurred in viewing the party's conduct in 1958 as overly
moderate, Petkoff and other younger Communists harped on the
criticism and in this way indirectly reproached the old-timers, who
had been completely in charge at the time, for the subsequent guerrilla fiasco.[10]

Not only did the young PCVistas defend the decision to engage in
guerrilla warfare as basically correct, but they actually glorified it as
one of the outstanding moments in the party's history. Petkoff, for
instance, wrote that only after 1959 did the PCV's "revolutionary profile" become apparent. The party's orthodox wing, which was led by
the old-timers, objected to this attitude and spoke of the need to
assign individual responsibility for the erroneous decision to take up
arms. In an oblique reference to Petkoff and his closest followers,

they pointed out that many of those PCVistas who shared Douglas Bravo's criteria of prolonging the guerrilla struggle, long after the defeat of that movement was evident, remained in the party following the expulsion of the Bravo group in 1966.[11] These attitudes were criticized as "retributive."

Much of the discussion on both sides regarding the errors committed was cast in personal terms. The young Communists, for their part, accused PCV secretary general Jesús Faría, along with other older comrades, of lacking courage and failing to speak out against the armed struggle. Faría rather unconvincingly attempted to defend his silence on grounds that party discipline prevented him from undermining a decision taken by the PCV, and that in any case his opposition to the guerrilla movement would not have altered the course of events.[12]

The internal debate on the armed struggle was related to the polemic that the future MASistas waged regarding the imminence of socialist revolution. Petkoff attempted to demonstrate socialism's immediate prospects by disproving the traditional Communist thesis that Venezuela was a semifeudal nation with incipient capitalist development. He maintained that clear-cut capitalist relations had come to characterize the most productive sectors of Venezuelan agriculture while increased communication between city and countryside diminished rural isolation that was a feature of precapitalism.[13] In short, the political strategy that the PCV had designed for a backward, semifeudal society had to be replaced by one that was based on the struggle against capitalism, with its all-pervasive influence in the nation.

Petkoff and his supporters opposed other traditional Communist positions that had discouraged the party from struggling on behalf of far-reaching goals. Most important was their rejection of the policy of popular frontism, in which an alliance with moderates around a set of specific reforms eclipses the party's socialist objectives. The pursuance of agreements with nonsocialist parties had been the centerpiece of PCV strategy since its founding in 1931, until the policy was rendered virtually meaningless (though it was still officially followed) by its commitment to the armed struggle in the 1960s.

Although the debate on strategies of revolutionary change focused mainly on objective conditions in Venezuela, the theoretical and philosophical implications were also explored, particularly in *Revolución sin dogma* by dissident Communist Freddy Muñoz. The book, a defense of Marxist voluntarism, attacks mechanical Marxists for assuming that revolutions can be predicted with absolute certainty and for always being taken by surprise by the "accidents of history." Muñoz recalls Zinoviev's opposition to the Bolsheviks' seizure of power in

October 1917 on grounds that "we do not have the right to take risks," and concludes by saying that, contrary to what some PCVistas currently believe, "revolutionaries have to take risks."[14] Although Muñoz did not refer directly to the guerrilla experience in Venezuela, it was apparent that between the lines he was defending the decision to take up the armed struggle on grounds that it was a calculated risk that at the time was worth taking.

New strategies held a special appeal to the younger Communists whose self-abnegation in the guerrilla struggle had been the greatest and were thus the most traumatized by the defeat. The situation they were in was similar to that of young people throughout history who participate in wars or other events that require great personal sacrifice and then find themselves subject to psychological distress when they try to readjust to their previous way of life. This feeling of bewilderment and emptiness was vividly described by the young Communist Angela Zago at the end of her *Aquí no ha pasado nada,* when she realizes that in Caracas, in spite of all the changes she has gone through as a rural guerrilla fighter, "nothing has happened."[15]

While the young PCVistas who were experiencing difficulty in readjusting to aboveground existence resisted returning to the past, the veteran party leaders were reiterating timeworn slogans. Furthermore, rather than analyze the recent period in order to distinguish the correct policies from the errors committed, many of the old-timers passed off the entire guerrilla struggle as one big blunder, thus belittling the sacrifice that had been made. It was natural, therefore, that the young Communists would be more receptive to the innovations proposed by the Petkoff group, especially because, as previously stated, they were allegedly deduced from the lessons of the guerrilla movement and called for recognition of the positive aspects of that experience.

Several other incidents related to the armed struggle would leave an indelible mark on those Communists who left the party in 1970 to form MAS. One was the deterioration of relations between the PCV and the Cuban government, which had so heavily influenced the Venezuelan left in its decision to take up arms in the first place. In order to avoid the internationalization of the Venezuelan conflict, the PCV leaders vetoed Che Guevara's proposal to participate personally in their nation's guerrilla movement. In March 1967 Fidel Castro in a famous speech openly sided with Douglas Bravo and assailed the top Venezuelan Communists by name for their cowardly abandonment of the armed struggle. The PCV leaders unanimously condemned Castro for his intrusion into the internal affairs of the Venezuelan left.

Most of the polemical responses to Castro's remarks were formulated by Pompeyo Márquez and other future MASistas who had previously been heavily committed to the guerrilla movement. They, rather than Gustavo Machado, Jesús Faría, and other PCVistas whose support for the struggle had been at best lukewarm were in a better position to win over party cadre who sympathized with Bravo and who felt a special attraction to Cuba. Machado, Faría, and other orthodox Communists maintained close ties with the Soviet Union, and thus may have been reluctant to argue with the Cubans who, despite outstanding ideological differences, were still aligned with Moscow. Some Venezuelan Communists were convinced that their party was a victim of international circumstances in that Castro's attack was really aimed at the Soviet Union, which Castro, for pragmatic reasons, preferred not to mention by name. For the future MASistas, the incident confirmed the notion that socialists in each nation should pursue their own course without interference from abroad.[16]

The experiences of dozens of imprisoned Venezuelan leftists whose sentences were commuted to exile during the presidency of Raúl Leoni (1964–1969) would also bear heavily on future events. Many young Communists settled in socialist countries where they were influenced by the winds of change generated by the French student movement as well as the reforms sponsored by the government of Alexander Dubček in Czechoslovakia in 1968. Living abroad for the first time, on the heels of a crushing military defeat, these young Communists suffered a cultural shock aggravated by the conditions they encountered, which clashed with their idealized notions of socialism. The Venezuelan representatives to the pro-Soviet world youth movement assumed positions that differed, albeit subtly, with those of the orthodox majority. The PCVistas usually voted with delegates from Vietnam, North Korea, Rumania, and a few other nations who maintained an independent line on matters such as condemnation of China. At one USSR Communist youth conference the Soviets tried to censure the speech prepared by the Venezuelan representative, Alexis Adam, who insisted on delivering the original version.[17] These incidents served as an important antecedent to the division of the PCV in 1970 in which the dissident faction stood for the autonomy of each Communist Party within the world Communist movement.

The Communist Youth and the "Academic Renovation" Movement

The student protests in Venezuela in the late 1960s coincided with and, to a certain extent, influenced the debate in the PCV that led to the founding of MAS. Communist student leaders upheld ideas that were shaped by their political experiences on campus and that were increasingly at odds with orthodox communism. The university protests, coming shortly after the shattering defeat of the guerrilla movement, seemed to demonstrate that the Venezuelan left could rely on a great reserve of popular energy in the struggle for revolutionary change. This optimism regarding the short-term possibilities of revolution in Venezuela was basic to the thinking of the future MASistas.

The student movement, influenced by its counterparts in France and elsewhere, proposed restructuring the universities under the banner of "Academic Renovation." The students called for "parity" between the student body and faculty in university governing councils (which up to then were controlled by the professors) and the redesigning of course programs in order to stress the study of Venezuela's condition as a dependent nation.[18] The Renovation Movement stressed the importance of examining all assumptions, regardless of how long-standing or sacred, a process embodied in the catchword *questioning*. The students resorted to takeovers of individual schools on campus and the convocation of open assemblies to facilitate widespread participation of the university community in decision making.

In spite of the extreme politicization of Venezuelan students, the initial thrust of the Renovation Movement was independent of political parties, and to a certain extent spontaneous. Nevertheless, confrontations between the PCV, MIR, and the social Christian COPEI—the three most influential parties among students at the UCV in Caracas and elsewhere—seriously undermined the movement's effectiveness. Violence erupted at the UCV as a result of clashes between PCV and COPEI militants in March 1969 when Alexis Adam, the Communist president of the main student organization on campus, the FCU, was shot and critically wounded. Later that year troops occupied the university, and shortly thereafter it was indefinitely closed.

The Renovation Movement, following the lead of New Leftist student groups that emerged elsewhere in the 1960s, denounced bureaucracies of all types for stultifying individual creativity and initiative. This critique of formally constituted organizational structures found its logical expression in the open assemblies, where both university authorities and the FCU were harshly criticized for not responding to the interests of their institutional base. In this way the PCV came under attack, in the first place because of its support for the rectoral administration at the UCV and other universities, and in the second because of its control of the FCU, which, in the argot of the Renovation Movement, was being "questioned" by the students.

The PCV's policy on campus in the late 1960s diverged significantly from that of MIR, which at the time was still committed to the armed struggle. MIR called for "taking the university to the streets" (*sacar la universidad a la calle*), which in effect would mean converting the universities into a support base for the guerrilla movement and other off-campus actions. The MIRistas, unlike the Communists, participated in the takeover of university buildings. The PCV stressed academic issues and made a conscious effort to moderate the tactics and rhetoric that had been associated with the armed struggle.[19] This new posture was clearly rewarded in student elections at the UCV in 1968 in which the PCV candidate for president of the FCU received 8,432 votes, whereas COPEI's vote was 6,875 and MIR's a mere 2,467.

Though PCV students criticized the most extreme expressions of Academic Renovation, they staunchly defended the general thrust of the movement. They not only supported the controversial system of "parity," equal student-teacher representation, but actually favored granting university employees participation in the decision-making process. The older Communist leaders, on the other hand, tended to write off the Renovation Movement as a manifestation of anarchy and confusion on campus. This disparagement, in the words of Communist Juvencio Pulgar, ex-president of the FCU at the UCV, was due to the failure of older party leaders to understand "that the University faces a crisis [which] it has to confront, in the sense of strengthening and expanding its autonomous and democratic structures."[20] According to Pulgar and other young Communists, Academic Renovation was not an invention of the ultra-left, as the old-timers believed, but rather a necessary response to pressing institutional problems.

A major source of tension within the PCV was the efforts of Communist student leaders to apply procedures employed in the Renovation struggle to internal party affairs. In the first place, the Communist Youth, inspired by the democratic impulse of the Renovation Movement and especially by the system of "parity," proposed reforms designed to democratize the party's internal structure. The young Communist leaders protested that the representation of the Communist Youth in the decision-making process of the party was merely symbolic. They also called for secret elections for selection and removal of members of the party's national leadership, and for making them accountable to the rank and file. Some young PCVistas advocated the abolition of the position of secretary general, whose authority was considered excessive, and its replacement by a three-member secretariat. Communist Youth members also complained that they had been denied access to the pages of the PCV's official organ, *Tribuna Popular*. As a response to this violation of internal democracy, Communist students at the UCV put out their own newspaper, *Deslinde,* which published articles of differing viewpoints on issues currently being debated within the party.[21]

The tendency to "question" conventional organizational structures and ideas, which the Renovation Movement encouraged, was applied by the Communist Youth to party politics. The hard-line Communists objected to this procedure since it implied placing in doubt basic features of Marxist orthodoxy. One leading PCVista protested that the younger Communists went so far as to "question" the socialist bloc countries, in the same way that they questioned university authorities.[22] PCV head Gustavo Machado was particularly forthright in rejecting the "obsessive questioning which characterizes the promoters of chaos." He went on to state: "It is inadmissible to me that the party's problems can be faced with procedures . . . under the heading of Renovation, in the manner that has been imposed by small groups of anarchists, adventurists and nihilists."[23] His statement reflects the old-timers' skepticism, if not disdain, toward the Renovation Movement.

The Communist Youth waged a polemical struggle on two fronts: against "ultra-leftism" and certain New Left doctrines represented by MIR, and against the dogmatic and outdated conceptions upheld by the orthodox leaders of their own party. On the one hand, the young Communists rejected the New Left view of the middle class as the main protaganist of social struggle, which in Venezuela was translated into inciting students to participate in the armed struggle both on and off campus. On the other hand, the orthodox Communist tendency to belittle the role of students and subordinate their struggles to those of the working class was also spurned.

Many of the arguments that the Communist Youth used against ultra-leftists for their defense of the armed struggle and confrontational tactics on campus were shortly thereafter employed to combat the "dogmatism" of the older PCV leaders in the internal debate that led to the division in 1970. Indeed, the phraseology subsequently used by MAS leaders was first formulated during this period in the polemics against the ultra-left. Thus, for instance, in the late 1960s PCV student leaders maintained that the MIRistas were tied to the past due to their "fetishism" of "sacred concepts" and were thus unwilling to abandon guerrilla warfare despite changing times. They also argued that the armed struggle had trapped the left in a "ghetto," making it impossible for leftists to reach out to the populace at large.[24] This same vocabulary was used by Petkoff and others in their struggle against the older PCV leaders who were accused of upholding rigid and antiquated political notions; and it subsequently made its way into Petkoff's *Proceso a la izquierda* (1976), which was directed against the twin hazards of dogmatism (as represented by the PCV) and ultra-leftism (as represented by MIR).[25]

Events Leading to the Division

Two areas of internal discord produced the division in the Communist Party in December 1970. In the first place, political differences pitted Petkoff's group, known as the "left-wing," against the orthodox members of the party. The most controversial issue was the Soviet invasion of Czechoslovakia in August 1968, while to a lesser extent discussion centered on certain theories put forward by Petkoff pertaining to revolutionary stages and social classes. In the second place, the attempt to establish sanctions against Petkoff for his public opposition to the invasion of Czechoslovakia redounded to his advantage by opening up an internal debate regarding party democracy. This second area of contention was much more heavily charged than the first. By defending party democracy and unity in the face of the orthodox Communists' insistence on expelling Petkoff from the Central Committee, the left succeeded in winning over numerous party members, including the overwhelming majority of youth activists. These PCVistas—who left the party along with the left wing—did not adhere to well-defined positions on the political issues under debate, but were moved and estranged by what they considered to be heavy-handedness on the part of the party's orthodox leaders.

The internal dispute in the PCV over Czechoslovakia was typical of the international Communist movement. Indeed, the Warsaw Pact–sponsored invasion, which undid the reforms of the Dubček government, helped erode the cohesiveness of the pro-Soviet camp. Some Communist parties manifested their unswerving adherence to Soviet policy by praising Moscow's decision, without reservation. At the other extreme, French Communist dissident Roger Garaudy (who ironically had previously served as spokesman for the PCF in its denunciation of the independent line of the Italian Communists) extolled the Dubček reforms as representing a new socialist model of worker participation in decision making.[26] Various Communist parties presented sharply critical analyses of socialist construction in Czechoslovakia, both before and after Dubček's assumption of power, to demonstrate that grave problems in the socialist world needed correction. Some of those who upheld this position, such as spokesmen for the Italian and Spanish Communist parties, concluded by condemning the invasion, whereas others, such as the equally critical Fidel Castro, extended qualified support for it.

In 1969 Petkoff published *Checoeslovaquia: El socialismo como problema,* which reflected Garaudy's stand in favor of the Dubček regime. Petkoff praised Dubček's moderation in resisting "pressure from the left flank" that called for breaking with the Soviet Union.[27] Petkoff's position was shared by his close followers in the PCV. One of them, Manuel Caballero, compared the Soviet invasion with Fidel Castro's intrusion in the internal affairs of the Venezuelan left in 1967, which was unanimously denounced by the PCV leadership.[28] While the Central Committee of the Venezuelan Communist Party supported the invasion, it also affirmed the right of each Communist party to puruse its own course.[29] Debate within the party was especially animated due to the presence in Czechoslovakia, at the time of the invasion, of dozens of Venezuelan Communists who happened to be returning from a youth festival in Sofia. These young PCVistas spoke with a degree of authority in refuting the assertions of their orthodox comrades that the arrival of Soviet troops in Czechoslovakia was widely acclaimed by the general populace.[30]

The 1968 national elections in Venezuela also served as a backdrop to the schism in the PCV. The proscribed Communist Party, through its legal front, the Union para Avanzar (UPA), coined the slogan "Neither AD Nor COPEI: Change!" and approached the various left-of-center parties that supported the presidential candidacies of Miguel Angel Burelli Rivas and Luis Beltrán Prieto Figueroa in hopes of convincing the parties to unite. Since unity was not forthcoming, the UPA chose to endorse Prieto Figueroa, the more progressive of the two, who was president of MEP, a recent split-off from AD. This decision was accepted by almost all the top PCV leaders, including Petkoff, who saw in Prieto's pledge to decree a general amnesty the possibility of providing Communists with breathing space in order to recuperate from the defeat of the guerrilla struggle.[31]

Communist Youth leaders unanimously criticized their party's support for Prieto. The younger Communists, who had been more profoundly affected by the guerrilla experience and had taken greater risks, recoiled at the idea of backing Prieto who, as president of the National Senate a few years before, had spoken out in favor of punitive measures against the allegedly terrorist left. Indeed, anti-AD sentiment ran deep among Communist Youth militants, who were thus loath to work on behalf of MEP, whose top leaders including Prieto had helped found AD in 1941. MEP inherited AD's anticommunism, as demonstrated by its insistence that Communists not openly support the Prieto candidacy, an attitude that influenced one small leftist group to support the allegedly less sectarian Burelli Rivas.[32] In opposing alliances with moderate parties, the Communist

Youth anticipated the position of Petkoff and other PCV dissidents at the time of the 1970 division. Petkoff (despite his stand in favor of Prieto in 1968) became the foremost opponent of popular frontism, whereby the left submerges its long-term socialist objectives in order to ally itself with parties to its right on a platform of moderate reforms.

The "left"-wing of the PCV put forward various heterodoxical concepts in articles in *Deslinde*, which Petkoff defended in his *Socialismo para Venezuela?* in 1970, and which were subsequently embraced by MAS. Perhaps the most far-reaching of these ideas was that, owing to Venezuela's socioeconomic evolution, the next stage in the nation's development would be socialism. Some orthodox Communists admitted that the upcoming revolution would produce changes in favor of socialism but characterized its basic thrust at the outset as anti-imperialist, directed mainly at the United States. Others challenged Petkoff's assertion that latifundism had been completely displaced by capitalist structures in the countryside and that therefore the banner of antifeudalism was obsolete.[33]

Some of Petkoff's positions evoked a particularly heated response from the orthodox wing of the PCV since they challenged long-standing and virtually sacred features of orthodox Communism. Petkoff viewed the "free play" of organized factions in the Communist Party and representation of minority opinion in the leadership as prerequisites for internal democracy.[34] In addition, he argued that the PCV should maintain its independence from the Soviet Union, and that to be truly "independent," the party had to be critical of the socialist bloc.[35] Finally, Petkoff, Muñoz, and other PCV "leftists" questioned whether the Communist Party was indispensable to the revolutionary process and pointed to the allegedly marginal role played by Communists in the establishment of socialism in Cuba.[36] This position was denounced as "liquidationist" by the orthodox Communists, even though Petkoff did not openly call for the liquidation of the party. Nevertheless, in private conversations Petkoff and his closest followers suggested that not only was the Communist Party dispensable but that it was actually incapable of leading the revolution in the first place.[37]

A third current in the party, known as the "center" and closely associated with Pompeyo Márquez, was critical of the "left's" unorthodox ideas but at the same time displayed a willingness to question and even modify established dogma. The centrists were staunch defenders of the Soviet Union and rejected the harsh criticisms of the socialist bloc formulated by Petkoff in *Checoeslovaquia*, but also warned against the error of "myth-making [with relation to the

USSR] which we fell into in previous years."[38] Márquez criticized the PCV "left" for having inherited the ingenuous belief of the guerrilla period that revolution was an immediate possibility, but at the same time affirmed the need for Communists to retain their "vocation for power," which guided their actions in the 1960s.[39]

Márquez also took a middle position regarding party organization, specifically, the norms for carrying out internal discussion. He criticized Petkoff for violating the Leninist principle of democratic centralism in publishing *Checoeslovaquia* before it was submitted to the PCV for consideration. Márquez wrote *La vigencia del PCV no está en discusión* ("The Continuance of the PCV is not in Question") to refute the notion that the revolution could be achieved without the Communist Party.[40] On the other hand, Márquez insisted that the PCV fully air the dispute within the party regarding Czechoslovakia and other issues raised by Petkoff and his followers, rather than take disciplinary measures against them. Indeed, shortly prior to the division in the PCV, Márquez made guarantees that reprisals would not be taken against Petkoff the condition for his continued presence in the PCV.[41] By fervently defending the right of dissent, the centrists helped place the issue of internal democracy in the center of debate; it came to overshadow the ideological positions that each side assumed. In the process, the centrists made common cause with the leftists, despite the sharp political differences between them.

Petkoff's original opposition to the PCV direction in the early 1960s was based on arguments regarding the incapacity and old age of the party's top leaders.[42] Immediately following the invasion of Czechoslovakia in 1968, Petkoff suggested to his closest supporters—Freddy Muñoz, Alfredo Maneiro, and Germán Lairet—that the party was not worth saving.[43] The Petkoff group then pursued a Machiavellian strategy of purporting to uphold the banner of party unity, even reiterating the phrase originally coined by Pompeyo Márquez, "the continuance of the PCV is not in question."[44] Future events would vindicate this strategy in that the leftists were able to win over a large number of party militants—perhaps a majority as was claimed—to the dissident faction that became MAS. Although the centrists rejected Petkoff's position on Czechoslovakia and other issues, they objected to the disciplinary measures the PCV leaders tried to impose, as well as the violation of internal party norms. Petkoff's limited following was concentrated in the Communist Youth, although the majority of its members, along with its secretary general Antonio José Urbina, followed an independent line that approximated that of the centrists.[45]

At the XV Plenum of the PCV's Central Committee in February 1970 the centrists succeeded in passing a compromise resolution that criticized Petkoff for publishing *Checoeslovaquia* while dropping disciplinary charges against him. The decision was hailed by all members of the party, with the exception of a small group of hardliners headed by Eduardo Machado and Guillermo García Ponce, who called for nothing short of Petkoff's expulsion from the Central Committee. Most orthodox leaders, however, shared PCV secretary general Jesús Faría's belief that the most valuable contribution that they could make to the international Communist movement was to maintain party unity. Faría was even willing to relinquish his leadership position and struggle within the party in favor of his ideas, if this was necessary to avoid a schism.[46]

The position of Faría, Gustavo Machado, and other orthodox leaders stiffened as a result of a lengthy article published in *Pravda* and signed by "Comrade A. Mosinev," which signaled the decision of the Soviet leadership to intervene directly in the internal PCV dispute (see appendix 2). The piece pointed to Petkoff's "special hatred of the Soviet Union, which he does not [attempt to] simulate" and went on to quote a pamphlet entitled "Anti-Socialist Ideas of T. Petkoff" written by García Ponce and Pedro Ortega Díaz, which represented the position of the hardliners. The immediate hardening of Faría's stand indicated the degree to which certain top Communist leaders continued to take cues from the Soviet Union. The influence of the article was even more pronounced in the case of hardliner Eduardo Machado, who claimed that it was tantamount to an "order" to take disciplinary measures against Petkoff, and that to do otherwise would jeopardize the PCV's standing in the international Communist movement.[47]

Although Faría continued to display a willingness to reach a compromise solution,[48] he now took steps to avoid being displaced, at all costs, by comrades whose commitment to Communist orthodoxy was open to question. This determination led to efforts to manipulate the PCV's upcoming Fourth Congress, whose delegates were nearly evenly split between the centrist and leftist groupings (headed by Márquez and Petkoff, respectively), on the one hand, and the orthodox wing of the party (which included both the hardliners and the somewhat more flexible Faría), on the other. At the Central Committee's XIX Plenum in November 1970, Faría recommended postponement of the Fourth Congress, intervention in the party's large sections of Caracas and the state of Miranda, and granting of special powers to the PCV's Political Bureau, which was controlled by the orthodox wing. In addition, for the first time, Faría insisted on Petkoff's suspension from the Central Committee for one year.[49]

Faría justified his call for putting off the congress on grounds that

Petkoff, who was the PCV's secretary general in Miranda, and his close followers had manipulated the selection of delegates both in that state and in the neighboring Federal District. Nevertheless, Faría's decision was undoubtedly dictated by the realization that, as a leading orthodox Communist admitted in one of the sessions,[50] the orthodox wing lacked the delegate strength to control the upcoming congress. Actually, the leftists had been calling for the prompt realization of the congress and the hardliners had been stalling even before Faría hardened his stand at the XIX Plenum, thereby lending credence to the claim of the future MASistas that they represented the Communist majority. By insisting on the immediate convocation of the congress, the leftists and centrists were drawn even closer together, at the same time that they were able to identify themselves with the twin objectives of party unity and internal democracy.

That organizational rather than political issues set off the polarization in the party was unfortunate for the orthodox wing, since a large majority of PCVistas preferred its ideological and programmatic positions to those of the left. Rather than recognize that they had been outmaneuvered by the leftists, the old-timers blamed the division on the betrayal of Pompeyo Márquez, whose decision to leave the party came as a surprise to them.[51] Shortly after the XIX Plenum, personal accusations were hurled at Márquez, in some cases recalling old incidents, in spite of his long and unimpeachable record of sacrifice and dedication.[52]

Another bitterly contested organizational dispute arose over the Communist Youth's scant representation in the upcoming congress. The overwhelming majority of Youth members did not technically belong to the PCV and were thus excluded from participation, with the exception of those who automatically became delegates to the congress by virtue of holding top positions. The young Communists felt that their quota of sacrifice during the guerrilla struggle had been sufficiently great as to warrant a proportionate input in decision making. The old-timers, for their part, accused Communist Youth members of trying to create a parallel structure. The knotty issue of the Youth's representation at the Congress was under discussion throughout 1970, but without any breakthrough in sight.

The Founding of MAS

Both the orthodox Communists and the dissidents held separate congresses in January 1971, one in the name of the PCV and the other, the Movement toward Socialism. Those who stayed in the party confirmed their commitment to orthodox Marxism at the PCV Congress by filling the vacancies created by the departure of the dissidents in large part with trade union and peasant leaders.[53] Three hundred regular delegates and two hundred "fraternal" ones attended MAS's convention. The positions MAS assumed were devoid of much of the heterodoxy that was associated with the Communist left and that was to become MAS's stock-in-trade in future years. Indeed, Petkoff was willing to make major concessions to the former centrists who, after all, had enjoyed more support in the PCV than had the leftists. Pompeyo Márquez became secretary general of MAS, in recognition of the great prestige he enjoyed both in and outside of the organization, and his close ally, Eloy Torres, was named subsecretary general. Upon Márquez's insistence, MAS retained the communist title by calling itself "MAS (New Communist Force)," and declared at the outset that "we are, more than ever, communists."[54] MAS's founding document eschewed the far-reaching revisions of Marxism found in Petkoff's *Socialismo para Venezuela?* It made no mention, for example, of Petkoff's postulation regarding the revolutionary nature of the middle class, and of his skepticism regarding the vanguard role of the working class,[55] and instead pointed to the "need to go to the working class [since we are] convinced that without it as the decisive force, no victory is possible."[56]

The founding MASistas did, however, stake out positions that differed, albeit subtly in parts, from those of orthodox Communism. MAS departed from traditional Communist Party policy by ruling out the possibility of an electoral pact with moderate parties for the upcoming 1973 elections, since it would at best lead to "reformism" instead of "revolutionary alternatives."[57] Although the free play of internal factions that Petkoff had called for in the Communist Party was rejected by MAS, the party did attempt to foster internal democracy at its founding convention. Thus the standard Communist practice of presenting an official slate was dropped, and nominations for candidates were encouraged from the floor, to the extent that sixty-three were made for the thirty-three-member Central Committee. Finally, MAS, in its founding document, committed itself to "elaborating a Venezuelan theory of the Venezuelan revolution." MAS went on to denounce the orthodox leaders of the PCV for "perceiving the party as an end in itself, as a narrow and dogmatic sect . . . [and for being] tied to a stereotyped 'Marxism' [which resembles] catechism."[58]

MAS also differentiated itself from the PCV by extending praise to different socialist and nationalistic governments throughout the world. The party's founding document exalted the examples of socialism in Cuba, the Soviet Union, and China, while claiming to be inspired by the struggles carried out by the anti-imperialist governments of Juan Velasco in Peru, Omar Torrijos in Panama, and the progressive Arab nations. The breadth of this identification was related to a trend over the previous two decades, which Petkoff and Muñoz had noted in their works published at the time of the division in the PCV: since the Chinese revolution in 1949, no revolutionary government had gained power with the active backing of a Communist Party.[59] Progressive, anti-imperialist, and even socialist regimes had come to power through diverse forms of struggle, often contrary to established Marxist dogma: military coups, in the case of Egypt in 1952 and Peru in 1968; guerrilla warfare waged by a small band that lacked the support of the local Communist Party, in the case of Cuba; and elections, in the case of the recently elected government of Salvador Allende in Chile.

This multiformity of experiences was not lost on the young Venezuelan Communists who founded MAS. Their assimilation of these developments would profoundly influence MAS in several important respects. First, MAS spurned the glorification of a particular socialist model, such as the USSR, Cuba, and China, and talked of individual "roads to socialism." Second, the failure of the Communist parties to achieve power anywhere over the past twenty years encouraged the MASistas to question the Leninist model of a tight-knit party, which had previously been considered a sine qua non for socialist revolution. And third, the revolutionary character of various military regimes in Latin America, Africa, and the Mid-East led MAS to reject the standard Communist notion that the upcoming anti-imperialist revolution in third-world nations would be democratic. MAS's fraternal relations with the Alianza Nacional Popular (ANAPO), which was formed by the followers of Colombia's ex-dictator Gustavo Rojas Pinilla and represented, according to the MASistas, "socialism a la Colombiana," was indicative of this new direction.[60] In succeeding years the MASistas would stress their commitment to democracy and would thus lose interest in groups like ANAPO.

Even though MAS's birth was inspired by developments in the non-Communist left, the early MASistas, and especially the ex-PCV centrists headed by Pompeyo Márquez, attempted to establish MAS's credentials in the international Communist movement. Shortly after the founding of MAS, Márquez headed a delegation of MASistas that visited Communist parties throughout the world. They were received by top party officials in Rumania and Yugoslavia, both of which enjoyed some independence from the Soviet bloc. In addition, they met with Santiago Carrillo of the PCE and Italian Communist leaders, though in France they conversed with Socialist Michel Rocard rather than with representatives of the more orthodox Communist Party. The equally pro-Moscow Communist Party of Chile snubbed the MAS delegation during its stay in that nation, evoking a firm response from Márquez: "We have no interest in polemicizing [with the Chilean Communists] but nobody can assume that they hold a monopoly on Marxism-Leninism."[61]

The PCE and a faction of the Greek Communist movement issued statements favorable to MAS. The other Communist parties that had moderately distanced themselves from Moscow upheld a neutral position and published both sides of the Venezuelan dispute in their presses. The Rumanian party, for instance, refrained from sending delegations and messages to either the MAS or the PCV conventions in January 1971. Jesús Faría formally protested the neutral stand of the Italian Communist Party and the objective coverage of the dispute provided by its newspaper, L'Unita. According to Faría, the principle of international solidarity ruled out the possibility of recognizing two Communist parties in one nation. As long as MAS upheld its claim to the title of "Communist," the international Communist movement was obliged to choose between it and the PCV.[62]

In private conversations with Venezuelan Communists prior to the 1970 division, top PCI leaders expressed support for the positions assumed by Petkoff. At the same time the Italian Communists tried to convince the leftist PCVistas to modify certain stands in order to preserve party unity and to work with patience from within to reorient party policy. This was the position of Renato Sandri of the PCI's international affairs department, who addressed the PCV Central Committee's XIX Plenum in an effort to avoid a schism. After the division MAS leaders were convinced that Sandri and others preferred their positions to those of the Venezuelan Communists, even though the Italians felt obliged by tradition to maintain special ties with the PCV.[63]

Pompeyo Márquez and others who shared his views saw the recent division as part of a worldwide trend toward renovation in the Communist movement. Eleazar Díaz Rangel, a leading MASista who had been a member of the PCV's Central Committee, traveled to Mexico and met with PCM head Arnoldo Martínez Verdugo in an effort to establish relations between the two parties. Díaz Rangel wrote that "renovation is flowering in Latin American Communism," after having been held up for a decade due to the Sino-Soviet dispute, which generated debate over issues that were unrelated to the concerns of the continent.[64]

It was evident that between Márquez's efforts to gain recognition from Communist parties throughout the world and Petkoff's belief—stated in private—that no Communist movement could bring about a revolution in Venezuela, MAS was born with two distinct ideological strains. During MAS's early months of existence Petkoff submerged his opinions and made major concessions to Márquez to ensure that the new party got off the ground. Only one member of Petkoff's inner core of supporters, Alfredo Maneiro, rejected Petkoff's efforts to draw close to the PCV centrists and, as a result, left MAS shortly after its founding convention. Maneiro argued that the presence of the centrists in the new party would hold it back from undertaking sweeping revisions of orthodox Communism.[65]

Petkoff's strategy of capturing the centrists for the party that he first envisioned creating in 1968 was a master stroke. His goal of dividing the PCV in order to create a new heterodoxical political organization was indeed a formidable challenge. Parties that split off from others invariably have a hard time passing the test of time, a predicament that is especially evident in the case of divisions in Communist parties. The identification with a long-standing political tradition as well as with one of the world's most powerful nations, and the enjoyment of certain material benefits, albeit limited, such as invitations to travel to socialist nations, are among the special attractions that party members grow accustomed to. The history of international communism since 1917 provides few examples, if any, of well-established political parties that emerged from Communist parties. The same history is replete with cases of desertions of intellectuals, both individually and in groups, with intentions of engaging in ongoing political activity, but who quickly fade from the political scene. Petkoff's group within the PCV consisted almost exclusively of university and former university figures, totally lacking in influence in trade unions or other off-campus organizations. The prospects for Petkoff's left faction at the time that he embarked on his schismatic strategy was thus not particularly promising.

Despite the proliferation of factions within MAS after its founding in 1971, the two basic ideological positions associated with Teodoro Petkoff and Pompeyo Márquez have remained. Petkoff's followers, who succeeded in becoming the dominant force in the organization by the late 1970s, were always haunted by the idea that perhaps Alfredo Maneiro was right in saying that the presence of the ex-PCV centrists in MAS would tie their hands and prevent them from developing a novel and innovative approach to socialism. MAS's painful setbacks in the 1978 and 1983 presidential elections, when its vote count was far inferior to what had been anticipated, seemed to confirm Maneiro's pessimistic prophesy. In both instances Petkoff's followers, by way of self-criticism, attributed MAS's poor showing to its failure to make a complete and thorough break with its orthodox Communist past. In private, some of them blamed their more orthodox party companions and either explicitly or indirectly defended the correctness of Maneiro's analysis regarding MAS's "original sin" of having lined up with the centrist leaders.

4   Ideology, Policy, and Style

MAS's Revolutionary Vision

MAS, upon its founding, was heavily influenced by the youth radicalism of the 1960s known as the New Left. This movement emerged outside of the established Communist parties, which up until then had virtually monopolized leftist politics and were sometimes even considered synonymous with the left. As the 1960s neared an end, it became apparent that the New Left exerted an influence on some Communist parties and that, far from constituting a homogeneous movement, it was ideologically dispersed in many directions.

The movement's common denominator was its critique of the established Marxist dogma upheld by most Communist parties. The New Leftists highlighted the role of the vanguard: they viewed the revolution as the work of revolutionaries and a tribute to their dedication and skill, and assigned objective conditions to a secondary role. Related to this voluntaristic notion was the rejection of the strategy that leftists pejoratively labeled "economism," whereby agitation over immediate demands is given priority over the ideological struggle of winning people over to the radical reorganization of society. New Leftists even devoted much time trying to describe the type of utopia they were endeavoring to bring about, an effort that at times appeared to be a futile exercise in predicting the distant future.

In all other respects New Left movements were torn by irreconcilable differences. At one end, anarchism was resurrected, with its notion of the facile overthrow of the existing order. At the other extreme stood the philosophy of Herbert Marcuse, which was pessimistic regarding the likelihood that the popular classes would comprehend their oppression and act against it. Similarly, one current of the New Left virtually dismissed class analysis as irrelevant to the task of making revolution. Other New Leftists defended Marx's view of the primary role of workers in the revolutionary process, though they were more generous regarding which sectors were to be included in that class. Still others maintained that professional wage earners were more conscious of their oppression and more likely to put forward truly revolutionary demands than members of the traditional working class.[1] All three of these viewpoints regarding social classes were expressed by MASistas.

One outstanding feature of the New Left reflected in MAS was its skepticism toward all-encompassing ideologies. The New Left was influenced by a group of social scientists who in the 1950s had declared that ideology had lost its relevance in postindustrial society, a dictum that was embodied in the phrase "an end to ideology." MAS's metamorphosis from its self-proclaimed Marxism-Leninism and identification with the world Communist movement to a party bereft of any ideological allegiance recalled the New Left's position. The MASistas decided to drop these labels, not so much as a result of any particular criticism of Marxism per se, but because they felt that official adherence to any ideology would obstruct the search for original ideas. One prominent MAS leader, Anselmo Natale, wrote that Marxism was an "unnecessary tag" that would stifle the "climate of freshness and openness" that had always characterized MAS's internal debates.[2] Marxism, it was felt, like other ideologies tended to discourage free and uninhibited inquiry and to oversimplify complex issues.

MAS divested itself of the Communist label a few months after its founding when it dropped the name "MAS (New Communist Force)." MAS student leaders also abandoned the name "Communist Youth" (JC), which had been the PCV's youth organization. The MASista youth had temporarily retained the JC title in order to demonstrate that they had inherited the organization by virtue of the fact that nearly all PCV youth leaders had joined MAS.[3]

The decision to cease calling itself "Marxist" was taken at the party's national convention in September 1974. Joaquín Marta Sosa, who had been an important leftist Copeyano student leader in the 1960s, argued that only by suppressing the Marxist label could MAS hope to attract progressive Christians. A different position was taken by the more orthodox Freddy Muñoz, who maintained that, although dropping the official identification with Marxism was undoubtedly a healthy move, the party's leaders should be in any case Marxist. In future years Muñoz would criticize MAS for failing to promote the study of Marxism among rank-and-file members.[4]

MAS also began to question its identification as a leftist party. The bifurcation of the Venezuelan political community into left and non-left, it was felt, was disadvantageous in that it created unnecessary obstacles to reaching people and bringing about a radical realignment in their sympathies. By the time of the 1983 electoral campaign MAS assertively attempted to distance itself from the Venezuelan left, in part to differentiate its candidate from José Vicente Rangel (who was supported by the traditional left but was widely associated with MAS). MASistas even began to feel uncomfortable with the socialist label, in spite of its being inherent in MAS's very name, because of the negative images that it often conjured up. The MASistas sought a way out of the predicament by broadening the definition of socialism to take in such diverse models as workers' control, democratic socialism, decentralization, and municipal autonomy.

MAS's fear that the leftist label represented a liability had a basis in fact, as demonstrated by public opinion polls such as that used by Enrique Baloyra and John Martz in their *Political Attitudes in Venezuela*. This survey showed that 21 percent of the population considered themselves leftist whereas 22 percent identified with the center and 31 percent with the right. Baloyra and Martz attributed this inclination to the right to the guerrilla struggle when Venezuelans came to associate the left with violence and the right with law and order.[5]

With MAS's move to the right in the late 1970s and the impressive growth of the Socialist parties of France and Spain, sentiment in MAS began to favor affiliation with the Socialist International (SI). Although the MASistas decided at their 1980 national convention to solicit entry into the SI (a request that AD, as a full-fledged member of the organization, was able to veto), a certain lethargy prevailed in MAS regarding the strengthening of ties with social democratic parties in other countries. The MASistas, like the New Leftists before them, were suspicious of ideological denominations. Their fear—perhaps more latent than overt—that the social democratic label would replace the Marxist one made at least some of them reluctant to link up formally with an international movement that was the apologist of yet another *ism*.

MAS's main reason for seeking membership in the SI was to use the organization's conferences as a forum to express opinions. The MASistas had no intentions of submitting to the discipline of an international organization and stressed that "membership in the SI does not signify an obligatory ideological definition nor uniformity of opinions; on the contrary, each affiliate party conserves its autonomy."[6]

The New Left's voluntaristic approach, expressed by the slogan "the duty of every revolutionary is to make a revolution," was shared by MAS, especially in its early years. MASistas frequently pointed out that only an active vanguard that was conscious of and motivated by a utopian vision could ensure the successful outcome of the revolution. This revolutionary leadership, it was felt, could overcome such formidable problems as the growth of a state bureaucracy, which had perverted the Soviet experiment. In general, the revolution's salient features were determined by the vanguard; as Luis Bayardo Sardi stated in an internal party forum, "the characteristics of socialism are molded above all else by the volition of the leadership component."[7]

The early MASistas also felt that the vanguard could replace the political party, which was important, but not essential, to the success of the revolution. In their writings in the late 1960s, Petkoff, Muñoz, and other dissident Communists pointed to the negligible role played by Communist parties in recent revolutionary processes. The attitude of the early MASistas toward the revolutionary vanguard was reflected in their effort to build an amorphous "movement of movements" (discussed in chapters 5 and 10), which was to transcend the limits of political parties.

The voluntarism of the early MASistas was also reflected in their optimism regarding the prospects for socialism in Venezuela. Parties like MAS that emphasize the subjective factor usually view revolution as a short-term possibility; unlike objective conditions that take time to mature, consciousness is an amorphous variable that can develop at any moment. Even before the founding of MAS, Petkoff had attacked official PCV ideology for its mechanical notion of revolutionary stages, which relegated socialism to the distant future. So vocal were the early MASistas in denying that revolution was a long-range proposition that they were accused of calling for "socialism now" (*socialismo ya*). MAS's leftist rival in the 1973 presidential campaign, Jesús Paz Galarraga, responded to the party's revolutionary haste by coining the phrase "socialism is not around the corner," although such a slogan exaggerated MAS's true position. MASistas denied that they favored "socialism now" and insisted that if they were to triumph at the polls, they would create conditions for bringing about socialism at a later date.[8] They added that socialism was realizable within their lifetimes and should thus be made the focus of party propaganda.

MAS's position on the transition to socialism was influenced by Eurocommunism and specifically by Gramsci's theory of the struggle for hegemony. According to this thesis, the working class and its party in nations with an extended democratic tradition would come to power, not so much through a forceful seizure as through an incremental process of gaining influence and control in civil society (which included such institutions as professional associations, schools, and the church).

This more gradualist approach led MAS to spurn what it derogatorily called the "cataclysmic" view of revolution in which a devastating
economic crisis produces intense social conflict, government repression, and eventually a popular upheaval. The MASistas rejected the
use of violence as inappropriate to Venezuela, which, because of its
similarities with the democracies of Western Europe, would be able
to achieve socialism through a gradual takeover of civil society. According to Petkoff, the highly interventionist role of the Venezuelan
government in all aspects of the economy resembled the welfare state
of Western European countries.[9] Most important, MAS leaders repeatedly pointed to Venezuela's sizable oil income as guaranteeing
the stability and endurance of the democratic system.[10]

Even though by the mid-1970s Venezuela was the most firmly
established democracy in Latin America, it was hardly the democratic
bulwark that the MASistas sometimes made it seem. Actually, of all the
nations in Latin America, Chile and Uruguay most resembled Europe
in the maturity of their political cultures and traditions, but both of
them were governed by repressive military regimes by the mid-1970s.
Argentina, whose people identified more with Europe than Latin
America, was also governed by a military government after 1976. The
MASistas failed to come up with cogent arguments to back their claim
to Venezuelan exceptionalism, or to explain why Venezuela was im-
mune to the militarization that had spread across the continent. Cer-
tainly oil wealth in itself was no assurance that democracy would
prevail. After all, the stability of the Venezuelan economy and institutions was as dependent on the export of a single commodity as was
that of any of the poorer third-world nations.

Gramsci's view of the gradual achievement of socialist hegemony in
civil society—which became an article of faith among the MASistas—
has produced debates among his followers over the revolutionary
content of the strategy. Carl Boggs, for instance, who has written
extensively on Gramsci, has criticized the Eurocommunists for envi-
sioning a progressive accession to power, devoid of the sudden rupture
with the past that inevitably takes place in the Gramscian scheme.[11]
Within MAS a similar polemic has taken place. The orthodox Freddy
Muñoz, while recognizing that the socialist dominance of civil society
is a drawn-out process, maintains that a revolutionary transformation
occurs at a given point. Muñoz denies that the key element at this
juncture consists of large-scale nationalization, and instead views
workers' control as a more viable locus of revolutionary change. In
contrast, the thinking of the social-democratic current in MAS is based
on an evolutionary path to socialism devoid of sudden transformations.

MASistas generally concur in viewing the achievement of socialism as fundamentally a process of broadening channels of popular participation and input in decision making. The emphasis on the perfection of democracy in the stage leading up to socialism contrasts, at least in degree, with the European social democratic parties, which stress economic reforms[12] and with the Eurocommunists who place the accent on the struggle against monopolies.[13]

MAS national leader Carlos Raúl Hernández, in *Democracia y mitología revolucionaria* (1977), attempted to detail the process of socialist transformation in Venezuela. Hernández stated that the implantation of socialism should take place within the confines of the nation's legal structure without revising the Constitution (a position also upheld by the PCI and other Eurocommunist parties). Although the process leading up to socialism was one of democratization, Hernández argued, socialism itself will transform the role of property in favor of the people. Banks, for instance, will modify their credit policies in order to serve popular interests. Hernández concluded his remarks on the new function of property under socialism by stating, "all of us will be property holders under a society like this."[14] Hernández rejected the model of distribution of company stocks to workers as "bourgeois." Like most MASistas, he assigned the government a limited role in the general supervision of society.[15]

MASistas envisioned the coexistence of workers' control and other forms of property arrangements under socialism. They debated among themselves the scope and feasibility of these systems. The MASistas failed, however, to specify the locus of ownership and of ultimate decision-making power in their version of socialism. The extended discussions that took place in MAS over the specific characteristics of Venezuelan socialism set the party off from its socialist counterparts elsewhere. At times, this examination appeared to be an idle speculative exercise, if not a form of utopian thinking. Nevertheless, it filled a gap in Marxism that dated back to Marx's own dismissal of the effort to predict the exact nature of socialism as futile.[16] Given MAS's propensity for dwelling on the socialist utopia, it was natural that the party would give priority to the task of winning people over to the idea of socialism, as opposed to agitation over concrete demands.

Class Analysis

The belief that industrial workers (the proletariat) will play the leading role in the socialist revolution is a key tenet of classical Marxism. Marx pointed to the factory as a veritable school where the workers would develop a sense of solidarity and discover new forms of struggle. Furthermore, he felt that the proletariat's ever greater concentration in workplaces would heighten its class consciousness and self-confidence. Marx assumed that the proletariat would come to constitute the vast majority of the population, while the middle class would all but disappear.

These predictions regarding worker consciousness and numerical strength were not borne out by time. It was this incongruity between theory and fact that New Left theorists addressed themselves to. Some of them broadened the definition of working class to take in technical and even professional workers, calling them the "new working class." Others postulated that professionals who were employed by private companies constituted a class unto themselves that in many respects was more revolutionary than the traditional working class with its obsession over bread-and-butter issues. Still others, like Marcuse, wrote off the working class as submissive and unable to transcend the controls that were built into the system.

All three of these general theories influenced MAS's thinking, which, needless to say, was also shaped by special considerations of class in third-world societies. Petkoff and other PCV dissidents in the late 1960s questioned the orthodox Marxist emphasis on the proletariat to the neglect of other social groups, an imbalance they pejoratively labeled *obrerismo* (workerism). In *Socialismo para Venezuela?* (1970) Petkoff recalled his own disappointment in the working class because of its failure to act decisively in the overthrow of Pérez Jiménez in 1958. Although the general strike called two days before Pérez Jiménez's flight from Venezuela was a success, "there arose doubts in many of us, regarding . . . the validity of the [Marxist] model" of the proletariat's revolutionary behavior. At one point in the book Petkoff insisted that Marcuse's view on the passivity of the working class in modern society was, to a certain extent, applicable to Venezuela. He also stated that in countries like Venezuela it is impossible to predict what class will be the most important in the revolution, since it could be the working class, just as it could be the petty bourgeoisie or the marginal class (those who lack steady employment).[17]

Upon the founding of MAS, Petkoff criticized the "Stalinist" Communist parties for underestimating the role of the middle class, especially in underdeveloped countries where its expertise was needed to help sever ties of dependence.[18] Some MASistas like Germán Lairet (and occasionally Petkoff himself) went beyond this position by stating that professionals and technicians had a greater capacity to grasp the nature of their oppression and to struggle against it than did the traditional working class.[19] Actually, the analysis that emphasized the revolutionary role of the middle sectors was not new to Latin American political thinking. Haya de la Torre, as far back as the 1920s at the time of the founding of APRA, had argued that the middle sectors and especially small property holders had the most to lose by imperialist penetration and would thus be more inclined to participate in the struggle for national liberation than either the working class or the peasantry.[20]

A second, more orthodox viewpoint within MAS was expressed by Freddy Muñoz, who, even before he left the PCV, noted in his *Revolución sin dogma* that the classical concept of the proletariat needed to be updated. Muñoz rejected the notion that unskilled workers in heavy industry should be assigned a special position in revolutionary strategy since technical and service workers would play an equally decisive role. He also made use of the Eurocommunist concept, first formulated by Gramsci, of an "historical bloc" in which the workers would rely on the active participation of middle sectors, the peasantry, and other social groupings in the struggle for socialism. Muñoz, like the Eurocommunist parties (but unlike the more heterodox Petkoff), noted that of all classes workers have the greatest revolutionary potential.[21] MAS's main trade union leaders also supported the view of the primacy of the working class while acknowledging the complementary role of other sectors in the revolutionary process.[22]

MAS's organizational growth was not matched by inroads in recruitment among members of the lower and working classes. Though MAS quickly emerged as the number-one party in the student movement and gained influence in professional organizations, its support in labor unions and peasant leagues was not proportionately greater than its standing in the national electorate. MAS did attract a larger number of low-income voters in the 1978 national elections than it had in 1973, but it failed to parlay this electoral sympathy into more active forms of participation.

Some political analysts have asserted that the transformation of European social democratic parties into multiclass organizations had a deradicalizing effect on them. (Other writers have pointed to the same process in the PCI, which, since the 1950s, improved its standing in the middle sectors while losing support in the lower strata.)[23] The connection between the increasing middle-class constituency and the rightward drift of European social democracy has been questioned by the Marxist writer Adam Przeworski. He argues that the decision to try to win over the middle class was a logical move, once it became clear that the working class had reached its numerical limit and that the middle class was not about to be reduced to insignificance, as Marx had predicted. Thus the social democrats' search for middle-class support did not imply in itself a retrenchment in commitment to radical social change.[24]

Przeworski's analysis, though plausible for the European setting, is not applicable to MAS. Unlike the European parties, MAS, ever since its founding, has lacked a base of support in the labor movement. MAS has failed to establish itself firmly in the working class in part because no consensus exists among MASistas that such an effort should be given priority. MAS's membership has always been predominately middle class, as demonstrated by its electoral successes in professional and student organizations. The party's decision to make a special effort to reach low-income groups in national elections does not in itself say anything about MAS's class priorities since these sectors represent, after all, the overwhelming majority of the electorate. Indeed, the electoral strategy of AD, COPEI, and other nonleftist parties has been shaped by the same consideration. In short, MAS's middle-class base and its multiclass analysis distinguishes the party in a fundamental way from the PCI and other European parties with large working-class followings.

Is there any connection, then, between MAS's rightward course, on the one hand, and its failure to move beyond its middle-class base, on the other? Membership in the middle class in Venezuela in the 1970s was synonymous with privileged—if not elite—status, despite the challenges and difficulties that such a position also entailed.[25] Professionals and small-business interests greatly benefited from the oil price hikes after 1973, and their incomes compared favorably with those of their counterparts elsewhere in Latin America, many of whom actually immigrated to Venezuela in search of employment opportunities. MAS's condition as a middle-class party thus translated itself into articulating the viewpoints, if not the interests, of relatively well-to-do sectors, a function that in time could not have helped but mean the abandonment of radical socioeconomic objectives and the acceptance of positions that downplay conflict and emphasize change through consensus. Had the party made a concerted attempt to alter its class composition, or had it attempted to reach out to the middle class after having first established itself in the working class (as was the case with the PCI), then it would have been less inclined to modify its ideology. MAS, however, as would have been the case with any left-wing party that emerged from privileged sectors and accepted its class make-up, was bound to move to the right in the course of time.

Economic Analysis and Policy

Teodoro Petkoff and other founding MASistas characterized Venezuela as a capitalist society and placed socialist revolution on the agenda for the medium-range future. The early MASistas maintained that the Venezuelan bourgeoisie was fully integrated into the world capitalist system and thus would not struggle against Venezuela's condition of dependency. They felt that members of the Venezuelan bourgeoisie should be singled out for special attack, as they constituted the main enemy in the upcoming stage.

This analysis and focus coincided with the version of the theory of dependency upheld by André Gunder Frank, a German-born economist who had received much recent acclaim in Venezuela. Petkoff (who is himself an economist) and other MAS political leaders deny having been influenced by Frank and point to his world system approach, which downplays differences among developing nations, as being at odds with MAS's emphasis on Venezuela's unique conditions.[26] Nevertheless, the similarity between Frank's analysis of capitalism and social classes in underdeveloped countries and that of the dissident Communists in the late 1960s would suggest that at least an indirect influence was exerted on MAS. (Petkoff's refusal to recognize Frank's theoretical influence is just one more example of MAS's tendency to view its brand of socialism as original and impervious to the influence of foreign models.)

A large group of Venezuelan economists, including some who would later join MAS, were indebted to Frank and offered him a particularly warm reception when he came to Venezuela in the late 1960s.[27] Hector Silva Michelena (a prominent economist who was identified with MIR) was most vocal in acknowledging this influence. Silva Michelena hailed the emergence of a "new school of social science," led by Frank and other *dependentista* economists, as representing a challenge to traditional Marxism, which has been "out of touch with ongoing reality."[28] Elsewhere, Silva Michelena wrote that the leftist establishment had dubbed Frank a "Trotskyist" and, along with conservatives, had opposed the diffusion of his ideas, thus explaining why his major work, *Capitalism and Underdevelopment in Latin America* (1967), had until then not been published in Spanish.[29] The PCV dissidents faced the same predicament: confronting well-established political movements, namely international communism, with original ideas.

During the mid-1970s MAS's position calling for a thorough break with capitalism in the not-too-distant future was modified in favor of an extended transitional period in which key features of capitalist society were to be retained. It was not clear to what extent elements of the transitional society would be conserved under socialism. Among the important economic policies that MAS proposed for the transitional period were the defense of small and medium-sized businesses, the fostering of cooperatives and workers' control of industry, the government's withdrawal from certain spheres of economic decision making and restraint in the takeover of private companies. MAS made clear that no one form of property relations would predominate and that both private and state ownership would coexist.[30]

Petkoff's interest in the plight of the small and medium-sized business owners was first evidenced in his staunch support for Alexander Dubček's socialist model in Czechoslovakia, which favored small and medium producers. By the mid-1970s the MASistas made a concerted effort to reach out to these sectors and pledged that a MAS-led government would exempt their firms from nationalization.[31] Nevertheless, it was not at all clear whether small-scale private property was seen by MAS as a permanent feature of socialist society or merely as a transitional form.

The MASistas frequently come to the defense of small and medium-sized business owners and thus, for instance, have called on the government to modify the credit policies of state-controlled financial institutions in their favor. When the government implemented a multitier system of foreign exchange in February 1983 (in which commercial firms were allowed to purchase undervalued dollars for certain nonluxury imports), MAS proposed that dollars be sold to small and medium-sized business owners at the preferential rates. MASistas also discussed the possibility of organizing the support of these business people within Fedecamaras, the nation's main business organization.[32]

Several doubts may be expressed regarding the viability of MAS's inclusion of small and medium property holders in its plans for socialism. Few Marxists have denied the revolutionary potential of the small business owner, who is classically referred to as part of the petty bourgeoisie. The affluence of the medium-sized business owners in Venezuela, however, is more pronounced than that of counterparts elsewhere in Latin America and, regardless of the precariousness of their position in the economy, they are unlikely to see socialism as amenable to their interests. More important, MAS's more recent emphasis on small-scale production, which would open up opportunities to small and medium-sized business owners, as well as its guarantees to members of that sector, leave open to question whether the party's program does not represent a return to nineteenth-century competitive capitalism.

MAS's avid support for workers' control is not surprising, as it has been generally defended by heterodoxical movements and rejected by orthodox Marxists.[33] MAS, along with other parties on the left, criticized the CTV for distorting the idea of *cogestion* (worker representation in management), which President Raúl Leoni had decreed for public enterprises in the mid-1960s. The CTV had limited *cogestion* to the appointment of trade union officials to the executive boards of state companies. Authentic *cogestion,* as opposed to what MAS called "symbolic *cogestion,*" implied more direct forms of worker participation. MAS also called for the establishment of a special bank in order to facilitate credit to companies that were run by the workers.[34]

The effort to define the parameters of workers' control and the industries that were suited for the system was a source of extended internal debate in MAS. Petkoff, for instance, denied that workers' control could be applied to the oil industry, where a relatively small number of employees, many of whom were not even workers, ran the nation's most important industry. Such inordinate power in the hands of a small group would violate the spirit of socialism.[35] Germán Lairet, on the other hand, defended workers' control in petroleum by arguing that the professional formation of a large number of employees in that sector would facilitate their participation in the decision-making process.

MASistas viewed workers' control as part of the "democratization" of property, which represented a higher stage than the democratization of the nation's political structure. Nevertheless, MAS failed to specify whether the owners of companies placed under workers' control would be dispossessed of their property. MAS's support for workers' control thus suffered from the same vagueness regarding ownership as the much-heralded "communitarian property" championed by COPEI[36] and the *cogestion* advocated by the AD-controlled CTV in its "Document of Porlamar" ratified at its Eighth Congress in 1980.

Another salient feature of MAS's economic program in its early years was its call for large-scale nationalization. This position was not surprising at the time, given MAS's criticism of orthodox Communism for its failure to stress socialist objectives. The fledgling MAS's support for the nationalization of the oil industry in 1971 preceded by several years the decision of COPEI, AD, and the PCV to support the same measure.[37] In its program for the 1973 presidential elections, MAS earmarked the property of twenty Venezuelan capitalist families for immediate expropriation. This plank was absent from the program of MAS's leftist rival, the New Force, whose call for nationalization encompassed mainly foreign interests in Venezuela. In addition, the MASistas called for socialized medicine.[38]

MAS modified its call for sweeping nationalization after 1973 as part of its emphasis on the dangers of excessive state bureaucracy, which was seen as an obstacle to democracy under both capitalism and socialism. The ideological currents that influenced MAS—the New Left, the Czechoslovakian experience of 1968, and Eurocommunism—also stressed the evils of bureaucracy. The PCI, for instance (unlike the PCF), ruled out the possibility of extensive nationalization and even favored the privatization of certain state companies in order to avoid the rampant growth of an uncontrollable state bureaucracy.[39]

The MASistas argued that the government's takeover of a firm would not necessarily improve conditions, either in that company or in the economy as a whole. This attitude was reflected in MAS's support for the "socialization" of the oil industry, which it called for at the time of the 1973 elections. According to MAS, the recent wave of nationalizations in third-world countries, very often with the tacit consent of the U.S. government, signified that nationalization had lost its revolutionary character. MAS maintained that the oil industry should not only be taken over but also socialized, so that its organization and policies would accord to the interests of the nation. In later years MAS extended the proposal of socialization to other sectors of the economy and began to insist that more important than the ownership of a firm (that is, whether it was state, private, or mixed) was its social function. MAS explicitly rejected nationalization of financial institutions and instead called on the government to closely monitor their activities to ensure that they favored both the public interest and small and medium-sized businesses, as against monopoly firms.

MAS was reluctant to burden the state with the ownership of enterprises with a limited or uncertain margin of profitability. The Venezuelan government since 1958 had assumed control of scores of faltering and bankrupt companies in diverse sectors, such as finance, tourism and cement production, which were not considered to be of strategic importance or priority interest to the state. In the 1983 presidential campaign MAS proposed the transfer of state companies to the private sector in order to put an end to the colossal losses incurred by government management of unprofitable firms.[40] This policy was, in fact, subsequently followed by the government of Jaime Lusinchi (1984–89).

MAS's support for payment of compensation to the oil companies whose holdings were nationalized in 1976 represented another departure from the policies of the traditional left. Among the parties of the opposition, the PCV and MIR (both of which labeled themselves Marxist-Leninist) opposed indemnification, whereas MAS, MEP, and COPEI favored it. MAS's national deputy and petroleum expert, Freddy

Muñoz, defended his party's stand in Congress, stating that the Venezuelan government was fortunate to have the resources to offer compensation and thus avoid unnecessary conflict. Muñoz claimed that MAS's position was "responsible," in contrast to that of the traditional left, which sought to generate conflict for the sake of conflict. He insisted that MAS's support for compensation was based entirely on pragmatic considerations, not on any moral commitment to respect the rights of property.[41] In addition, the nation's constitution did not contemplate confiscation of property without due cause, and thus payment of compensation would avoid a knotty and undoubtedly protracted legal ordeal.[42]

MAS's opposition to confiscation and its reservations regarding nationalization contrasted to the position traditionally upheld by Communist parties. Orthodox Communists have invariably hailed government takeovers of industry by both socialist and nonsocialist regimes.[43] They have also insisted that foreign interests receive but minimum reimbursement, if any at all, for their property.[44] In Venezuela, in spite of the government's failure to completely sever relations with multinational oil firms, the nationalization in 1976 was welcomed by the Communist Party as a step in the right direction.

In the 1970s a radical critique of nationalization was formulated in Venezuela and elsewhere, inspired in large part by dependency theory, with its concern over the emergence of new forms of foreign control. This view was put forward by the mazagine *Proceso Político*, published by a group of young social scientists and political activists, which offered a thorough and well-documented criticism of the nationalization of petroleum. According to this thesis, Venezuela's position as a satellite in the world capitalist system was actually fortified rather than undermined by the takeover of the industry.[45] MAS's oil policy during its early years was similarly critical, especially in its concern that structures of dependency would survive nationalization. MAS insisted that nationalization be accompanied by complementary measures designed to facilitate the autonomy of the industry and to ensure that the nation's true interests would be served.

By the latter part of the 1970s MAS modified its position and toned down its radical rhetoric. The party supported payment of compensation to the oil companies, opposed widespread nationalization, and stressed the constructive role that U.S. companies had to play in oil and other industries. Related to these policies was MAS's tendency to assign greater significance to the social function of property than to its ownership. In doing so, the MASistas accepted a viewpoint originally formulated by the German Social Democrat Edward Bernstein, who downplayed the significance of ownership and maintained that "the basic issue of socialization is that we place production, economic life, under the control of the public weal."[46] This focus shaped MAS's main formulations in the area of economic policy. In short, following its early years MAS minimized the importance of nationalization in the revolutionary process and left open the possibility that private property would survive under socialism.

Foreign Policy

At its founding MAS viewed itself as part of a renovation tendency within the world Communist movement that included Eurocommunist parties, the Rumanian Communist Party, and others that maintained a degree of independence from Moscow. In its founding document MAS called itself an "international force" on the side of the Soviet Union, China, Cuba, and other nations that were constructing socialism and combating imperialism.[47] In addition to identifying with the world Communist movement, MAS projected a third-worldist image, as demonstrated by its fraternal ties with the followers of ex-dictator Gustavo Rojas Pinilla of Colombia, who were grouped in ANAPO, and by its fervent support for the government of Juan Velasco in Peru. Pompeyo Márquez branded ANAPO—a nationalist organization with an ill-defined ideology—"socialism a la colombiana."[48]

During its first few years of existence MAS distanced itself from the socialist bloc. MAS leaders occasionally expressed doubts whether socialist countries could be considered truly socialist and referred to them by invoking the term *chucuto* (sham) socialism. MAS did not hesitate to criticize Cuban intervention in Africa and viewed mistakes committed by that nation as the logical outcome of its "totalitarian" structures. On the other hand, the party lauded certain aspects of Cuban society and recognized that Cuba maintains a relative autonomy within the socialist bloc.[49] In addition, MAS leaders occasionally pointed to the role played by the Soviet Union in the spread of socialism, though their praise of that nation was highly qualified.[50]

The MASistas have been less restrained in their praise of the U.S. democratic system[51] than of the Soviets and have even ridiculed the tendency of the left to attribute all setbacks of socialism to the machinations of the CIA. In party circles Petkoff argued against the thesis that the anti-imperialist struggle should be directed mainly against the United States because of its greater hold over all facets of Venezuelan society. Petkoff and other MASistas maintained that precisely because of the U.S. position of dominance, MAS should display greater flexibility and establish ties with influential North Americans in order to deter a possible U.S. intervention against Venezuelan socialism.[52] MAS has made a concerted effort to convince Washington that a MAS-led government would be amicably disposed to the United States and would not endanger its supply of Venezuelan oil.[53] The exceptionally cordial relationship between Petkoff and U.S. ambassador William Luers until his replacement in 1982 is one indication that at least the moderates and liberals in the U.S. State Department do not lump MAS in with traditional leftist groups that are considered hostile to U.S. interests. When Luers—at the time subsecretary of state for Latin American affairs—traveled to Venezuela in April 1975 to make preparations for a visit by Secretary of State Henry Kissinger, he chose to meet with MAS's presidential candidate José Vicente Rangel, among others.[54]

By the late 1970s MAS's greater stress on democratic goals was reflected in its positions on foreign affairs and its attitude toward parties abroad. By that date MAS no longer maintained close ties with or extolled parties like ANAPO or governments like that of Velasco in Peru, whose commitment to democracy was open to question. Instead, MAS took special note of developments in France, Spain, and Greece, where socialist parties came to power through elections. MASistas expressed hope that the success of these regimes would point to the viability of a new model in which true socialism and true democracy were to be achieved simultaneously. MAS's interest in a new brand of socialism more authentic than European social democracy and unaffiliated with the world Communist movement led the party to organize the conference entitled "From Existing Socialism to New Socialism," held in Caracas in May 1981. Socialist delegates from throughout the world gathered to exchange ideas regarding implementation of original socialist models. Several years later Petkoff, MAS's presidential candidate for the 1983 elections, traveled to Colombia to meet with Luis Carlos Galán, head of the New Liberalism faction of the Liberal Party; the two leaders declared their support for common objectives. The encounter was widely commented upon in the press in both nations. These initiatives, however, were not followed up in further conferences or meetings, evidence of MAS's reluctance to form close attachments with political movements in other countries.

MAS was also hopeful that the leftist regimes that came to power in Grenada and Nicaragua would point the way to novel forms of popular and democratic participation. With the overthrow of Somoza in 1979, MAS called on the Venezuelan government to support the Sandinistas in order to reduce tensions and enable them to carry on with their democratic initiatives and maintain independence from both the U.S. and Soviet camps. According to the MASistas, the strengthening of nonaligned regimes in Nicaragua, Grenada, and elsewhere would provide Cuba with greater maneuverability vis-à-vis the two blocs and enhance the credibility of MAS's position in favor of a truly neutral stand. By focusing their attention mainly on the Sandinistas' commitment to democracy and neutrality (rather than on the struggle against imperialism), the MASistas left the impression that their support was conditional upon the continuance of those policies.[55]

The public statements on foreign affairs delivered by Petkoff and Pompeyo Márquez revealed differences in style and positions. Márquez more strongly condemned U.S. foreign policy and was less critical of the socialist bloc than was Petkoff. Nevertheless, MAS has consistently favored third-world struggles for independence from super-power domination and opposed all foreign intervention, whether in Afghanistan, Poland, or Nicaragua. MAS has staunchly defended its right to criticize Cuba and other socialist regimes for violating democratic norms and for compromising their independence by aligning themselves too closely with the Soviet camp. MAS's critical posture has been publicly denounced by other leftist parties, including MEP, MIR, and, of course, the PCV on grounds that criticism should be tempered, if not completely withheld, as a result of the extenuating circumstances faced by those governments. Moisés Moleiro, for instance, the secretary general of MIR, which supported Petkoff in the 1983 presidential elections, scored MAS at the time for maintaining "a type of ongoing critique of the Cuban revolution."[56]

The declarations of two young outspoken MASistas, Carlos Raúl Hernández and Jean Maninat, who were identified with the renovation faction in MAS headed by Bayardo Sardi, ran counter to the party's official position, which placed the main part of the blame for the crisis in Central America on the Reagan administration. Hernández and Maninat, in *Cuba-Nicaragua: Expectativas y frustraciones*, published on the eve of the Nicaraguan elections of 1984, lashed out at the Cuban and Sandinista leaders as well as at the United States. Few Venezuelan politicians, if any, absolve the United States of major responsibility for the situation in Central America, and thus Hernández and Maninat, in denouncing both sides in the dispute in nearly equal terms, assumed a conservative position in the context of Venezuelan politics. The authors argued that the presence of 4,000 Cuban advisors in Nicaragua "plays an important political-ideological role," while the skepticism of the Sandinistas regarding what they pejoratively call "bourgeois democracy" raises doubts about the seriousness of their commitment to open and honest elections.[57]

Hernández and Maninat were publicly rebuked by Pompeyo Márquez for the harshness and inopportuneness of their attacks, while MAS's executive secretary, Manuel Isidro Molina, denied that the authors' remarks in any way represented the party's official position. In spite of these criticisms, Petkoff attended the book's "baptism" (a promotional gathering in which the work is formally presented to the public), where he congratulated the authors for their journalistic accomplishment.

As in other cases of public declarations by MASistas that contradicted the party's official position (such as those of Manuel Caballero, discussed in chapter 7), two possible explanations for MAS's failure to take disciplinary measures against the authors can be offered. MAS may have justified its flexibility on grounds that, unlike other parties such as the PCV, AD, and COPEI which were organized on the basis of a centralist structure, MAS was truly democratic and thus permitted and even encouraged its members to articulate their own opinions. A second explanation is that the dissenters might actually have been expressing the viewpoints of top party leaders, in this case Petkoff, who for pragmatic reasons chose not to identify himself publicly with their positions.

Quite ironically, the most strongly worded rebuke of the authors came from Manuel Caballero, who threatened to resign from MAS if they were elected to the national committee at the party's upcoming convention (which they were not). According to the well-known historian and journalist, the publication of *Cuba-Nicaragua* committed MAS to a position that was clearly unacceptable to the majority of its members and thus could not go uncensured, "not even in the name of tolerance."[58]

The evolution of MAS from the "orthodox" to the "responsible" left was manifest in its position on Venezuela's territorial disputes with neighboring Colombia and Guyana. At the time of MAS's founding, Pompeyo Márquez published in *Deslinde* a standard traditional leftist explanation that viewed Venezuela and Colombia as proxies of multinational firms, in this case Exxon and Shell, whose manipulation of the conflict was due to Venezuela's refusal to grant them concessions.[59] In viewing Venezuela and Colombia as victims of imperialist machinations, Márquez dismissed the actual claims of both nations as being of secondary importance. The focus and content of the article greatly contrasted with Márquez's *En peligro la integridad territorial de Venezuela* published ten years later, which was a detailed defense of Venezuela's position based on a legal and historical analysis.[60] Márquez's new stand was dictated by the realization that the traditional left in Latin America, in adhering to an "international" line on territorial disputes among third-world countries, had lost credibility among the general populace and was branded "anti-national." Nevertheless, MAS stopped short of utilizing jingoistic language and called for an equitable solution to the problem. Its moderation was attacked at least on one occasion by a representative of Venezuela's miniscule right wing, Pedro José Lara Peña, who accused MAS of betraying national interests.

MAS, in arriving at these positions on foreign affairs, attempted to reserve for itself a political space uncluttered by either the traditional left or AD and COPEI. Unlike its leftist rivals, MAS defended its right to be unrestrained in its criticism of existing socialism. At the same time its staunch opposition to interventionism set MAS off from AD and COPEI, which, with the exception of a few leading politicians (such as Carlos Andrés Pérez), have failed to speak out against U.S. foreign policy except in the most mild of terms. MAS's policy on international affairs, at its best, can be seen as original for a Latin American leftist party, unfettered by sentimental attachments or special commitments to Cuba or other international idols, and intent on putting forward constructive criticism of those nations from a socialist perspective. At worst, MAS's stands can be seen as vacillating and subject to a mechanical and awkward policy of balancing criticism of the United States with that of the Soviet Union. In addition, it may be argued that MAS's efforts to occupy a center-left position on foreign policy and other issues is doomed to failure, as that space has already been fully staked out by AD and COPEI.[61]

Attitude toward the Armed Forces

Left-wing military coups in third-world countries, beginning with that of Egypt in 1952, that promoted far-reaching reforms and confronted former colonial powers motivated leftist political theorists to reexamine long-accepted attitudes and assumptions regarding the armed forces. In the traditional leftist concept based on the Bolshevik experience in 1917, the armed forces represented a bulwark of the established system that revolutionaries attempted to subvert by pitting common soldiers against their officers. This model was unsuitable to explain the Egyptian coup in 1952 or any of the scores of subsequent ones in which the military as an institution, headed mainly by junior officers, spearheaded a movement in favor of radical change.[62]

One of the first leftist theorists to offer a new vision of the role of the armed forces in third-world countries was Jorge Abelardo Ramos, an eclectic Argentinian neo-Trotskyist, whose favorable view of the military was shaped by his characterization of *peronismo* (which emerged from within the armed forces) as nationalistic and anti-imperialist. Ramos pointed to the original liberational impulse of his nation's military, symbolized by San Martín, and argued that its "true tradition" continues to be "nationalist, popular and democratic." Ramos accused Argentinian traditional leftists of being unable to grasp the nature of the military's revolutionary mission because of their ideological dependence on European thinking that denigrates the role of the armed forces.[63] By the 1960s Soviet theorists, undoubtedly influenced by their nation's support for Arab socialism, also revised the Bolshevik dogma but were particularly cautious lest the armed forces be perceived as a substitute for the Communist Party in the revolutionary process. Soviet writers were wary of the concept (which had been proposed by Italian Communist writers, among others) of the military's relative autonomy vis-à-vis powerful economic interests. According to the Soviets, the armed forces under an oppressive regime may be receptive to radical ideas, but upon gaining power its elite status will set it off from the popular will; thus, authority must be quickly transferred to a Communist party.[64]

At the time of the division in the PCV in 1971, the gap that existed between the theory and practice of the Venezuelan left regarding the armed forces was typical of third-world countries. At the PCV's most recent congress in 1961 the military had been described as "subordinate to the policies of North American imperialists, the oligarchy and the commercial bourgeoisie."[65] Nevertheless, this harsh characterization did not accord with the military's role and the left's own behavior in modern Venezuelan history, which was replete with examples of reformist and even radical movements in the armed forces: the October 1945 coup, whose objective was universal suffrage and direct elections; the military conspiracies fomented by the clandestine AD against the dictatorship of Pérez Jiménez in the 1950s; the January 23, 1958, coup, which reestablished democratic rule; and the military uprisings in Carúpano and Puerto Cabello in 1962 in which members of the PCV and MIR actively participated. Thus the proposal to reconsider the role of the armed forces in Venezuelan society announced by the newly created MAS was long overdue.

MAS labeled the armed forces along with the church and other institutions the "living forces" that had a rich potential to contribute to the nation's development.[66] The MASistas pointed out that the democratic commitment of Venezuelan military officers contrasted with the attitudes of their counterparts in other Latin American nations. For instance, the Venezuelan military (unlike that of Colombia in more recent years) did not forcefully oppose the amnesty that the Caldera and Pérez governments conceded to guerrillas.[67] MAS rejected the widely held notion that the military was confined to a "ghetto" and was divorced from the socioeconomic and political life of the nation. MASistas cited the instances in which the armed forces participated in the struggle for democracy and the active interest military personnel had in politics. On this basis, MAS called for "de-mythologizing the apolitical nature of the military."[68] José Vicente Rangel, shortly after running as MAS's presidential candidate for the second time, wrote in the final passage of *Seguridad, defensa y democracia: Un tema para civiles y militares:*

> Just as it would be suicidal [to advocate] a strictly military strategy as an alternative [for the nation], it is stupid to continue to believe in an anachronistic apoliticism of the armed forces and an aseptical institutionality which serves but the defiled objectives of powerful groups and the crystallization of a hypocritical image of national institutions. Why not, then, analyze the role that, given the complexities of the State in modern society, an institution like the armed forces can play?[69]

MAS called for specific measures in order to facilitate the military's further integration into society, some of which were undoubtedly viewed as detrimental and even threatening by the military hierarchy. To encourage public debate over issues related to the armed forces, MAS proposed that the defense budget be submitted to Congress for approval. According to Petkoff, the Ministry of Defense's prerogative of drawing up its own budget without parliamentary approval is an "anti-democratic privilege that does not exist in any civilized country."[70] Petkoff also called for universal military service on grounds that the current practice of confining recruitment to the sons of the poor creates resentment and perpetuates an "aristocratic non-democratic vision" among officers.[71] The most important and controversial reform MAS supported—as did the rest of the left, though less vocally—was the military's right to vote. MAS's program in the 1978 presidential elections called for the implementation of this measure as part of the "democratization of the armed forces." It also called for the participation of junior officers "in some decision making" within the institution.[72]

Adecos and Copeyanos also favored the incorporation of the military in civic and developmental projects and boasted of the number of officers who had been appointed to administrative posts when their parties were in power. Nevertheless, the scope of this participation was never defined, as demonstrated by COPEI's criticism of AD for including a military officer in its slate in the elections for the Association of Economists (Colegio de Economistas).[73] In addition, AD and COPEI insisted that the participation of military personnel in elections violated the principle of the apolitical status of the armed forces, which was consecrated in the constitution. In general, AD and COPEI were not as fervent and outspoken as MAS in favoring military participation in civilian society.

Luis Esteban Rey, a journalist and leading AD member, warned that MAS's zeal in formalizing and systematizing the military's role in the public sphere pointed in the direction of a collegiate (or corporatist) system, which would require far-reaching constitutional modifications, despite MAS's claim to the contrary. Rey also took exception to MAS's effort to link the armed forces' institutional concerns with certain nationalistic policies. Thus he attempted to refute José Vicente Rangel's claim that the Venezuelan military had an inherent interest in excluding foreign capital from the oil industry in order to safeguard national security.[74]

MAS's advocacy of military reforms and its stress on the vital role of the armed forces provoked the alarm of certain AD and COPEI leaders. Rómulo Betancourt, among others, denounced MAS for trying to subvert the armed forces in order to encourage military intervention in politics.[75] The MASistas feared that these accusations, formulated after the 1973 elections when MAS emerged as the most promising leftist party, would be the opening salvo in a campaign to associate MAS with the disloyal left. There was a certain irony in the charge's coming from Betancourt, who first arrived at the presidency as a result of his participation in the October 1945 coup.

MASistas have often lauded the Venezuelan armed forces for its capacity to guard against the corruption and inefficiency in its own ranks that are rampant in other institutions. At times MASistas have actually pointed to the exemplary behavior and outstanding qualities of the military that would suggest that it is destined to play a special and unique role in the nation's development.[76] In more recent years MAS has failed to participate as actively as it once did in the exposure of cases of corruption in the armed forces. MAS's statements regarding the moral integrity of the armed forces—though not as unqualified as those of AD and COPEI[77]—lend credence to the party's thesis regarding the need to facilitate the integration of the armed forces in the nation's political and administrative life. MAS's position may also be related to its efforts to cast itself as the "responsible left" and abide by the rules of the political game set by AD and COPEI. According to these rules, criticism of the armed forces is virtually taboo, and the institution is ardently praised on a periodic basis by politicians.

Nevertheless, MAS's portrayal of the rectitude of the armed forces is somewhat exaggerated, as demonstrated by various national scandals that broke out in the early 1980s. At that time several officers, the most prominent of whom was Lieutenant Colonel Luis Alfonso Godoy, accused their superiors of refusing to act on persuasive evidence regarding misuse of military funds.

The rest of the left has been less restrained than MAS in its public remarks, and some sectors have actually attempted to make a case for institutionalized corruption in the armed forces.[78] Significantly, José Vicente Rangel, after expressing MAS's favorable attitude toward the armed forces, shifted his position when he became the frontrunner of the parties of the traditional left (the PCV and MEP) in the 1983 elections. Rangel supported the efforts of Lieutenant Colonel Godoy's mother to bring her son's case to the attention of Amnesty International and accepted her request to adopt Godoy as a "prisoner of conscience." Rangel also brought to the nation's attention alleged attempts of the extreme right to convince the military to intervene prior to the 1983 elections, an accusation that, because it implicitly questioned the loyalty of sectors of the armed forces to the democratic system, invited sharp rebuttals from government spokesmen.

MAS has accurately pointed out that the apoliticism of the Venezuelan military is a myth. Officers actively discuss diverse political issues, which find a prominent place in the courses taught in military schools. Although MAS does not state it publicly, many military officers are closely identified with one of the two main political parties of the establishment, and this tacit affiliation is virtually a sine qua non for steady promotion at the higher level.[79] The legitimization of political activity in the military, as championed by MAS, would lessen the control that conservative superior officers exert over the more free-thinking junior ones under the guise of guarding against politicization. It may be hypothesized that MAS's support for this process is partly designed to enable the party to carve out its own influence and to ensure against reprisals taken against its military followers.

MAS has made clear that it is interested in winning military personnel over to socialism and not just fortifying the institution's loyalty to the democratically elected government, regardless of its ideological commitment. Throughout his political career Petkoff has expressed faith in the revolutionary potential of officers. In 1962 Petkoff, along with several other young Communists, participated in an abortive plan to instigate an uprising at a military base at La Guaira.[80] As a dissident Communist shortly before the creation of MAS, Petkoff continued to speak of "progressives" and "leftists" in the armed forces.[81] MAS inherited this optimism and contrasted Venezuela's military favorably with that of Chile, which it described as being based on a veritable caste system.[82]

MAS's position on the armed forces must be placed in the context of the party's general political approach dating back to the division in the

Communist Party in 1970. The MASistas, like the New Left in other countries, harped on the need for leftists to be open and emphatic about their political goals and to break with the tendency of the traditional left to hide behind rigid and dogmatic formulations, which only created uncertainty and suspicion regarding its true intentions. The Venezuelan youth movement in the 1960s and the Communist Youth in particular considered frankness and straightforwardness to be great virtues. Support for this approach was reflected in MAS's extensive efforts to define long-term socialist objectives and the priority that it assigned to their diffusion. It was also manifested in MAS's decision to accept organized factions and allow party members to express openly their differences with the official party line. In doing so, MAS maintained that it was only recognizing a phenomenon that was inevitable in all political organizations, namely, the emergence of internal currents of opinion.

MAS's military policy contained the same elements of respect for openness of expression and recognition of a de facto situation that the nation's politicians had long tried to suppress. MAS called on the nation to accept that military personnel in Venezuela were already politicized and took an active interest in the political destiny of the nation. Just as MAS attempted to shatter myths perpetuated by dogmatic Marxists, among others, the party talked of the need to expose falsehoods regarding the apoliticism of the armed forces, which had deprived military officers the opportunity to pursue their political interests just as any ordinary Venezuelan citizen.

Style and Rhetoric

In recent years students of political parties in Latin America have addressed themselves to the role of style and the utilization of cultural forms in politics. Several of these researchers have noted that analysis of the popular symbols that parties draw on opens up a world of information regarding the appeal of political movements and the nature of their followers.[83] The importance these writers assign to style would suggest that style and content constantly act on one another and are intricately connected. Thus, for instance, leaders who lightheartedly threaten the use of violence as an attention-getting device may end up resorting to violence because they are trapped by their own rhetoric. Similarly, political leaders who employ cultural symbols in order to legitimize radically new and untested goals may find it difficult to reconcile the old and the new, to the extent that they are forced to tone down their radicalism and tailor it to the nation's traditions.

Populist parties have been especially prone to utilize popular culture in order to bolster their claim to represent the people.[84] One historian has pointed out that populist reliance on folkways and art forms from distinct periods creates a "living museum" of the discontinuities and uncompleted processes of social change in third-world nations.[85] Not only populist parties but also Eurocommunist ones under the influence of Gramsci perceived the need to incorporate national symbols into their propaganda. According to Gramsci, the proletariat in European countries had to create its own version of national culture in order to challenge that of the ruling elite. In doing so, the working class would be able to attract other classes, which up to then accepted the dominant culture, to an "historical bloc" committed to social change. By viewing national culture as the cement of the revolutionary alliance, Gramsci departed from the tendency, especially pronounced in the early Marx, to discard nationalism as antithetical to working-class "internationalism."

The writings of Gramsci and the example of AD during its populist period in the 1940s influenced MAS to explore the nation's culture in search of relevant symbols. This interest became marked following the 1973 presidential elections, when MAS made a concerted effort to abandon the abstract leftist rhetoric that until then had characterized the party's propaganda. In analyzing the vote for MAS, which fell short of expectations, party leaders concluded that MAS's pitch had suffered from "essentialism." This term referred to the tendency to attribute all social ills to capitalism without making an effort to analyze the specifics of the problems confronting the nation and offering efficacious, albeit short-term, solutions. In addition, party propaganda, it was felt, insulted the sensibilities of Venezuelans by attacking in personal and even vulgar terms capitalists, trade union bureaucrats, and others who were held responsible for the nation's problems.[86]

In February 1974 MAS's Central Committee ratified a document drafted by Luis Bayardo Sardi entitled "A New Mode of Being Socialist" (see appendix 3). According to this thesis, MAS should attempt to reach people at their own level by modifying the language typically associated with the left and by avoiding slogans that are jarring, intimidating and difficult to grasp. The document reprimanded MASistas for failing to comprehend the concrete problems of the nation and for possessing a "superficial knowledge of real people . . . their everyday life and their hopes for change."[87]

"A New Mode of Being Socialist" signaled a radical change in MAS's style. The party dropped its practice of making frequent reference to members of the Venezuelan financial oligarchy by name as part of its anticapitalist approach. MAS's propaganda, rather than conjuring up images of internecine conflict, austerity, and human suffering in the tradition of the orthodox left, attempted to convey optimism regarding the positive changes that socialism would bring about. MAS posters avoided gray and yellow, which evoke unpleasant associations, and instead utilized bright colors to convey exuberance and hope. Furthermore, party propaganda and rallies for the 1978 and 1983 presidential campaigns were designed to produce a euphoric mood that sharply contrasted with the gatherings organized by MAS's leftist rivals, which often took on the character of mass protests.

MAS spoke of socialism as natural and imminent rather than as the result of a distant catacylsm.[88] This message was embodied in the slogan "socialism is an idea whose time has come." MAS's efforts to describe in concrete terms what socialism in Venezuela will be like was meant to demythologize the concept, which, according to some non-Marxist writers, has been obscured by traditional leftists who view it as a veritable Second Coming.[89] Rangel expressed MAS's intentions in his final remarks at a campaign gathering for the 1978 elections: "We are not in the presence of either a messianic idea, a magic word, or a utopia. The process of construction of socialism is something of this world not heaven. It is not mythology, nor infantile adventure, rather an expression of maturity and responsibility."[90]

"A New Mode of Being Socialist" also influenced MAS to revise its attitude toward the two main parties of the establishment. As Communists in the 1960s, the MASistas had been particularly hostile to AD for unleashing the repression that had induced the left to take up arms. After 1973, however, MAS avoided the intransigence of the traditional left by offering the AD administration constructive criticism. MAS not only did not hesitate to endorse AD and COPEI policies but even praised the two parties for their defense of the democratic system and the democratic values of the nation.[91] Indeed, this posture was more generous and flexible than that of AD and COPEI toward each other.

According to many MASistas, AD owed its success to its populist style, which was easily grasped by the general populace. Bayardo Sardi wrote, "to be anti-Adeco is to disdain popular culture."[92] It was this Venezuelan culture, as well as AD's interpretation and utilization of it, that the MASistas proposed to study as part of the "New Mode of Being Socialist" approach.[93]

Throughout its history MAS has emphasized the originality of its policies. Such MAS catchwords as *newness, freshness,* and *discovery* capture the idea that the party is embarking on an untrodden course. Thus, for instance, following the 1973 elections MAS boasted that "*for the first time* a party with a well defined policy" in opposition to capitalism had come in third place in national elections. MAS also stated that up until then "a socialist opposition has *never* existed."[94] During this period MAS began to use the slogan "the *new* majority" to describe its efforts to reach out beyond the traditional clientele of the left. Referring to the strategy laid out in "A New Mode of Being Socialist," Freddy Muñoz commented that *"for the first time* in the political history of the nation, socialism has been incorporated into the political culture" (italics added).[95]

MAS's emphasis on originality can be seen as part of its New Left inheritance and also as a legacy of the generational conflict in Venezuela in the 1960s, which led to the formation of MAS. The New Left had attempted to engage in new forms of struggle based on a totally new outlook and so discarded past issues as irrelevant. Petkoff shared this ahistorical perspective and argued, at the time of the formation of MAS, that Venezuela had entered a new stage in which such traditional leftist strategies as popular frontism and the "revolution of national liberation" prior to socialism had become obsolete. MAS's attraction to the idea that it represented something new and unique led it to examine and revise its positions constantly and to undergo radical changes in an effort to strike out in new directions.

MAS's style was influenced by the New Left and the youth movement of the 1960s in two other respects. In the first place, its attempt to be direct and straightforward was to a certain extent a throwback to the 1960s, when young people considered these attributes a prime virtue. Thus, for instance, in the 1983 campaign MAS asserted that "Teodoro [Petkoff] says what he thinks and accompanies his words with action."[96] In the second place, MAS's optimism regarding the short- and medium-range possibilities of socialism in Venezuela reflected the same voluntarism that led young leftists in Venezuela to take up arms in the 1960s. This confidence about the future was embodied in the MAS slogan "Indeed We Can" (*si se puede*).

MASistas have not viewed the "New Mode of Being Socialist" as a mandate for a sharp transformation in the party's style, but rather a call for the reexamination of practices and an ongoing effort to grasp the nation's political culture. This vision was reinforced by MAS's follow-up statement to the New Mode document, known as the "Declaration-80," which was debated at MAS's national convention in 1980. In a self-criticism of the party's attempts at innovation since the 1973 elections, the document stated: "Far from considering that the ideas laid out in the New Mode of Being Socialist have already completed their mission, we believe that it has become urgent to develop a new consciousness with regard to their significance and to make a new effort much more concentrated than before to . . . facilitate the insertion of our message in the popular conscience."[97]

The Declaration-80 conceded that the consolidation of Venezuelan democracy since 1958 had produced significant political gains but added that the process was incomplete. As a remedy, the document advocated reforms encompassing judicial, legislative, and executive authorities and announced the party's willingness to support any nonsocialist government that promoted democratization and social change.[98] The Declaration-80 set the tone for MAS's participation in the 1983 elections. The institutional reforms advocated by the document became formal proposals in the campaign of Petkoff, MAS's presidential candidate. Themes related to democracy, which MAS began to emphasize following the 1973 elections, now overshadowed the party's socialist message.

Many of the slogans MAS devised for the 1983 elections had vague meanings, for example, "For a Venezuela Which Is Necessary" (*una venezuela necesaria*) and "Change," which became MAS's main catchword in the campaign. In addition, MAS stressed Petkoff's unattachment to powerful economic interests, his history of personal sacrifice, and the fact that he had never shared power and thus could not be held responsible for the nation's problems.[99] This emphasis on honesty, independence, and commitment to democracy at the expense of socioeconomic definitions was illustrated by a card that was distributed during the campaign. It displayed a colored photograph of Petkoff on one side and a capsule statement of what he represented on the other:

> I believe in Liberty. The change in Venezuela which democracy should guarantee is the right of free thought, [and] the certainty that jails are for delinquents and not for those who struggle for their ideas.
>
> I have fought against dictatorships and against injustice and for that reason am an ardent enemy of all repression. I situate myself in a position against capitalism, which promotes and protects dictatorships, and against the Soviet regime which concedes privileges to a minority and imposes the absolute power of a party which is increasingly totalitarian. . . .
>
> I believe in the greatness of Venezuela. This country can put itself together and be an example for the world. This is the nation . . . which I am sure of reaching.[100]

MAS has attached much importance to the development of effective publicity techniques, and for this purpose the party's National Commission of Propaganda has organized work sessions known as Jornadas Nacionales de Propaganda. Because of its considerable influence in intellectual circles, the party has been able to rely on many talented and even nationally prominent photographers, painters, and journalists. MAS's Jacobo Borges, an internationally recognized artist, as well as Pedro Zapata and Régulo Pérez, worked on street murals in the 1973 and 1978 presidential campaigns, which were masterpieces in their own right. Unlike AD, COPEI, and several smaller establishment parties, MAS refuses to hire U.S. electoral publicity advisors and prints "Made in Venezuela" in small letters on campaign material.[101]

MAS's relations with the nation's main national dailies were particularly poor. Members of MAS's propaganda team who worked in the 1983 campaign complained that *El Nacional,* whose co-owner Miguel Otero Silva maintained close relations with the Communist Party, provided the Rangel candidacy with more extensive coverage than it did Petkoff's.[102] To protest this unfair treatment, MAS at one point ceased sending press releases to that newspaper. In addition, *Diario de Caracas,* which alloted Petkoff considerable space, played up MAS's internal problems and gave its journalist Pastor Heydra, a former MAS student leader (and ex-president of the FCU at the UCV) who left the party embittered, complete liberty to smear the party.

MAS attempted to compensate for this liability by putting out its own periodicals. Its greatest efforts were in the mid-1970s with the publication of the daily *Punto;* various magazines including *Para la Acción* and *Reflexiones,* which contained analytical and highly original articles; and newsletters published by the MAS fractions of different labor and professional organizations. In subsequent years these efforts tapered off, until the 1983 elections, when the party resumed publication of a weekly magazine entitled *Seminario.*

MAS's leftist critics such as Moisés Moleiro in his *Izquierda y su proceso* (which was a response to Petkoff's *Proceso a la izquierda*) belittle the party's stylistic refinement on grounds that it represented mere technical improvements based on emulation of the parties of the establishment. MAS responded by claiming that its publicity techniques were designed to reach people at their own level and to draw on the nation's cultural symbols, and thus could not be dismissed as nonsense or sophistry.[103]

The modifications in MAS's style following the New Mode of Being Socialist document in 1974 were advantageous to the party in some respects and disadvantageous in others. On the positive side, the party countered the stereotype of leftists as intransigent and excessively critical, at the same time that it continued to adhere to socialism. That MAS made less frequent reference to socialism in the

1983 campaign than in the previous two did not mean that it had abandoned its commitment to the system. Changing the party's style and searching for new ways to reach large numbers of people who were up to then unreceptive to leftist ideas did not necessarily entail sacrificing the party's long-range goals.

On the negative side, MAS failed to uphold its previous image of staunch critic of the ruling elite and the capitalist system. By frequently praising the government and offering constructive criticism in place of virulent attacks, MAS was outflanked not only by the other parties of the left but by AD and COPEI when they were in the opposition. MAS's soft-line approach was initiated during the administration of Carlos Andrés Pérez when a wide range of popular reforms were implemented and general prosperity set in. MAS's policy was perhaps compatible with the general mood of the times. It was less fitting, however, in the 1980s, when economic contraction, largely the result of falling oil prices, triggered widespread discontent. In this new context MAS was considered by many to be too compliant and therefore unsuited to play a leading role in the defense of popular interests.

Conclusion

MAS has always stressed commitment to ideology and its diffusion to large numbers of Venezuelans. During the party's early years the MASistas infused their propaganda with an anticapitalist and socialist message, whereas after the 1973 elections they began to play up their democratic convictions. MAS's commitment to ideological purity and openness regarding its long-term objectives has been contradicted in practice in a fundamental way. The MASistas since even before the founding of MAS have displayed a keen sense of pragmatism and political realism. As PCV dissidents, they feigned adherence to communism and engineered the split in the party in the name of Communist unity. Later, the New Mode document led MASistas to submerge certain beliefs and practices and eliminate others in order to reach people at their own level. During the 1983 electoral campaign, MAS leaders put forward proposals to fortify the nation's democratic structures in part because they appreciated the necessity of—in the words of Petkoff—"defining the struggle according to the values accepted by the majority . . . [and] no political value in Venezuela is as important as that of democracy."[104] Finally, MAS's effort to perfect its style and employ well-established cultural symbols could not help but reshape the party's message.

The MASistas have also emphasized the originality of their ideas. As has been suggested in this chapter, to a certain extent this claim is exaggerated; MAS borrowed heavily from Eurocommunist and New Leftist movements. The MASistas not only prided themselves on the thoroughness of their search for new ideas, but on their party's internal democracy, which facilitated the search. As a result, MAS's positions were in constant flux. As has been shown, MAS's attitudes toward U.S. imperialism, the role of social classes in the revolutionary process, the nationalization of industry, and the short-term prospects of socialism were thoroughly revised during its fifteen-year history. Furthermore, these and other issues were the source of conflicting public statements by party leaders. This ambiguity and indefiniteness could not help but undermine MAS's ideological cohesiveness.

In short, MAS's effort to win people over to its ideological formulations was flawed in two respects. First, the MASistas revised certain positions that they felt the majority of Venezuelans could not understand or were not ready to accept. At times their behavior bordered on sophistry in that they seemed to be more concerned with perfecting the art of persuasion than engaging in ideological struggle. MAS paid heavily for this apparent deceptiveness; in public opinion polls MAS leaders scored lower in honesty and sincerity than spokesmen of other parties on the left.[105] Second, MAS failed to achieve ideological clarity in spite of the importance it assigned to the realm of ideas. The problem was compounded by the tendency of MAS leaders to publicly contradict the official party position. This lack of cohesiveness detracted from MAS's ability to attract and retain the support of leftists who looked askance at the party's ideological vacillation and lack of firmness.

5 MAS and Unity of the Left: A Comparative Perspective

Unity of the Left in Venezuelan History

The efforts of Venezuelan leftists to devise a strategy of interparty alliances have been a major source of debate and conflict on the left ever since the founding of the first modern political organizations in 1936. Ever since 1936 the left has been confronted repeatedly with new challenges related to interparty relations. A small sample of these disputes will serve to highlight the history of the polemic and to show how elusive the goal of unity has been. In 1936 the fusion of various political organizations into the "Single Party of the Left" provoked intense discussion over whether leftists should openly call for socialism. The recently founded AD and a PCV legal front group formed a joint slate for the municipal elections in Caracas in 1942 and then squabbled over the planning and carrying out of the campaign, in the process seriously embittering relations between the two left-wing organizations. The PCV's call for mass mobilizations in defense of the AD government of Rómulo Gallegos shortly before the November 1948 coup drew conflicting responses from the governing party.[1] During the early years of the Pérez Jiménez regime, mutual suspicion between the PCV and AD undermined united action, and only after 1954 did they attempt to set up a common front against the dictatorship. And in the 1960s the clandestine PCV and MIR tried to convince the various parties of the moderate left to unite behind one candidate for the 1963 presidential elections on a platform of civil liberties, but these efforts to promote unity were rejected, not only at the time but in subsequent years.[2]

Since 1936 leftist opposition to unity has come from two sources, what can be called a *left position* and a *right position*. The *left position* spurns alliances with the nonsocialist (or moderate) left, whereas the *right position* avoids formal arrangements with certain parties on the far left. These terms can be best illustrated by considering examples of attitudes and agreements between the socialist and nonsocialist left throughout Venezuelan history and in other historical contexts. Since the founding of AD in 1941 until 1958 (when it could no longer be considered part of the Venezuelan left), Rómulo Betancourt was that party's leading exponent of the *right position* regarding unity of the left. In the late 1930s Betancourt had proposed to his closest followers that they challenge their main leftist rival, the PCV, on ideological grounds without relying on heavily charged anti-Communist rhetoric. Betancourt, however, subsequently went against this pledge of moderation by harshly lashing out at the Communists. He rejected unity with the PCV on grounds that it was a politically insignificant organization and thus any agreement with it would pay but limited dividends that would hardly compensate for the risks incurred. Betancourt feared that an alliance with the Communists would tarnish AD's image as a nationalistic party since it would be associating itself with the foremost champions of the Soviet Union in Venezuela.

Betancourt called on his trade union followers in 1944 to leave PCV-dominated unions and set up parallel structures, a policy he defended with the slogan "to divide is to locate." The phrase implied that Venezuelan workers should be given the opportunity to choose between clearly identified AD and PCV labor organizations. According to Betancourt's line of reasoning, AD could gain control of the labor movement if it were careful to maintain its separate identity, in which case workers would decide between its labor leaders and Communist ones on the basis of ideological rather than trade union issues.[3] This argument was typical of the *right position* of other periods, when leaders of the moderate left opposed alliances with the far left out of fear that such agreements would blur ideological differences, to their own natural disadvantage. In short, those who adhere to the *right position* are moderate leftists who are apprehensive of being discredited by association with Communists and other "authoritarian" Marxists.

The *left position* was typified by the PRP(C) during its brief existence of 1947–52 (as discussed in chapter 2). PRP(C) leaders refused to work within the AD-dominated Confederation of Workers of Venezuela (CTV) on grounds that it was undemocratic and instead established their own parallel labor organizations. At the time of the November 1948 coup the PRP(C) refused to rally to the defense of the leftist AD government of Rómulo Gallegos, which it considered to be a tool of U.S. imperialism.[4] In general, the *left position* of groups like the PRP(C) spurned unity with the moderate sector of the leftist camp (in this case,

AD) on grounds that those parties were amenable to the interests of the ruling class. In addition, those who defended the *left position* emphasized their party's far-reaching socioeconomic objectives while disdaining the reformism of the moderate left.

Unity of the Left in Other Nations

The most systematic supporter of the *left position* for decades was the Trotskyist movement, with its miniscule constituent parties in almost all countries throughout the world. In the 1930s Trotsky and his followers in Spain and elsewhere fought against the Comintern line known as "popular frontism," whereby Communists united with the nonsocialist left in order to halt the spread of fascism. The Trotskyists criticized the Communists for making major concessions to their nonsocialist allies by basing the alliance on a moderate reformist platform rather than a revolutionary one. The configuration of the left in most nations where popular fronts were formed undoubtedly influenced Communist policy. The moderate left generally enjoyed widespread electoral support, and it was thus logical that unity would be based on terms favorable to its interests.

By the time of the founding of MAS in 1971, however, a new correlation of forces less favorable to the moderates had emerged in Venezuela and most other nations. This situation became evident in Chile at the time of the formation of the Unidad Popular (UP) coalition that brought Salvador Allende to power in 1970. The Communist Party of Chile as well as many sectors of the Socialist Party favored inviting nonsocialist groups to join the coalition in order to tip the delicate balance of electoral power in favor of the left. This strategy was opposed by a sector of the Socialist Party headed by secretary general Raúl Ampuero, who felt that inclusion of the moderate leftist Radical Party and factions of the Christian democratic movement in the alliance would undermine its socialist content. Ampuero left the Socialist Party to found the Socialist Popular Union on the basis of a purely socialist program.

The conflict between Ampuero and the UP over the policy that socialists should pursue toward the moderate left differed from the clash between Communists and Trotskyists in the 1930s in Chile and elsewhere. The moderate left in Chile in 1970, typified by the Radicals, was a junior partner in the coalition and was dwarfed by the Socialist and Communist parties. In contrast, the Popular Front coalition that came to power in 1938 in Chile was led by a much larger Radical Party (which, as in 1970, represented the moderate left) and included the Communist and Socialist parties to its left.

Thus in 1970 the nonsocialist or moderate left was not likely to wield considerable influence within the leftist coalition, as it had in 1938. For this reason, the UP program in 1970 was much bolder than that of the popular front period of the 1930s and even envisioned structural reforms leading to socialism.[5]

MAS's Positions on Unity of the Left

These examples of the *right* and *left positions* are useful for understanding MAS's relations with both the moderate and socialist left. Throughout its history MAS has been reluctant, if not loath, to unite with other parties close to it on the political spectrum. At the time of its founding MAS assumed a *left position* with regard to intraleft relations, a stand similar to those of the PRP(C) and Raúl Ampuero. By the mid-1970s the party, though not completely abandoning the *left position* arguments, adopted the *right position* in opposition to unity of the left.

The experiences of young Venezuelan Communists (the future MASistas) after 1958 shaped their negative attitude toward alliances with parties to their right and accounted for their *left position* during MAS's early years. Petkoff and other PCVistas of his generation were retrospectively critical of their party's support for interparty unity in 1958, which was aimed at consolidating the nation's fledgling democracy. The young Communists asserted that the PCV should have channeled the effervescent mass movement on a radical course rather than complying with a tacit agreement with other parties to its right in order to maintain order. In the 1960s Petkoff and other PCVistas were disappointed at the timid efforts of the moderate left to halt government repression aimed at the guerrilla movement. After years of infighting that undermined its effectiveness, the moderate left by the end of the decade finally engaged in discussions of unity that the orthodox PCV leaders were anxious to encourage. The young Communists, on the other hand, criticized these plans as based on electoral rather than programmatic objectives, and were skeptical of the intentions of the moderate leftists.[6] These misgivings were expressed in 1970 by Petkoff and Freddy Muñoz in their *Socialismo para Venezuela?* and *Revolución sin dogma,* both published in the heat of the PCV's internal debate. Petkoff attacked the popular front strategy as giving the enemy a "respite," and Muñoz wrote that the parties to the PCV's right were characterized by "opportunism and sham politics."[7]

MAS inherited this *left position* critique of unity and from the outset spurned the electoral talks initiated by the moderate leftists by announcing its intentions to run its own candidate for the 1973 presidential elections on an explicitly socialist program. The MASistas emphasized the socialist content of their message, a policy incompatible with electoral cooperation with the nonsocialist left.[8] They maintained that interparty agreements among socialist and nonsocialist leftist parties invariably suffered from "programmatic indefinition and vacillations at the moment of confronting the system."[9]

MAS's opposition to interparty unity in its early years was reflected in its conceptualization of its role as a "movement of movements." According to this idea, MAS should be more of a movement than a party, amorphous and ample enough to attract militants of other parties without obliging them to renounce their party membership. This strategy was based on the realization that the nation's two main political organizations, AD and COPEI, were mass parties that had succeeded in instilling in their members a deepseated loyalty and identification. If MAS was to become truly a "new majority," as it proposed, it had to recognize this national reality by reaching out to the rank and file of AD and COPEI. The movement-of-movements concept thus envisioned unity at the base of the establishment parties (referred to in other contexts as the "united front from below") and in doing so ruled out unity from above in the form of interparty alliances.[10]

The correlation of forces consisting of center, moderate left, and socialist left changed significantly by the mid-1970s, leading to MAS's shift from a *left* to *right position* on interparty unity. The moderate left ceased to represent a viable alternative or to play a significant role, either in elections or politics in general. Parties that had occupied that space in the 1960s redefined their positions and veered either to the left or the right. Thus the Fuerza Democrática Popular (FDP) supported COPEI's candidate in the 1973 and 1978 presidential contests, as did the URD in 1978, while another party of the moderate left, the MEP, radicalized its stands by embracing an explicitly socialist doctrine. Meanwhile, although the electoral showing of the socialist left (the PCV, MIR, MAS, etc.) was not particularly impressive, its presence in the universities and, to a lesser extent, in the labor movement as well as its prodigious literary output made it an important pole of attraction. The falling out of the moderate left in the 1970s fortified both the socialist left and the center. Thus the combined vote of the moderate left (consisting of the Partido Revolucionario Nacionalista, FDP, MEP, and URD) was 28 percent in the 1968 congressional elections while five years later that sector (consisting only of URD) received a mere 3 percent. The socialist left (represented by the PCV), on the other hand, in 1968 received 3 percent while five years later the socialist parties (now consisting of the PCV, MIR, MAS, and MEP) polled 12 percent.

As a result of this reconfiguration, popular frontism, in which the socialist left plays a subordinate role in an alliance with the moderate left, was no longer a plausible option. The *left position*, which attacked the popular-front strategy as a sellout to the moderate left, thus lost its relevance. In rejecting leftist unity, MAS continued to attack popular frontism but it had in effect become a straw man, whose image was conjured up for the sake of argument.

By the mid-1970s MAS's target in opposing unity of the left shifted from the moderate left to parties like the PCV, which were fully committed to socialism (see figure 5-1). MAS turned down proposals for a united left candidacy for the 1978 presidential election, as it had for that of 1973, and actually rejected support offered by other leftist parties for its own candidate. In doing so, the MASistas embraced a *right position*. MAS began to stress the democratic side of socialism as well as its commitment to a neutral foreign policy. Like Betancourt, who also maintained a *right position* in the 1940s, the MASistas feared that an alliance with the PCV—with its pro-Moscow line and adherence to "totalitarian socialism"—would create confusion regarding their party's professed goals of democracy and nonalignment in foreign affairs. In short, the thrust of MAS's argument against interparty unity during its early years was that it would detract from the achievement of radical objectives (that is, it took the *left position*) but by the mid-1970s MAS's main concern was maintaining a democratic and neutral image, which association with certain socialist parties ran the risk of undermining (the *right position*).

Another aspect of MAS's relations with other parties on the left by the mid-1970s recalls Betancourt's *right position*. Shortly after severing ties with the Communist movement in 1937, Betancourt favored carrying out an open debate with the PCV devoid of anti-Communist rhetoric, a pledge he did not live up to in subsequent years. Similarly, after leaving the PCV, the MASistas refused to engage the Communists in petty bickering and later called for airing differences with the rest of the left without resorting to "scandalous attacks."[11] In practice, however, MAS frequently attacked leftist adversaries in personal terms. Not only were Communists lambasted for their loyalty to the Soviet Union, but MEP leaders were criticized for their past membership in AD and for being "old-time leftists."

MAS's negative attitude, at times contempt, toward other socialist parties was related to another aspect of MAS's reorientation in the mid-1970s. MAS leaders scrapped the movement-of-movements concept and began to emphasize the need to fortify MAS as a party. Rather than viewing a broadly based movement as the main vehicle of social change, MASistas underlined the importance of the political party.

1973 ELECTIONS

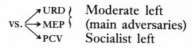

Parties to the Right of MAS

MAS (left position)   vs. URD ⎱ Moderate left
                                  MEP ⎰ (main adversaries)
                                  PCV   Socialist left

1978 AND 1983 ELECTIONS

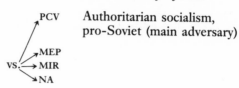

Parties to the Left of MAS

                              PCV   Authoritarian socialism,
                                    pro-Soviet (main adversary)

MAS (right position)   vs. MEP
                                   MIR
                                   NA

Figure 5-1 MAS's Position among Leftist Parties
in Three Presidential Elections

The nation's political culture, it was maintained, had reserved a dominant role for parties through which all important change had been channeled.

According to this new outlook, of all parties in Venezuela MAS represented the nation's only hope for achieving true socialism. MAS's slogans "Venezuela Needs a MAS Government," "Now It's Time for MAS to Govern," and "To Be a Patriot Is to Belong to MAS" recalled the equally divisive phrase coined by the Alianza Popular Revolucionaria Americana (APRA) during that party's early years: "Only APRA Will Save Peru." The MASistas argued that the highly amorphous state of the rest of the left, with its host of miniscule parties, limited its possibilities. The position of the left would be greatly strengthened if it were exclusively represented by its largest party, namely, MAS. Indeed, the MASistas talked of the need to create an electoral "tripolarity," in which the electoral options would be limited to AD, COPEI, and MAS.

In at least one respect MAS was consistent throughout the decade. The MASistas never abandoned the conviction that the rest of the Venezuelan left in all its varieties (both the moderate and socialist left) was unsuited for the task of achieving true socialism. They viewed their leftist rivals as tied to a long-standing political strategy that had never proved successful in Venezuela. The MASistas had faith in their own capacity to lead the struggle on the basis of new ideas and a thorough break with the past. This optimism had always characterized the two generations of Communists who had come of political age immediately before and after the overthrow of Pérez Jiménez in 1958, and who now formed the backbone of MAS's leadership. Such an outlook was considered arrogant by MAS's leftist rivals. Thus, underlying the varied and somewhat contradictory arguments against unity based on the *left* and *right positions* was MAS's hostility toward fellow leftists that stemmed from a generational resentment against the "old left" that had failed to establish itself as a major force in the nation. This disdain would mean that, even at moments when MAS considered the possibility of joining in a leftist alliance, it was highly unlikely that enduring unity would result.

The 1973 electoral campaign represented a watershed in recent Venezuelan history. The heated issues of government repression and amnesty for political prisoners, which were the focus of public attention in the violence-ridden 1960s, were largely left behind. The two major presidential candidates, Carlos Andrés Pérez of AD and Lorenzo Fernández of COPEI, proposed that the government play a strong interventionist role in the economy to promote rapid economic growth, and both hinted that the state might run the oil industry in the not-too-distant future. Both these pledges were fulfilled by President Pérez (1974–79), who took advantage of the windfall in oil revenue derived from the sharp increase in oil prices in the months following his election.

The left put up two presidential candidates. Jesús Paz Galarraga, who had been AD's secretary general in the 1960s and who spearheaded the split in 1967 that gave rise to MEP, was nominated by the New Force. Besides MEP, the Paz candidacy had the support of the PCV as well as a sizable group of renowned independent leftist intellectuals. The other candidate, the independent José Vicente Rangel, was endorsed by MAS and, after gaining legal status in 1972, MIR.

The New Force was initiated by the moderate leftist parties—MEP, URD, and FDP—in an attempt to avoid a repetition of the disappointing results of the 1963 and 1968 presidential elections, when competing moderate candidates splintered the vote of the moderate constituency. Inspired by the election of Salvador Allende in 1970, the moderates attempted to broaden the base of the New Force to include the entire left by accepting the PCV. The inclusion of the Communists radicalized the New Force and opened up encouraging prospects for broad-based unity for the 1973 elections and beyond.

The leftist drift of the New Force, particularly the participation of the Communists, was rejected by many moderate leftists, who instead opted to support either AD or COPEI candidates. The FDP refrained from formally joining the New Force and ended up backing COPEI's candidate in return for leading positions in that party's congressional slates. Most of those moderates who endorsed the AD candidate had previously left that party in divisions that had occurred in 1962 and 1967. Raúl Ramos Giménez, who had led the 1962 split, chafed at the "numerous ideological somersaults and unjustified changes in position"[1] of the moderates and proceeded to draw close to AD, before he unexpectedly passed away in early 1973. Other defections occurred in MEP, though on an individual basis rather than all at once. Many MEPistas rejected unity of the left and called on their party to abandon the New Force after the other moderate parties had withdrawn from the coalition. They favored the nomination of MEP president Luis Beltrán Prieto Figueroa as candidate, and, as had occurred in 1968, the exclusion of Communists from participation in the campaign.[2]

The URD left the coalition following the New Force's convention in July 1972, when Paz was selected over URD's standard-bearer, Jóvito Villalba. The balance of power for nominating the presidential candidate at the convention was held by a group of independent leftist delegates who were selected by the coalition's constituent parties, the URD, MEP, and PCV. Enough of the PCV-chosen "independents" voted for Paz to tip the balance in his favor. Although Villalba pledged himself at the close of the convention to work diligently in favor of the Paz candidacy, he was later won over to withdrawal by URD leaders who had been loath to cooperate with the Communists from the beginning. These URDistas accused Paz's supporters of foul play at the convention in the form of a secret pact between the PCV and MEP in favor of Paz. This charge may have been based on fact, but Villalba's history of clashes with the PCV, particularly during the period of guerrilla warfare, made it probable that the Communist-appointed independents would have sided with Paz in any case, with or without instructions from the PCV.

The emergence and radicalization of the New Force was a promising development for the left. The formation of similar alliances in Chile and Uruguay in recent years pointed to a new strategy based on electoral unity embodying far-reaching objectives. In Venezuela until then, unity had been so frequently espoused but then frustrated by the course of events that its achievement now seemed like a long-awaited, momentous event. The New Force united the PCV with the most "advanced" leaders of the moderate left, who spurned the anticommunism preached by some of their party companions. The coalition's platform called for "democratic-socialist actions and transformations" upon gaining power, including the nationalization of basic industry. The New Force's program was thus more radical and broader in scope than any previous electoral pact in the nation's history.

The unity the New Force embodied began to extend itself beyond mere electoral objectives. In labor organizations and universities the PCV joined the parties of the moderate left in electoral slates, some of which bore the name "New Force." "Popular Committees of the New Force" were also established in slum dwellings to lead the struggle around grass-roots issues. Unity, however, was not forthcoming in all student and labor organizations. In the case of the steel workers' union in the Guayana region, ATISS, the PCV tried to capitalize on its considerable support by running its own candidates for the elections in April 1971, after being excluded from the slate led by a MEPista and backed by URD and FDP. Where the PCV did not enjoy significant backing and was left out of the moderate grouping, as in the Medical Federation of Venezuela, the Communists refused to support any slate. (Throughout the period under study the national leaderships of leftist parties—such as those of the New Force—have generally refrained from imposing policies regarding alliances on their fractions in individual worker and student organizations. Nevertheless, unity from above has usually been reflected in interparty agreements at lower levels.)

MAS's selection of its own presidential candidate in opposition to the New Force was the organization's first important decision, made shortly after its birth in January 1971. Given the groundswell of enthusiasm for the New Force and its radicalization, MAS's rejection of unity was a bold move. MAS's secretary general, Pompeyo Márquez, expressed doubts regarding its advisability but was quickly won over to the idea.[3] One argument in favor of launching a separate MAS candidate was that it was imperative for MAS's survival as a recently founded organization to project its own image, rather than throwing its lot in with the more well-established parties of the New Force.[4] Throughout the campaign MAS viewed the New Force as a timid opposition, though this argument lost cogency once the coalition began to offer far-reaching solutions.[5]

The MASistas differentiated themselves from the New Force, in spite of its move to the left, by explicitly denouncing capitalism and stressing their own commitment to socialism. Some of MAS's statements left the impression that it was advocating the immediate implantation of socialism, though this intention was denied by the party.

MAS's constant reference to socialism was meant to correct the traditional leftist practice of focusing on the gloomy and negative features of society and its problems without leaving room for hope. MAS frequently attacked members of the Venezuelan bourgeoisie by name, and its newspaper *Bravo Pueblo* published articles detailing the histories and life style of individual capitalists. Such slogans as "the poor to power, the rich to the sewers" were also intended to dramatize MAS's message.[6]

MAS's program was more far-reaching than that of the New Force. MAS called for government takeover of the enterprises of the nation's twenty largest "supermillionaires."[7] In addition, the party attempted to go beyond the proposal for nationalizing the oil industry that the New Force and even URD candidates put forward. The MASistas claimed that nationalization in itself was no longer a truly revolutionary slogan, as imperialism had learned to work around and even benefit from government takeovers. Thus MAS advocated the "socialization" of the oil industry whereby its structure and policies would be designed to directly benefit the general populace.

MAS's emphasis on the struggle against capitalism contrasted with the New Force's anti-imperialist focus. The MASistas felt that the general populace could more readily grasp the perniciousness of individual Venezuelan capitalists than it could that of a remotely based imperialist system.[8] On a theoretical level MAS defended its approach by denying that the overthrow of imperialism was a prior stage to—or was more urgent than—the establishment of socialism. MAS's subordination of the anti-imperialist message and its emphatic support for a neutral, as against pro-Soviet, foreign policy held implications that would become evident in future years when the party softened its stand toward the United States and downplayed the struggle against imperialism.

The nomination of José Vicente Rangel as MAS's presidential candidate was a fortunate choice that gave the party an advantage over its rivals in the New Force. Unlike the uninspiring Paz Galarraga, Rangel possessed considerable charisma. In making their selection, the MASistas took into account the fact that Rangel represented the type of Venezuelan that their party was trying to win over. In the 1960s Rangel had been a leading member of the URD and then (after his expulsion in 1964) the Partido Revolucionario de Integración Nacionalista (PRIN), both of which belonged to the nonsocialist moderate left. Since the dissolution of PRIN, Rangel had retained his status as an independent. With this background Rangel seemed to embody the "emerging currents," which the MASistas talked of in reference to those Venezuelans whose outlooks had been shaped by mainstream politics, but who now were coming around to accepting socialism.[9] Furthermore, Rangel, as a moderate leftist, had never succumbed to the anticommunism of many of his party companions. Indeed, as a national deputy, Rangel had gained recognition for his exposure of the assassination of Communist guerrilla leader Alberto Lovera at the hands of Digepol, the military police unit.[10] Rangel was so highly regarded by the left that he was invited to address one of the plenums of the PCV's Central Committee in 1970, where he made an impassioned plea for the preservation of party unity.

MAS's reluctance to reach an understanding with other leftist parties either on behalf of its own candidate or else a commonly designated one was also characteristic of its attitude in the two subsequent presidential elections in 1978 and 1983. With URD's withdrawal from the New Force and MEP's acceptance of an explicitly socialist program for the Paz candidacy, an agreement with MAS became a definite possibility. The New Force's leftist course seemed to invalidate MAS's arguments against unity, which rested on the need to emphasize radical solutions. MAS, however, was not even receptive to the New Force's call for formal conversations about the possible withdrawal of both candidates and support for a mutually accepted independent. As in 1978 and 1983, MAS vacillated toward the rest of the left and made only half-hearted efforts to establish a dialogue. MAS waited until mid-1973 to agree to enter negotiations with MEP but failed to indicate whether it was willing to talk with the PCV.

The New Force's fervent support for unity was applauded by a large group of independent leftists who ended up backing Paz. Miguel Otero Silva, the renowned writer and co-owner of the nation's leading daily, *El Nacional,* typified the attitude of other independents. Otero Silva announced that he was endorsing Paz because the New Force had staunchly defended unity. An active participant in leftist politics for nearly fifty years, Otero Silva somewhat nostalgically reviewed the left's historic efforts to achieve unity. According to him, the unity put into practice in 1936 and 1958 had been limited to agreements from above involving party leaders, but now the New Force represented a more all-encompassing commitment that took in the rank and file.[11]

In addition to their stormy relations with the New Force, the MAS-istas failed to develop a working rapport with MIR, which supported the candidacy of José Vicente Rangel. During the campaign MIR publicly complained of the unfair treatment it received from the MASistas. In *Tiempo de verdades,* published shortly before the 1973 elections, Rangel denied that MAS monopolized his candidacy, which he claimed was open to other parties.[12] Rangel's attitude created discomfort among some MAS leaders, who insisted that MAS exercise even greater control over the campaign. They claimed that Rangel was a MASista candidate in spite of his independent status and opposed MIR's use of its own banners and slogans at election rallies.

The 1973 elections initiated a period of two-party dominance in Venezuelan politics, which contrasted sharply with the fragmentation and small pluralities that characterized national elections in the 1960s. AD and COPEI received over 85 percent of the vote, a situation that was to be repeated in the presidential contests of 1978 and 1983. During these years the electorate was virtually polarized between AD and COPEI; many Venezuelans who sympathized with the smaller parties were carried away in the heat of the campaign to vote for one of the two larger ones with a realistic chance of winning. The left could not help but be influenced by this new national reality. In the 1960s leftists had denounced political and labor leaders of AD and COPEI for being tools of U.S. imperialism and lacking popular support. The success of both parties after 1973 induced the left, and MAS in particular, to tone down its rhetoric and look for ways to emulate their style. The electoral strategy of the MASistas was designed to break the polarization of the electorate between AD and COPEI by convincing voters that MAS represented a viable alternative and was prepared to govern in the not-too-distant future.

MAS's showing in the 1973 national elections represented a modest success, considering the recentness of the party's founding and the generally adverse state in which the left found itself following the guerrilla fiasco. MAS's 5.3 percent of the congressional vote compared favorably to MEP's 5.0, as well as the 1.2 and 1.0 of the PCV and MIR, respectively (see table 6-1). Rangel, who undoubtedly attracted a large number of votes for MAS's congressional slates, was nevertheless outpolled by Paz, 5.1 percent to 4.3 percent. The electoral results were far below the party's general expectations, which one leftist commentator calculated to be about 13 percent, or two and a half times greater than what the party actually received.[13]

MASistas have generally viewed electoral results as a basic measuring rod that determines the correctness of the party's positions. This attitude is undoubtedly related to the party's emphasis on the quest for power and its criticism of the PCV and other leftist parties for practically abandoning hope of ever governing. The MASistas have always harshly criticized the traditional left for working within a political ghetto, whereby leftist parties vie for the support of those who have always identified with the left without striving to win over a majority, let alone an overwhelming majority, of the population. A consistent improvement in MAS's electoral showing is seen as proof

Table 6-1　Results of National Elections of 1973

Major parties and presidential candidates	Percentage of votes	Deputies elected
Left		
MAS	5.3	9
MEP	5.0	8
MIR	1.0	1
PCV	1.2	2
URD	3.2	5
Center		
AD	44.4	102
COPEI	30.2	64
Right		
CCN*	4.3	7
Left		
Paz	5.1	
Rangel	4.3	
Villalba	3.1	
Center		
Fernández	36.7	
Pérez	48.7	

*Cruzada Cívica Nacionalista.

that the party is avoiding following in the footsteps of this moribund traditional left. This outlook, however, has definite pitfalls in that the relative success of a given policy cannot be measured solely on the basis of its short-term acceptance among voters. Party stands can be rejected in an upcoming election but be proven correct in the long run, either at the polls or in another context.

MAS's tendency to dwell on the significance of electoral returns became strikingly clear in Petkoff's *Proceso a la izquierda*, where he devoted considerable space to diagnosing each party's vote in the 1973 contests. Petkoff emphasized MAS's superior showing over the PCV and MEP in the congressional election, although MAS's edge over the latter party was slight. For Petkoff, MAS's vote in comparison to that of the PCV was a clear vindication of the positions that he and other dissident Communists had assumed at the time of the 1970 division. MEP was also singled out because its sharp electoral decline reinforced Petkoff's argument that the traditional left was doomed to stagnation, if not virtual disappearance. Petkoff wrote that MEP, in spite of having greater financial resources at its disposal, received fewer congressional votes than MAS because it "relied on a rhetoric which the left—in all its variants which bridge an arch which extends from the PCV to the Trotskyists and includes MIR, the Bandera Roja [a guerrilla organization] and distinct university groupings—had saturated the country with during the last forty years. This was not what the young Venezuela wanted to hear." Petkoff went on to state that MAS's participation in the elections "presented the opportunity to prove whether an unmistakably revolutionary socialist force could leave the leftist ghetto and initiate the struggle to win over the masses to socialism."[14]

The empirical approach of Petkoff and other MAS leaders in arguing for the viability of their policies on the basis of electoral results would prove to be risky. In the two subsequent presidential elections, 1978 and 1983, MAS failed to make substantial inroads, and in the second of these contests the party's percentage declined. The 1983 "calamity," as those elections were called, produced considerable disillusionment among MASistas. Similar frustration would have prevailed in any party whose vote was so far below its expectations. What made the blow especially severe in the case of MAS was that for the previous ten years party members had been convinced that the most cogent argument in favor of MAS's policies was success at the polls. MASistas were thus unprepared for the disappointing returns, which influenced some of them to abandon the party and others to call for a thorough revision of its policies.

Although MAS leaders viewed the party's showing in the 1973 elections as a partial triumph, they were not completely satisfied with the results. Their reexamination of their policies and self-criticisms following the elections brought about a profound modification in the party's policies and conduct. Now MAS moderated and refined its rhetoric, expressed an open hostility toward orthodox Communism, and showed a willingness to support and even cooperate with AD and COPEI in order to achieve specific objectives. The necessity for these changes was accepted by almost all MAS leaders, a consensus that was especially surprising given the firmness with which the founding MAS-istas had embraced their original positions. Nevertheless, the revisions produced a certain amount of dissension as some party heads wanted to go further than others in revamping policies. Though MAS was born with two ideological currents, each one associated with one of its two main leaders, Teodoro Petkoff and Pompeyo Márquez, internal debate during the party's early years was carefully limited and controlled. After 1974, however, the controversies erupted into heated discussion and eventually the emergence of organized factions.

In toning down its rhetoric and discarding intransigent stands, MAS was influenced by two unrelated events that took place in 1973: the overthrow of the government of Salvador Allende in Chile and the oil price hikes decreed by OPEC. Petkoff's thorough analysis of the Chilean coup in his *Proceso a la izquierda* and elsewhere was typical of the interest of top MAS leaders in the lessons which that experience offered. In their view, the major errors committed by the coalition that backed Allende—specifically, the excessively militant rhetoric and the rapid pace of radical reforms, which alienated middle sectors—was of an ultra-left brand. The general prosperity that prevailed in Venezuela after 1973 also influenced MAS to pursue a moderate course. The quadrupling of oil prices in 1973–74 made possible far-reaching popular measures and led to improved living conditions for all the population. It also greatly strengthened the position of the nation's two main moderate parties, AD and COPEI, which established a near monopoly over the electorate. MAS leaders concluded that the party should place its emphasis on electoral activity and moderate its style, as a strategy based on mass mobilization and confrontation was not appropriate to the changed setting of the 1970s. Only in the mid-1980s when declining oil prices led to a deterioration in the general standard of living did MAS harden its stand.

In 1974 MAS addressed a major problem faced by all leftist parties that base their rhetoric on the struggle for socialism and revolution. The predicament is this: After stating in so many ways that only socialism can solve society's ills, what else can the party say? A party that does not deal with this question runs the risk of losing the ear of the public with the incessant repetition of slogans and formulas that are variants of the same anticapitalist message. Worse yet, in order to avoid this endless reiteration, the party may escalate its rhetoric, a dynamic that eventually leads to advocacy of the use of violence.

In an effort to solve this problem, MAS's Central Committee ratified a document in February 1974 drafted by Luis Bayardo Sardi and entitled "A New Mode of Being Socialist." Bayardo was among those MASistas who believed that MAS would have scored a substantially higher vote in the 1973 elections had it not committed the error, known as "essentialism," of reducing all problems confronting the nation to the need to achieve socialism.[1] As an antidote, the "New Mode" called on MAS to communicate to Venezuelans at their own level, and not to assume that they possess an advanced political consciousness. The MASistas were urged to offer viable, albeit short-term, solutions within the framework of the capitalist system rather than hold out socialism as a panacea.[2]

A corollary to this thesis was the concept described as "accompanying the people in their experiences." According to this strategy, the left avoids assuming a hardened attitude toward nonsocialist governments that raise popular expectations and enjoy widespread support. Even though the failure of such governments' policies are inevitable and predictable, the left should extend them qualified support until the population at large sheds its illusions and realizes that the measures are not going to produce the desired results. This approach was applicable to the reforms carried out at the outset of each presidential term, which raised hopes among the majority of the electorate, especially those who had voted for the party in power. By supporting these initial policies, the MASistas hoped to become closely identified with the popular mood and to ensure that they would not be held responsible later for the failure of the government to achieve its stated objectives.

This strategy was initially put into practice during President Carlos Andrés Pérez's first year in office in 1974. As minister of the interior in the administration of Rómulo Betancourt in the early 1960s, Pérez had been held responsible for repressive actions against the popular movement and the left, and in ensuing years he was closely associated with the conservative *betancourista* wing of AD. Pérez surprised the nation and particularly the left when, shortly after being elected president, he defied his mentor Betancourt by supporting nationalistic and radical policies. Pérez immediately requested and received emergency powers from Congress and carried out such measures as the nationalization of iron and petroleum, controls on foreign investments, salary increases, and a price freeze on articles of basic necessity. Pérez's pro-third-world foreign policy included material and political support for the Sandinista guerrillas, militant calls for a New World Economic Order, and renewal of diplomatic relations with Cuba. These stands led some commentators to postulate that what was happening in Venezuela demonstrated that populism, which has generally been viewed as a transitional phenomenon bridging traditional and modern societies in the 1930s and 1940s,[3] was still a viable force.

The populist and third-world thrust of Pérez's policies met diverse reactions from the Venezuelan left, which still harbored resentment against him for his actions as minister of the interior. Two diametrically opposed positions manifested themselves on the left, with a series of gradations between them. On the one hand, several leftist political organizations viewed Pérez as representing the most reactionary sector of the ruling class, and AD as the left's principal enemy.[4] According to one such thesis, Pérez was an agent of those capitalists who were attempting to promote a new accommodation with U.S. imperialism, whereby Venezuela would play a more central role in the world system and would be transformed into a "subimperialist" power in the Caribbean region.[5] On the other hand, some leftists, including several important MAS leaders, maintained that Pérez's reforms were sufficiently radical and far-reaching that the left should back the government and try to reach a formal agreement with it.

Though unwilling to extend official support to the Pérez administration, MAS did staunchly back its program. MAS voted in favor of President Pérez's request for emergency powers even though, as the rest of the opposition pointed out, the nation was not in a crisis situation that would have required emergency measures. MAS accepted Pérez's rationale that the government should take immediate advantage of the windfall in oil revenue by allocating funds by presidential decree rather than relying on the slower legislative process. MAS's support of the Law Against Unjustified Layoffs was typical of its position on other government initiatives in that MASistas refuted some of the left's objections to the enactment while dismissing others with the argument that the law was, after all, better than nothing.[6]

MAS's flexibility toward the government and abandonment of its previously intransigent leftism was evident in its support for Pérez's planned takeover of the oil industry. MAS no longer characterized nationalization as a superficial measure and instead called for the prompt ratification of Pérez's proposal. Unlike the other parties of the left, MAS voted in favor of nearly all the clauses of the Law of Nationalization, which was approved by Congress in August 1975. MAS spokesmen defended the terms of compensation and warned that failure to reimburse the oil companies adequately would invite U.S. government retaliation. MAS pointed out that confiscation of property held by private companies was not contemplated in existing Venezuelan legislation and would thus necessitate the promulgation of a constitutional amendment, which would hold up the measure for some time.[7]

The other leftist parties accused MAS of being "pro-Adeco" and of granting the government "unrestricted" support. MAS defended its position by stating that it was opposed to the traditional leftist practice of carrying out opposition for the sake of opposition. The MASistas claimed that the lukewarm attitude of most leftists toward the government's reform program was due to the fact that it had been initiated by nonleftists.[8]

MAS's backing of government policies was also criticized by COPEI, which denounced Pérez's reforms as unconstitutional and demagogic. Actually, both COPEI and MAS, in different ways, benefited from the diametrically opposed positions they assumed toward Pérez. COPEI's hardened and vocal opposition served to invigorate the party's base, which had been demoralized by the thorough and unanticipated defeat it suffered in the 1973 presidential elections. The flexibility of MAS's approach toward the government and the originality of its arguments enhanced the party's image as a heterodoxical party intent on going beyond the left's traditional clientele. In one respect, however, MAS clearly failed to achieve a stated objective. In supporting Pérez's reforms in 1974, MAS had committed itself to large-scale mobilizations to ensure prompt and effective implementation, a pledge the MASistas admittedly fell short of fulfilling.

By 1975 the Pérez administration modified its reformist impulse and, as oil prices tapered off, was reluctant to consider additional measures that favored the working and marginal classes. MAS reacted to this change by assuming a hardened position toward the government. Unlike some leftists who were influenced by Pérez's progressive foreign policy, the MASistas voted to condemn him on the various charges of corruption that were brought before the National Congress. MAS leaders characterized Pérez's rule after 1975 as "developmentalist." These policies, they maintained, not only sacrificed the interests of the underprivileged classes but were designed to achieve a spectacular rate of economic growth by opening up the nation to multinational control and fostering ties of dependency.[9]

Petkoff and MAS historian Manuel Caballero labeled President Pérez's position after 1975 "social democrat," in contrast to his stands in 1974, which represented a throwback to AD's earlier populist stage. In the 1940s the nascent AD had been characterized by ideological vagueness and commitment to popular reforms, both trademarks of populism. According to Petkoff and Caballero, AD's affiliation with the Socialist International and identification with the social democratic movement in the 1970s signaled a greater emphasis on ideology, in contrast to the party's former populism. This change obliged socialists to react in kind by emphasizing socialist ideology. Thus Venezuela (after 1975) entered a new stage in which the struggle for reforms was subordinate to the effort to establish ideological hegemony. Caballero, addressing a MAS conference, pointed to the significance of AD's transformation from populist to social democrat: "To combat . . . Acción Democrática now with the same arms that were used to combat AD populism is like trying to fight a modern war with the outdated arms of an old war. In opposition to the social democratic AD of today, socialist forces should adopt a new policy based on . . . the deepening of their socialist character, message and content."[10] This analysis was used to justify MAS's emphasis on the ideological struggle, which was the keystone of the party's political strategy.

The Nomination for the 1978 Presidential Elections

Although the duration of national electoral campaigns in Venezuela was limited by law to ten months, the 1978 race got under way midpoint in the presidential term of Carlos Andrés Pérez. Unlike the United States, where party primaries take place the same year as the election, in Venezuela presidential contenders promote their candidacy years before the elections in order to consolidate support in their party for the purpose of securing the nomination and projecting themselves before the public. Both AD's candidate, Luis Piñerua Ordaz (who faced a mild challenge for the nomination from Jaime Lusinchi), and COPEI's Luis Herrera Campíns (whose bid for the nomination went uncontested) precipitated the race and converted it into a drawn-out extravagant affair, made possible by the nation's newly acquired oil wealth. The MASistas attempted to keep pace with AD and COPEI by initiating their campaign in 1976, first in the selection of a candidate and then in the effort to secure votes. This activity gave MAS the lead over leftist rival parties, which did not choose their presidential candidates until late 1977. Having invested so much effort at an early stage in the campaign, the MASistas were reluctant later on to withdraw their candidate in order to search for one who was acceptable to all the parties on the left.

MAS organized elections in order to select its candidate for the 1978 elections. As in the few other cases in Venezuelan history where political parties have implemented this system for nominating their presidential candidate, the internal elections in MAS were bitterly contested and undermined party unity. The polemical interchanges between the two contenders—José Vicente Rangel and Teodoro Petkoff—and their supporters centered on the role of MAS as a party. By the latter part of the year Petkoff recognized the far greater support enjoyed by his only rival and bowed out of the contest. Rangel's victory, however, was pyrrhic. During the campaign Petkoff's followers were placed in key party positions and, as a result, Petkoff's views regarding interparty relations became the official line. At the same time, some of Rangel's closest backers were forced out of the organization.

The main argument in favor of Rangel's nomination was that it reinforced MAS's image as a pluralistic party intent on opening itself up to the majority of Venezuelans who were politically unaffiliated. Not only was Rangel an independent but he had until recently been ideologically uncommitted, having belonged to the left-leaning but pragmatic URD and PRIN. An additional point in Rangel's favor was that during the 1960s he had unequivocally condemned violence perpetrated both by the government and the guerrilla left. Rangel was thus in a better position to counter the notion that—as one important survey demonstrated[11]—had been fixed in people's minds during the guerrilla years: that all socialists advocated and engaged in violence. Petkoff, on the other hand, had participated in the guerrilla movement, and his rapid speech, quick gestures, and somewhat disruptive appearance seemed to embody the leftist stereotype that MAS was trying hard to live down.

Rangel's standing as an independent, which became a central issue in the internal campaign, also worked to his disadvantage. Petkoff's supporters charged that Rangel planned to accept support from other leftist parties for his presidential candidacy, in which case MAS would lose control of the campaign, risk blurring its positions in the eyes of the public, and stumble into an alliance with other leftist parties that would not necessarily be to its benefit. In order to reassure the MAS-istas that he would not act independently, Rangel pledged himself to a special relationship with MAS. Not only would he uphold whatever policy MAS pursued toward other leftist parties, but, if defeated in the primaries, he would back the Petkoff candidacy. Rangel also asserted that despite his being an independent he agreed with MAS on all ideological issues.[12] In a final attempt to affirm his loyalty to MAS, Rangel pledged himself, in closed meetings, to joining the party following the 1978 elections.[13]

The central argument in favor of Petkoff's candidacy was that the selection of an independent as the most important spokesman for the party would weaken MAS's efforts to achieve greater ideological clarity and coherence. An independent as candidate, regardless of his vows to respect the party's decisions regarding the conduct of the campaign, would only symbolize the transformation of MAS into a patchwork organization that lacked clearly defined positions.[14]

Petkoff's supporters (the *teodoristas*) also pointed out that choosing a candidate who did not represent MAS's stands 100 percent resembled the popular-front approach in which party policies were submerged and concessions made. Obviously, Rangel and MAS disagreed on some points; otherwise, he would have joined the party. Specifically, Rangel's voting record in Congress on President Pérez's reforms in 1974 fairly well matched that of the other parties of the left, which were more critical of the government at the time than MAS.[15]

The *teodoristas* viewed Rangel's nomination as a concession to social democratic ideas that were allegedly upheld by several leading Rangel supporters, Germán Lairet and Antonio José Urbina in particular. Indeed, Petkoff had pejoratively labeled Lairet a "social democrat" because of his proposal that MAS reach a formal agreement with the AD government. Actually, Petkoff's harsh words for Lairet may well have been meant for Rangel. The *teodoristas* pointed out that Rangel had emerged from the ranks of the URD and PRIN, neither of which were socialist parties, and that thus his socialism could be considered more social democratic than truly socialist. They also maintained that Rangel's "bland" approach would hasten a rightward drift toward social democracy in MAS, a process that Petkoff, with his more polemical style, would be able to avoid. In contrast to Rangel's "nice-guy" image, which transcended ideological definitions, Petkoff was alleged to be more clearly identified with the positions that MAS was trying to assume, such as the acceptance of pluralism, the inevitability of class struggle and socialist revolution, neutrality in foreign policy, workers' management, and the struggle against bureaucracy.[16]

Actually, the *teodorista* view that Rangel's candidacy smacked of popular frontism and social democracy rested mostly on subjective arguments. Selecting an independent as candidate would not have prevented MAS from achieving greater ideological precision, as long as he was disposed, as Rangel allegedly was, to defend the party's program. Unlike the popular-front candidates of the 1930s who shied away from socialist objectives, Rangel pledged himself to support MAS's brand of socialism. Furthermore, the fact that Lairet backed Rangel did not imply that the two upheld identical positions. Indeed, Lairet was accused of being a social democrat because he favored closer relations between MAS and the "social democratic" government of Carlos Andrés Pérez, whereas Rangel was criticized for lining up with other leftist parties in opposition to many of Pérez's proposals. In short, the distinctions that the *teodoristas* made between Petkoff and Rangel were based mainly on the contrasting images that the two leaders projected rather than concrete political differences.

Freddy Muñoz, a leading *teodorista*, presented another argument in favor of Petkoff that was important for what it revealed about MAS's attitude toward leadership. Muñoz admitted that MAS had erred in allowing itself to become identified in the public eye with one individual, Rangel, who had no direct input into, and was not directly responsible to, party decision making. This tendency to entrust the party to one leader who was not accountable to others fell under the Latin American tradition of *caudillismo*, which MAS, according to Muñoz, should try to avoid. Petkoff, who was an "insider," was more likely to represent the party's collective leadership than Rangel, the "outsider."[17] Muñoz's line of thinking had been prevalent for some time among those who had been attempting to renovate the Communist movement. Support for the idea of collective leadership was found in the anti-Stalinist impulse in the Soviet Union prior to Khrushchev's consolidation of power, when the nation was governed by a troika. It later was articulated—though hardly put into practice—by the Eurocommunists, and then it was inherited by MAS. In future years MAS would try to achieve this goal by divesting the position of secretary general of its all-encompassing power and implementing other organizational reforms (to be discussed in chapter 10).

MAS and the 1978 National Elections

At the time of Rangel's formal nomination at MAS's national convention in July 1977, the MASistas refused to accept support from other leftist parties for their candidate, much less consider the possibility of a united leftist slate. Some top MAS leaders such as Luis Bayardo Sardi maintained that MIR's endorsement of the Rangel candidacy in 1973 had been a liability for MAS at the polls.[18] Rangel privately expressed his support for a united approach and met with MIRistas to try to encourage this possibility,[19] but his hands were clearly tied because of his vow to accept MAS's policy on interparty relations.

The other major leftist parties vocally called for unity of the left, though each pursued the goal in a different manner. The MEPistas stated that they would support a united candidacy only if MAS endorsed it and that otherwise they would launch their own candidate. The PCV also warned against partial unity in the form of its own exclusion, which it feared that MIR leaders, among others, favored.[20] The MIRistas, for their part, were particularly outspoken in their support for unity but were wary of a repetition of their experience in the 1973 campaign, when they were snubbed by MAS. Thus they were reluctant to support Rangel without reaching a previous agreement with MAS regarding the running of the campaign. By late 1977 MAS's obdurate stance had made unity virtually a lost cause, at which point MIR, MEP, and the PCV selected their own presidential candidates, each one of whom were leaders in their respective parties.

In Venezuela in the 1970s and 1980s leftists have frequently raised the banner of unity, and those parties who have most closely identified themselves with it have been rewarded at the polls. This pattern became evident in 1977 when MIR, which had been most fervent in its support for a candidate of the united left, won a series of spectacular victories in student and even trade union elections. MIR outpolled MAS, which was until then the most influential party among university students, at three of the nation's five main autonomous universities (the Central University, the University of Carabobo, and the University of the Andes). The MIRistas also won elections at two important oil workers' camps (Tía Juana and Cabimas) and made impressive inroads in the iron and steel workers' unions of the Guayana region.

Until this point MAS had somewhat unconvincingly tried to assure the public that it, too, favored unity, but the word was evoked only to refer to the effort to unite with the masses of people outside of their respective parties.[21] As a result of MAS's electoral defeats on campus and MIR's sudden ascendance, the MASistas reconsidered their position. In a public letter to MIR, MEP, and the PCV, Pompeyo Márquez proposed the establishment of an ongoing "Coordinator of the Left," which would meet to iron out differences among leftist parties and attempt to reach an electoral agreement. In the early months of 1978 the coordinator considered two proposals for selection of a united candidate for the presidential elections in December. MAS called for a "national consultation" (in the form of a survey or referendum among leftists) to select the candidate of the left among the four who had already been nominated, or anyone else. MIR and MEP, on the other hand, proposed the simultaneous withdrawal of the four leftist candidates and the selection of a mutually acceptable independent. MAS's plan was rejected by the other leftist parties on grounds that it was too elaborate to be worked out at such a late date in the campaign.

MAS, for its part, refused to reconsider Rangel unless it could be empirically shown that another leftist could perform better. The MASistas pointed out that Rangel's campaign had been under way for a year and that the remaining months until December were too short a period to introduce a new candidate to the public. MAS laid great stress on the mass turnout at rallies in support of Rangel as well as the results of public opinion surveys that pointed to his lead over his three leftist rivals. On this basis, the MASistas argued that Rangel, who was in any case the only independent among the four leftist candidates, was the natural choice to represent the united left at the polls.[22]

MAS was accused by many of being insincere in its support for a united candidacy. MAS's about-face after opposing interparty unity for some time seemed contrived. The party's refusal to withdraw its own candidate, as MIR, MEP, and the PCV offered to do, left the impression that its interest in unity was less than authentic. In addition, Pompeyo Márquez's bungling of a secret proposal introduced by Miguel Otero Silva also contributed to the general skepticism regarding MAS's alleged interest in unity. Otero had suggested that the left announce its support for the Rangel candidacy, but that it work out beforehand an agreement that would guarantee equitable participation in campaign decision making and proportional representation in united slates for the state legislatures and national Congress. Márquez, however, for unexplained reasons revealed the plan to the public, after which an irate Otero Silva withdrew it, arguing that it could only have been worked out behind the scenes in the absence of outside pressure.[23]

The modification of MAS's position in 1978 was not a completely futile gesture. The discussions in the Coordinator of the Left did serve to harmonize relations on the left and tone down the heated interchanges between the MASistas and other leftists. Furthermore, plans were made to coordinate the left's campaign for the municipal elections in June 1979, as well as the trade union elections scheduled for early 1979. Although labor unity did not materialize, the left did establish united slates for the municipal contests. Finally, MAS accepted the support offered Rangel by four small political groups—the Liga Socialista (LS), El Pueblo Avanza (EPA), the Vanguardia Comunista, and the Grupo de Acción Revolucionaria (GAR)—which were generally to the left of MAS. Not only did the MASistas welcome this endorsement but they incorporated members of the four organizations in their slates for the national Congress and state legislatures in the December elections.

The MAS campaign of 1978 contrasted both in content and style with that of 1973. In a general sense this was due to MAS's constant examination of its goals and pursuit of more effective ways to convey its message. MAS's emphasis—which at times bordered on an obsession—on breaking with the traditional left and achieving a "great leap forward" at the polls and a dramatic ascendance in the nation as a whole led the party to engage in an ongoing search for radically new formulas. In addition, as a result of their general disdain for unity on the left, the MASistas were encouraged to strike out in new directions in order to distinguish themselves from the rest of the left and justify their go-it-alone approach.

Guided by the thesis of the "New Mode of Being Socialist," MAS discarded the 1973 campaign practice of portraying capitalism as the embodiment of all evil and socialism as the panacea. In the 1978 campaign MAS went to the other extreme in offering technical solutions that were unrelated to socialism and in many cases divorced from political criteria. Thus a gap existed between the specific proposals in MAS's program and its frequent reminders to the public that MAS was a socialist party.[24]

The results of the 1978 presidential elections, as those of 1973, were disappointing to the MASistas, who had been generally confident of at least doubling the party's previous vote (see table 7-1). The mere increase of .9 decimal points was hardly the "great electoral leap forward" MASistas had talked about achieving. On the positive side was the spread of MAS's vote by region and class. On a state-by-state basis the party's vote was more equitably distributed than in 1973, when it was heavily concentrated in the Federal District and Barquisimeto. Indeed, MAS's percentages improved in nineteen of the nation's twenty-three voting districts.[25] In addition, electoral studies carried out by the party demonstrated that it made inroads among nonprivileged sectors since the 1973 elections, when the nascent MAS was largely unknown to undereducated Venezuelans and received most of its support from the middle sectors.[26]

Table 7-1 Results of National-Municipal Elections of 1978 and 1979

Major parties and presidential candidates	Percentage of national votes (1978)	Deputies elected	Municipal vote (1979)
Left			
MAS	6.1	11	9.7
MEP	2.2	4	2.1
MIR	2.3	4	3.3
PCV	1.1	1	1.2
Center			
AD	39.7	86	30.2
COPEI	39.7	86	49.1
Left			
Martín	1.0		
Mujica	0.5		
Prieto	1.1		
Rangel	5.2		
Center			
Herrera	46.6		
Piñerua	43.3		

The Municipal Elections of 1979

For the first time since 1958, the municipal elections were independent of those for Congress and were held on a separate date—in June 1979, six months after the national elections. The four main parties of the left, along with the four smaller ones that had supported the Rangel candidacy, agreed to put up a common front in the nation's 191 districts. The representation of each party on the slates was based on its percentage of votes in the December congressional elections. In addition, it was decided that the elected councilmen and their substitutes would rotate in office according to the relative vote of their respective parties. Thus, for instance, if MAS received 50 percent of the left's vote in a given district, its councilman would serve for half the term. Finally, a national committee was constituted to coordinate the campaign and another to be in charge of publicity. The left decided to base its electoral pitch on local issues, rather than ideological or national ones, and to highlight the problem of corruption, which was rampant at the municipal level. In addition to this common publicity, each party was free to launch its own propaganda as long as, of course, it was not directed against the rest of the left.

MAS increased its percentages in the municipal elections over the presidential ones by 90 percent, while its leftist partners made similar gains (see table 7-1), but in absolute numbers the left's vote did not improve substantially. The pro-MAS political scientist Pedro José Martínez, in an article in the scholarly journal *Politeia*, interpreted the electoral returns as indicating that unity of the left did not produce the desired results in that MAS failed to attract new voters. According to Martínez, the major difference in voting patterns between the December congressional elections and the June municipal ones was that in the second case a large number of AD supporters, disillusioned by their party's upset in the presidential contests, did not bother to go to the polls. As a result, both the left's vote and that of COPEI improved in proportion to the number of votes cast.[27]

Martínez's thesis is based on certain assumptions regarding the behavior of the Venezuelan voter. AD and COPEI are highly clientelistic, and consequently the willingess of their members to engage in campaign activity and go to the polls is closely related to their party's electoral prospects. In the municipal race the leftists, whose political commitment is not conditioned by material rewards, and the Copeyanos, who were buoyed by the results of the national elections, maintained their previous level of participation while that of the Adecos dropped off significantly.

Martínez's thesis notwithstanding, the electoral gains registered by the left over a six-month period impressed not only leftists but the nation as a whole. MAS leaders in particular hailed their party's showing in June as a great success and evidence that the party now occupied a significant place in Venezuelan politics.[28] Nevertheless, they failed to echo the conclusions their counterparts in other leftist parties reached, namely, that unity of the left had created a groundswell that swung over voters who had previously been skeptical about the left because of its constant infighting. Indicative of MAS's attitude were the statements by Pompeyo Márquez regarding the "tripolar" situation that had emerged from the municipal elections: the three "political points of reference" in the nation were now AD, COPEI, and MAS.[29] This analysis, which minimized the rest of the left and highlighted MAS, was too optimistic; MAS's 9.7 percent hardly compared with COPEI's 49.1 percent and AD's 30.2 percent. In addition, a comparison of the municipal elections of 1979 and the congressional—as opposed to presidential—ones of 1978 demonstrate that a sizable portion of the Venezuelan electorate favored unity of the left. While

MIR, MEP, and the PCV, which had supported unity all along, did not improve their standing significantly, MAS was handsomely rewarded for its revised position in favor of unity, with a 59 percent increase in its vote.

Pompeyo Márquez's statements regarding the new "tripolar" political system reflected MAS's confidence that it would virtually eliminate the other leftist parties. The refusal of the nation's largest socialist party to recognize the continued existence of its smaller leftist rivals was perhaps fitting for a nation like Italy where the Communist Party virtually monopolizes leftist politics, but Márquez's proclamation was at best premature for Venezuela. The choice of that moment for trumpeting MAS's dislodgement of the rest of the left was particularly inappropriate in that the formation of united leftist slates, according to most political commentators (Pedro José Martínez being an exception), had just proved to be a resounding success. Indeed, most sectors of the left drew just the opposite conclusion to that of Márquez, namely that unity of the left was the order of the day.

8   The Elections of 1983–1984

MAS's experience in the 1983 presidential campaign was in many ways a repetition of 1978 and even 1973. As in both previous elections the MASistas were unwilling, for ideological reasons, to throw in their lot with the rest of the left and support a united candidate. To avoid being blamed for the disunity on the left, MAS participated in discussions with other leftist parties and was disposed to accept the support of several of them for its candidate, as it had in 1978. The MASistas were confident that they would substantially increase their share of votes over the 1978 elections and thus achieve a "great electoral leap forward." This optimism regarding socialism's short-term prospects was also evident in the 1978 and 1973 contests and had been expressed prior to MAS's founding by Petkoff and other dissident Communists. The MASistas radically modified their electoral and political strategies in both the 1978 and 1983 campaigns in an effort to find a formula that would allow the party to fulfill these vaulting expectations at the polls. In contrast, other leftist parties were not as set on achieving dramatic short-term electoral gains, nor did they predicate the validity of their political strategy on the number of votes they received. Consequently, they were not as inclined to revamp their policies in response to their disappointing showing.

The three elections were similar in another respect: MAS's performance in each was the source of endless debate in the party. In 1973 MAS, being a recently founded organization, interpreted its vote as an outstanding success and a vindication of its policies, even though it polled far less than what it had anticipated. The 1978 and 1983 elections, on the other hand, were viewed as unmitigated failures. The results of 1983, in particular, threw the party into disarray and set off mass defections at all levels. Other leftist parties, which did not harbor illusions regarding impressive gains in the near future, were not nearly as traumatized by their equally unsatisfactory vote.

U.S. Reaction to MAS's Ascendance on the Left

At the time of its founding in 1971 MAS was carefully watched by leftists throughout the world, and especially by Moscow, because of the ideological challenge that the MASistas represented. With the consolidation of MAS's position as the largest party on the left and the third largest in the nation in the 1978–79 elections, observers in the United States, and Washington in particular, began to take a special look at the organization. This interest was reflected in articles on MAS in the State Department's *Problems of Communism,* the *New York Times* and elsewhere that formulated the hypothetical question of what the U.S. response should be to a MAS-led government in Venezuela.[1] The article in *Problems of Communism,* by Venezuela specialist David Myers, noted that the efforts of Petkoff and other MASistas to convince U.S. audiences that MAS's ascent to power would not jeopardize U.S. security have been fairly well received.[2] Other articles indicate that MAS's message has forced many Latin American area specialists to reexamine assumptions regarding U.S. interests and inter-American relations that date back to the early years of the Cold War.

That MAS was able to develop amicable relations with William Luers at this time was significant, though not everyone in the State Department shared the U.S. ambassador's views. Luers's attitude and that of other diplomats were shaped by international developments and changes in U.S. foreign policy in the 1970s. The Republican administrations of the 1950s and the Democratic ones of the 1960s upheld a polarized view of the world in which nationalist movements that did not closely identify themselves with Washington were dismissed as hostile to U.S. interests.[3] The Nixon administration, which assigned Latin America a role of secondary importance, showed less interest in exercising control over political movements in the continent. This attitude coincided with a relative lessening of U.S. economic interests in the area as well as the emergence of a multipolarity on the world scene in place of the dichotomy of the Cold War years.[4] It is ironic that the more pluralistic outlook was initiated by Nixon, whose political career up until then had been marked by strident anticommunism. Naturally, Presidents Nixon, Ford, and Carter in the 1970s stopped short of passively accepting Communist advances. Thus, for instance, Carter made clear that Communist Party electoral triumphs in France and Italy would be considered antithetical to U.S. interests. Nevertheless, during these years certain parties on the left not closely aligned with Moscow were given a different treatment than in the past.

The attitude of Luers and others toward MAS may have also been influenced by the State Department's relations with Venezuela's two major political parties. Traditionally, Washington has maintained special ties with AD. AD worked closely with State Department–backed labor leaders in an effort to wrest control of the international labor movement from the Communists at the outset of the Cold War, and later President Betancourt was one of the foremost Latin American champions of the Alliance for Progress. COPEI, on the other hand, has failed to develop a similar rapport with either embassy officials in Caracas or Democratic or Republican political leaders in Washington. The absence of a close bond is undoubtedly related to the staunch third-worldist and anti-U.S. rhetoric of the Latin American Christian Democratic labor movement, whose headquarters are in Venezuela. Because of the persistent efforts of MASistas to offer Washington assurances regarding their intentions, some U.S. diplomats may have viewed MAS as a welcome alternative to COPEI as AD's principal competitor in the nation's two-party system.

MAS and the Rest of the Left

Following the 1978 elections Teodoro Petkoff attempted to block José Vicente Rangel's bid to represent the united left in the 1983 presidential contests. Petkoff and his followers relied on the same arguments used against Rangel in the MAS primaries for the 1978 elections, and especially harped on the need to choose a party member rather than an independent as candidate in order to achieve greater ideological clarity.[5] In addition, the *teodoristas* stressed Rangel's disappointing showing in the 1978 contests. They pointed out that despite Rangel's charisma and the support he received from four smaller leftist parties, his 5.1 percent of the vote was below the 6.1 percent obtained by MAS in the congressional elections.[6] (Actually, the MIR, MEP, and PCV candidates fared worse in that they drew half or less than half of their party's congressional vote; clearly, many of those who supported leftist congressional slates preferred to cast their vote for one of the two presidential candidates with a realistic possibility of winning.)

The *teodoristas* also attacked Rangel for refusing to carry through on his pledge to join MAS. As they had done in the primaries for the 1978 elections, the *teodoristas* made an issue of Rangel's stands that were different from those of MAS. This time, however, the *teodoristas* not only maintained that Rangel, being an independent, could not be trusted to represent MAS's positions. They now pointed out that Rangel "opportunistically" shaped his stands in order to gain allies among parties on the left whose support he hoped to secure for his candidacy.[7] For example, the *teodoristas* chided Rangel for failing to condemn ex-President Carlos Andrés Pérez on charges of corruption involving the overpriced ship *Sierra Nevada*, a position that represented a flip-flop from his previous hardened opposition to the Pérez administration in 1974. This leniency toward Pérez, it was pointed out, coincided with that of several other leftist parties (specifically the PCV and a faction of MIR), which offered to back Rangel in his new bid for the presidency.

Petkoff's influence in MAS was greatly enhanced because of the success of his followers in occupying leadership positions in the party. During the MAS primaries for the 1978 elections Petkoff proved more adept at gaining organizational control than winning over the party's rank and file to his candidacy. By the party's Fifth Convention in May 1980 the balance of power between Petkoff and Pompeyo Márquez had shifted in Petkoff's favor. Some of Márquez's followers, such as MAS's general subsecretary, Tirso Pinto, denied that Petkoff's majority at the convention represented the will of the party's base. Márquez, who since his last years as a PCV leader had tended to downplay controversial internal issues that jeopardized party unity, preferred to defer to Petkoff rather than put up a hardened fight in favor of his own presidential nomination or that of José Vicente Rangel.[8]

MAS participated in lengthy negotiations with the other leftist parties in the Coordinator of the Left, where it helped draft a common program. Nevertheless, its lack of genuine interest in unity was even more apparent than in 1978. MAS's public attacks against its leftist rivals were sharper than ever before, in part because the party's prime objective was differentiating itself from the rest of the left. The MAS-istas harshly criticized and at times derided parties like MEP—despite its moderate brand of socialism—and prominent independent leftists, such as Miguel Otero Silva, once they announced their support for Rangel. The MASistas attempted to discredit the Rangel candidacy on grounds that it was based on the backing of a welter of miniscule parties (the largest ones being the PCV, MEP, and a faction of MIR), which they branded the "decadent left." According to the MASistas, Rangel was a virtual "caudillo" who presided over a situation of anarchy involving a host of parties with widely differing and even conflicting policies. Rangel acted as a demagogue in claiming to be able to reconcile these diverse positions, a task that was in fact impossible. In contrast, MAS had put together a concrete program and possessed sufficient organizational strength to be able to deliver on its promises.[9]

MAS's public support for a united left candidate for the 1983 elections was also viewed as insincere because of the public declarations of some of its leaders in opposition to unity. Although MAS's Political Commission in September 1980 prohibited party members from criticizing the rest of the left in public, this order was disobeyed by several prominent MAS leaders. The polemical Manuel Caballero used his column space in *El Nacional* to attack personalities on the left, and eight other MAS leaders issued the "Document of the Eight," which called on the party to drop out of the Coordinator of the Left. These MASistas were not censured by the party's national directorate, though disciplinary measures were taken against Tirso Pinto for his open support for Rangel. This inconsistency reinforced the impression that supposed dissenters like Caballero were, in fact, expressing MAS's real positions.

MAS's ambiguity and vacillations reflected the differences among the party's national leaders regarding relations with other parties on the left. Those who identified with Pompeyo Márquez were disposed to accept a united left candidacy but only under the condition that MAS, by virtue of being the largest party, have the main input in the selection of the candidate and the formulation of his program. The *teodoristas* were even more averse to joining other leftist parties on equal terms. Not only did they rule out any understanding with the PCV because of its alignment with the Soviet Union, but some of them (including Senator Bayardo Sardi) accepted partial unity of the left, not as a valid strategy in its own right, but as a necessary evil whose sole objective was to avoid being branded divisionist.[10]

The MASistas were well aware that the party would pay a price, especially on campus, for openly rejecting unity of the left, as it had before the 1978 elections. It was this pragmatism, more than any genuine interest in unity, that accounted for MAS's participation in the Coordinator of the Left for several years. Nevertheless, the fact that MAS's interest in unity was half-hearted, if not feigned, was apparent. Rangel called MAS's bluff when he stated, after months of fruitless negotiations over the type of system to be used for choosing the united leftist candidate, that he was willing to accept any method. Clearly, MAS could not agree to this offer because most top party leaders rejected a priori a united front that included the PCV.

In private, MASistas justified this Machiavellian approach by saying that, after all, "politics is politics." Petkoff and other leading MASistas were familiar with such a strategy, having employed it in the late 1960s when, as dissident Communists, they openly called for maintaining PCV unity when in fact they were determined to split the party. On that occasion the simulation of interest in unity had proved successful. In the early 1980s, though, MAS's talk of unity was less convincing, and it only created doubts in the public mind regarding the coherence of MAS's positions. After the 1983 elections some leading MASistas would attribute their party's disappointing showing to its protracted participation in the Coordinator of the Left.

The 1983 Electoral Campaign

In their dispute with Rangel the MASistas emphasized that they would openly advocate socialism in the campaign and that Rangel, who was intent on attracting small moderate parties such as the URD, would be forced to soft-pedal socialist ideas.[11] Actually, Rangel failed to receive the endorsement of any of the moderate groups, but even when he was attempting to secure their support, he clearly identified himself with socialism. MAS's pledge to base its campaign on the advocacy of socialism, as the party had done in 1973 and 1978, won over MIR (which was convinced that MAS was to the left of Rangel) to the Petkoff candidacy.

Nevertheless, the Petkoff campaign was marked by moderation and emphasis on MAS's commitment to democracy, which eclipsed the party's anticapitalist message. MAS devised a list of proposals for reforming the state in order to facilitate and perfect popular participation in public decision making. These propositions included direct election of governors, prefects, and judges, selection of candidates individually rather than by slate for all elective bodies, and the scheduling of municipal elections in the middle of presidential terms rather than simultaneously with or shortly after national elections. With much fanfare, Petkoff addressed different organizations, including AD, COPEI, the main labor confederation (the CTV), and the main business organization (Fedecamaras), to formally expound on his party's proposals. Although other leftist parties had long advocated similar reforms, MAS decided to carry out the campaign on its own.

MAS's decision to stress concrete proposals to fortify the nation's democracy was designed to expose the two major establishment parties where they were particularly vulnerable. Both AD and COPEI had always tried to score political capital out of the left's fateful decision to take up arms against a popularly elected government by portraying themselves as the only true champions of democracy. Nevertheless, certain features of the Venezuelan political system that Petkoff proposed to modify, such as the long time span between elections, were far more retrogressive than in other democratic third-world nations.

AD and COPEI leaders hesitated to commit themselves to revising these outmoded practices. Though at times they unconvincingly tried to identify themselves with the types of reforms proposed by Petkoff, on other occasions they claimed that Venezuela was not yet ready for such far-reaching changes.

MAS attempted to equate democracy with socialism and in doing so played down those features that are traditionally associated with the latter, such as nationalization and centralized planning. This emphasis on the political rather than the economic or social dimensions of socialism was evident in MAS's electoral program, which was subtitled "More Democracy for Venezuela":

> Our program and our socialism have as their basis the transformation of Venezuela in order to eliminate social injustice and economic inequality. Our socialism is . . . profoundly democratic, both with regard to its respect for political liberties and human rights as well as to the amplification of channels of popular participation in public affairs. It is said that democracy without dissidence, democracy without respect for minorities, democracy without opposition is not democracy. We maintain that socialism without dissidence, socialism without respect for minorities, socialism without opposition is not socialism.[12]

MAS's effort to deemphasize socialism and to redefine the word to rid it of its controversial connotations was the result of a conscious decision by the party[13] and was strongly supported by Petkoff's campaign manager, Luis Bayardo Sardi. According to Bayardo Sardi, the word *socialism* conjured up negative images that would seriously prejudice the Petkoff candidacy. Since MAS's socialist commitment was evident in its very name, the party's stress on socialism in the campaign was superfluous. Actually, this thesis regarding the disrepute of socialism was based on impressionistic rather than empirical evidence regarding political attitudes in Venezuela. A survey used by John Martz and Enrique Baloyra in *Political Attitudes in Venezuela* revealed just the opposite, namely, that those Venezuelans who identify with socialism outnumber those who support capitalism by almost two to one.[14] A second possible fallacy in Bayardo Sardi's thesis is that inclusion of the word *socialist* or *socialism* in a party's name does not in any way signify commitment to that system, as is demonstrated by the numerous social democratic organizations, among others, that have the word *socialist* or *revolutionary* in their name but that lost interest in radical change long ago.

MAS's restraint in calling for socialism and its efforts to disassociate

itself from the word's negative implications facilitated the incorporation of a small group of businessmen in the Petkoff campaign, some
of whom actually figured in the party's electoral slates. The MASistas
greatly valued this support, which they viewed as evidence that the
party was making inroads among small- and medium-sized business
owners, to whom a good deal of MAS's propaganda was directed. The
most renowned member of the group was Reinaldo Cervini, president
of the progressive business organization Asociacion Pro-Venezuela.
Another less prominent businessman who formed part of MAS's congressional slate was Gonzalo Ramírez Cubillán, who had previously
belonged to conservative business and political organizations.

Over the years MAS had attached increasing importance to the
cultivation of its image as a responsible party, which, unlike the
orthodox left, was willing to cooperate with the government in order
to contribute to the nation's general welfare. This attitude was demonstrated by the party's acceptance of austerity measures that implied
sacrifices for the popular, as well as privileged, classes. The Herrera
Campíns administration rewarded MAS for upholding these positions
by formally consulting it on certain matters along with AD and COPEI
and, in doing so, recognized MAS as one of the nation's three major
parties, thus enhancing its legitimacy in the eyes of the public.

MAS attempted to project this image in the presidential campaign,
as was demonstrated by its main electoral slogan "The Possible Venezuela" (*la Venezuela posible*). The term was designed to counter the
common belief that socialists were interested only in revolutionary
upheaval and would settle on nothing less than the achievement of its
utopian vision. In addition, MAS avoided use of heavily charged language against AD and COPEI (a policy that those two parties did not
follow in their attacks on one another) so as not to insult or alienate
the rank-and-file members of both organizations.[15] Campaign manager Bayardo Sardi also insisted on utilizing what he termed "the
norms of electoral sociology," a euphemism for public relations techniques. MAS financed public opinion surveys—a standard practice
followed by AD and COPEI—in order to exaggerate Petkoff's support
and counter the notion that he did not have a chance of winning.[16]

The style and content of the Petkoff campaign contrasted sharply
with that of José Vicente Rangel in several respects. First, Rangel was
backed by a host of smaller parties in addition to the PCV, MEP, and
the "New Alternative" (which consisted mainly of ex-MIRistas).
Rangel constantly cited the names of all the organizations that supported him in order to stress the pluralistic nature of his candidacy. In
the same vein, he helped publicize the congressional slates of each of

the parties that backed him and even addressed several of their national conventions. This acceptance of diversity contrasted with Petkoff's emphasis on the organized strength of MAS and MIR, which he frequently referred to as the two largest parties on the left.

Second, the slogans and banners used by Rangel's supporters were designed to convert their campaign rallies into social protests. The MASistas, on the other hand, attempted to create a festival atmosphere at their gatherings in order to reinforce the notion that socialist change would, from the outset, bring joy rather than violence and sacrifice. MAS's leftist rivals denounced these mass meetings as veritable "electoral carnivals."[17]

A third notable difference between the Petkoff and Rangel campaigns could be found in the programs, and in particular the proposals for structural reforms, put forward by the two candidates. The Rangel candidacy inherited the positions assumed by the PCV and MEP in the 1973 and 1978 elections. Rangel called for nationalization of financial institutions and basic industry and singled out U.S. imperialism as the principal enemy. Not only was direct reference to North American imperialism conspicuously absent in the Petkoff program, but in campaign literature the Soviet Union was held to be at least equally responsible for the problems facing third-world nations. Rather than stress nationalization, MAS's platform called for "new forms of economic organization" that would promote worker participation in decision making and strengthen ownership of small- and medium-scale property.

Expectations among the MASistas ran as high, if not higher, than in the 1978 contests. In no other election in Venezuelan history had a leftist party spent such large sums of money in media publicity. Furthermore, most MASistas had come to accept the *teodorista* argument that by launching its own candidate and distancing itself from the rest of the left, MAS would achieve a "great electoral leap forward."

MAS's tally, however, was half of the 10 percent party members believed would be the very minimum it would receive (see table 8-1). Not only did the vote disappoint party members but it surprised international observers such as political scientist Howard Penniman of the American Enterprise Institute.[18] A comparison of the congressional and presidential results of the 1978 and 1983 elections (see figure 8-1) shows that Petkoff's performance was particularly poor. Though MAS's congressional percentage declined just 7 percent, its presidential one was 19 percent less than that of 1978. In contrast, Rangel's showing in 1983 was superior to the combined vote of the presidential candidates of MEP, MIR, and the PCV in 1978.

Table 8-1 Results of National-Municipal Elections of 1983 and 1984

Major parties and presidential candidates	Percentage of national votes (1983)	Deputies elected	Municipal vote (1984)
Left			
MAS	5.7	10	7.2
MEP	2.2	3	2.7
MIR	1.6	2	1.4
PCV	1.8	3	2.1
Center			
AD	49.9	112	52.6
COPEI	28.7	61	21.7
Left			
Petkoff	4.1		
Rangel	3.3		
Center			
Caldera	34.6		
Lusinchi	56.9		

The Aftermath of the 1983 Elections

Just days after the 1983 national elections a large number of MAS leaders left the party. Some of them accepted government positions or drew close to AD or COPEI. The most important desertions included Alexis Ortiz (MAS's deputy from Anzoátegui); Walter Boza (the head of MAS in Caracas's eastern district); Antonio José Urbina (MAS's delegate to the Supreme Electoral Council), who was appointed Venezuelan ambassador to Sweden; and Germán Lairet (who had belonged to Petkoff's inner core of Communist supporters in the 1960s), who was appointed ambassador to Rumania. Urbina's and Lairet's request for permission from the party to accept their designations was rejected on grounds that it would be interpreted as part of a formal agreement between MAS and the government.

Nearly all of those who left MAS belonged to the party's "renovation" wing headed by Bayardo Sardi. Typical of the alleged motives for withdrawal was Walter Boza's statement that "it makes no sense to be a democrat in MAS when the party is led by a closed group of Marxist-Leninists."[19] These MASistas undoubtedly feared that the failure of the Petkoff campaign, which was led by Bayardo Sardi, would strengthen the hands of the party's more orthodox leaders.

The defections had a second motive besides the ideological one. Many who left MAS in December 1983 undoubtedly felt that their own political ambitions would not be well served in a party whose growth potential had proved to be so limited. Personal ambition always plays a role in politics, but there is evidence that it was the key factor in this case. The fact that the departures occurred on the heels of an electoral fiasco indicates that the resigners were moved more by MAS's disappointing results than by any shift in ideological forces within the party. Furthermore, had ideology been the overriding factor, the discontented MASistas would have left the party as a group and issued a single document justifying their decision. Instead, most of the important leaders who withdrew did so individually. MAS had always rejected the Leninist model of a close-knit party based on iron-clad discipline and in recent years had come to accept personal ambition among its members as a legitimate political motivation that should be encouraged rather than repressed. MAS's reorganization over the previous five years (discussed in chapter 10) was designed to foment competition for internal positions, an activity that absorbed a great deal of party energy. This philosophy and practice, as well as the conviction consciously nourished by party leaders that MAS's future would be one of spectacular growth, encouraged many MASistas to look forward to personal gains in the years ahead. MAS's electoral stagnation prompted them to question their continued presence in the party.

Figure 8-1 MAS's Electoral Showing, 1973–1984

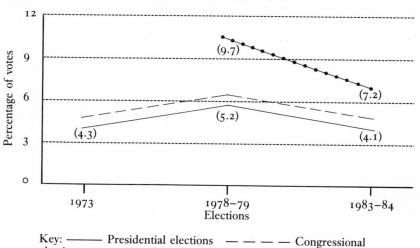

MAS's National Council responded to the December electoral fiasco by replacing the party's entire national leadership with three ad hoc committees that were to take charge of the party until its next national convention, due to take place within a year. At the same time the party turned inward by analyzing past errors and undergoing a protracted internal race for the party positions that were up for election at the upcoming convention. This introspective process produced a proliferation of factions, as was reflected in the competition for the post of secretary general; no less than six prominent national leaders announced their candidacies. The party's internal affairs throughout 1984 and early 1985 were marked by incessant questioning stemming from the same predicament that produced the mass defections: because MAS had always harshly attacked the traditional leftist parties for having abandoned all hope of achieving short-term success, now its own electoral stagnation seemed to put in doubt its raison d'etre.

The explanations individual MAS leaders offered for the party's poor showing in December reflected their own political thinking. The renovation faction headed by Bayardo Sardi, which had been critical of MAS's association with the traditional left, attributed the party's poor showing to its extended participation in the Coordinator of the Left and its alliance with MIR. Carlos Raúl Hernández, who defended this position, pointed to MIR's aggressive attacks against AD's deceased historic leader, Rómulo Betancourt, which offended the sensibilities of many Venezuelans and clashed with the more mild tone set by MAS in the campaign. Freddy Muñoz, on the other hand, who headed MAS's hard-line faction, criticized the policy followed by Petkoff's campaign manager, Bayardo Sardi, of diluting MAS's socialist message.

MAS's national leadership issued a statement that traced the party's electoral disaster to its failure to sufficiently distinguish itself from AD, COPEI, and the traditional left. This self-criticism had been generally recognized by MASistas for some time. Another widely held explanation was that MAS's decision to formally accept and actually encourage the existence of organized factions had seriously undermined the effectiveness of party work. A related assertion was that MAS's organizational weakness induced the party to rely too much on the mass media, especially in the form of paid advertisements.[20]

Shortly after the December national elections Petkoff pronounced himself in opposition to an alliance with other leftist parties for the municipal elections of May 1984. His statements "the rest of the left does not interest me in the least" and "we have nothing to look for in that world [of the left]"[21] were expressions of personal opinion. Petkoff pointed to MAS's bitter experiences after the 1979 municipal contests, when other leftist parties reneged on their agreement regarding rotation of city councilmen on the basis of the votes received by each party, thus depriving MAS of the opportunity to serve on several councils.

Petkoff's position met opposition within MAS, which ended up authorizing the party's organization in each municipality to set its own policy. In the vast majority of districts MAS's local leaders chose to run a separate slate. By including a large number of independents who were identified with community problems in the MAS tickets, the party endeavored to differentiate itself from the rest of the left by projecting an image of flexibility and open-mindedness.

The other parties on the left (including MIR, which had supported Petkoff in December) formed united slates for the municipal elections. Some leftists favored going beyond the terms of unity of the municipal contests of 1979, when leftist parties were represented individually on the ballot even though they all supported the same tickets. The proposed system, known as the *tarjeta única*, would have provided voters with just one possible selection for the leftist slate, while eliminating the names of the individual leftist parties. The plan, however, was vetoed by MIR. It is possible that the *tarjeta única* would have paid handsome dividends in the form of votes from a large number of independents who were skeptical of the intentions of the leftist parties because of their long history of infighting. As it turned out, in the oil town of Cabimas in Zulia and in several other municipal districts where the united leftist slate included MAS, the left fared especially well.

With the exception of the PCV, which registered a 43 percent increase over the 1979 municipal elections, the percentage of votes received by the leftist parties did not notably improve (see table 8-1). The PCV's dramatic increase was largely due to the firmness of its commitment to orthodox Marxism, which appealed to many leftists at a time when MIR and other parties replaced orthodoxy with a more ideologically eclectic approach. For the MASistas, their electoral stagnation only reconfirmed what the December contests had already made evident, namely, that party policies were in dire need of revision.

MAS's Political Strategy and the Venezuelan Electorate

The transformation in MAS signaled by the "New Mode of Being Socialist" document in 1974 can be seen as an effort to tailor policy to the general conditions and attitudes prevailing in Venezuela at the time. The economic prosperity that was triggered by OPEC's oil price hikes has already been mentioned as an important factor in explaining changes in party positions. In addition, general attitudes toward the political system and government policies, as measured by public opinion surveys, influenced the MASistas. Not only have MAS leaders assigned the "subjective" factor a determining role in the revolutionary process, they have shown great interest in opinion polls, especially with regard to electoral preferences. Numerous surveys have been undertaken by U.S. and Venezuelan firms and by individual teams, many contracted by AD, COPEI, and MAS. Studies based on these findings have been undertaken by distinguished U.S. and Venezuelan social scientists, including Enrique Baloyra, John Martz, David Myers, Robert O'Connor, Arístides Torres, and Kenneth Coleman.[22] These works and the statistics that they utilize give an idea of the general attitudes that have influenced MAS and the perceptions that are characteristic of the MASistas themselves.

Many of the studies highlight the apparent contradiction between the faith of Venezuelans in the nation's political party system, on the one hand, and their growing disillusionment with politicians, political parties, and government policy, on the other. Venezuelans view politicians as "predisposed to lie at every turn" (81.2 percent), and political parties as exclusively concerned with elections (79.9 percent) and controlled by "small oligarchical groups" (74.4 percent).[23] The government also scored low on its performance, particularly in the area of economic policy. Sixty-five percent of those interviewed in one survey carried out in the metropolitan area of Caracas in 1982 thought that the cost of living was "very high" and another 27.5 percent "high," and responses to questions regarding unemployment and public security were nearly as negative.[24] Respondents to another survey on the eve of the 1978 elections singled out the management of public services as particularly deficient.[25] Still another poll, in more recent years, shows that a majority of Venezuelans point to the failure to solve pressing economic problems as the major shortcoming of the Lusinchi administration: unemployment (31.4 percent), cost of living (20.2 percent), foreign debt (14.4 percent), and the economic situation (6.6 percent) were the main areas of concern.[26]

Disillusionment with government policy was reflected at the polls and explains why incumbent parties are invariably losers in presidential elections. Robert O'Connor, in a study of voting behavior in the 1978 elections, noted the correlation between shifts in voter preferences during the campaign to the advantage of COPEI and the government's loss of popularity. Those uncommitted voters who opted for

COPEI were especially moved by economic issues. O'Connor concludes that the outcome of the elections reflected general dissatisfaction with the administration of Carlos Andrés Pérez more than they expressed positive or negative attitudes toward either the COPEI or AD candidates.[27]

Growing widespread dissatisfaction with the performance of the last three governments in Venezuela did not seem to undermine confidence in the nation's political system. Only 11.3 percent of the respondents of a survey carried out by a team of MASistas assigned the major responsibility for the problems besetting the nation to the democratic system, whereas 20.9 percent blamed the previous government (of Herrera Campíns), 13.6 pointed to the current Lusinchi government, 19.6 percent to the economic situation, and 24.9 percent, political parties.[28] In another survey cited by Baloyra, 82.2 percent responded affirmatively to the question, "Do you prefer democracy like the one of the last 25 years" over dictatorship?[29]

Furthermore, despite sharp criticism of political parties, most Venezuelans closely identify with them. Almost twice as many respondents of one survey indicated that they had always sympathized with the same party than those who stated the contrary.[30] Political scientist Arístides Torres used empirical data to show that strong party loyalty pervades all sectors of society, a finding that rules out the possibility that a new movement can establish itself by attracting a large number of independents in a particular social group. Torres adds that Venezuela resembles the advanced democratic nations where a majority of citizens belongs to a given party, as against third-world countries like Colombia where cynicism and apathy prevails.[31]

The profile of the leftist voter that can be constructed from the results of public opinion surveys is helpful for understanding the challenges faced by MAS. In spite of MAS's success in drawing votes from low-income sectors in the 1978 elections, the party continued to be based on well-educated, urban youth.[32] The major preoccupation of leftists in general, and MASistas in particular, was education-related matters, unlike the population at large, which was more concerned with economic issues.[33] Although highly critical of the government, the leftists were not as negative as a group of cynics with low levels of political participation and ill-defined ideological beliefs. The MASistas had a high sense of their own efficacy, especially when compared with the cynics, who felt politically ineffective, and, to a less extent, with members of all other parties, including those of the left.[34]

The MASistas carefully analyzed general attitudes as they were recorded in political surveys. They drew the following conclusions, which were reflected in the party's reformulations after 1973: (1) The

Venezuelan public, with its overriding faith in democracy, would not be receptive to a leftist frontal attack on the established system. MAS-istas should thus cast themselves as defenders of the nation's democracy and the party's program should be designed to strengthen the political system rather than undermine it. (2) MAS had to go beyond its original constituency by offering immediate solutions of a technical nature to economic problems, which were the largest area of popular dissatisfaction. (3) The honesty of MAS candidates should be emphasized in campaigns in order to capture the votes of the large number of Venezuelans who question the ethical conduct of elected officials. (4) Loyalty toward AD and COPEI transcends the complaints that people have of their performance when in power. MAS should thus avoid sharp personal attacks on AD-COPEI leaders and be disposed to collaborate with both parties, at least on occasion. (5) The tenaciousness of the political party system and party loyalties obliged MAS to build the party rather than work through an amorphous "movement of movements." (6) The negligible and declining number of Venezuelans who identified with the "left"[35] convinced many MASistas of the necessity of dropping the leftist label and maintaining relations with the rest of the left at arm's length.

Conclusions Regarding MAS and Interparty Relations

In Venezuela, as in other nonsocialist nations, interparty unity has emerged as a paramount issue on the left over the past twenty-five years. The proliferation of socialist models set off by the Sino-Soviet dispute and accentuated by the rise of Eurocommunism has prompted many leftists to accept diversity and to call for a pluralistic approach to socialism. Those who defend the coexistence of distinct models for achieving socialism have been most vocal in their support of unity of the left. A few of them have proposed organic unity whereby leftist parties coalesce into one organization.[36] In Venezuela in recent years various smaller leftist parties have followed this approach, and even the larger MEP and MIR have considered the possibility of fusion.

A second form of unity consists of interparty accords for running common candidates. José Vicente Rangel personified this strategy in the 1983 elections. On that occasion Rangel identified himself with the spirit of unity by recognizing the individual identity of the parties that supported him and providing each one with publicity.

MAS, in spite of its embracement of ideological pluralism as a principle, has spurned unity with leftist parties that do not accept its version of the democratic peaceful road to socialism. MAS's insistence on running its own candidate and the refusal of many of its leaders to unite with the Communist Party under any circumstances have undermined leftist unity. Leftist leaders of various organizations have stated that interparty unity in which the largest party on the left, namely MAS, is not included is not worth pursuing. It was for this reason that in the 1978 campaign the left ran as many as four presidential candidates. Both MIR and MEP preferred to run their own candidates rather than form part of a coalition that, because of MAS's nonparticipation, could not have been considered representative of a truly united left.

MAS has employed heavily charged rhetoric in its polemics with the rest of the left. Its attacks on the PCV have been responded to in kind, in contrast to the explicit policy pursued by MEP, among others, of avoiding personal accusations against fellow leftists and playing down criticism of other parties on the left.

MAS has stayed clear of coalitions in order not to dilute its message in any way. During its early years the party attempted to identify itself with the struggle for socialism and thus assumed what we have called a *left position* of rejecting alliances with nonsocialist parties. The relative strength of the moderate left at the time would have given it the upper hand in an alliance with MAS, which would have been obliged to make major programmatic concessions. By the mid-1970s MAS emphasized its support for democracy, pluralism, and neutrality and, in the process, adopted a *right position* with regard to interparty relations. MAS was reluctant to associate itself with leftist parties such as the PCV, whose defense of the Soviet Union and the dictatorship of the proletariat was antithetical to these principles.

MAS's adherence to both *left* and *right positions* stemmed from the party's commitment to long-term ideological considerations. MAS has always subordinated the struggle to achieve reforms, whether they be improved benefits for workers or price controls, to the task of emphasizing the type of society that it is trying to create. MAS's short-term objectives approximated those of the rest of the left and would have thus been well served by a strategy of alliances with those parties. Nevertheless, the MASistas feared that participation with the orthodox left in coalitions based on immediate reforms would have blurred MAS's democratic image. Its tendency to stress far-reaching ideological goals and relegate reforms to secondary importance contrasts with orthodox communism. Most Communist parties have generally allowed immediate objectives related to bread-and-butter issues and support for the Soviet Union to overshadow their commitment to socialism. This orientation has led them frequently to ally themselves with parties and movements to their right with whom they have profound ideological differences.

The MASistas have played down agitation and mobilization centered on reforms in part because such activity would have forced MAS to work together with other leftist parties that support the same measures. Rather than emphasizing struggle over concrete issues, MAS's energy has been channeled largely into the arena of electoral politics. Winning elections has been its highest priority.

A sizable group of independent leftists has been consistently vocal, more so than any of the political parties, in favoring leftist unity. These independents have undoubtedly been MAS's most effective critics since no one can claim that their criticism of MAS's stand against unity was attributable to partisan loyalty. In the 1973 campaign most independents supported the New Force, which was firmer in its support for leftist unity than was MAS. In 1978 the independents played a key role in the creation of the Coordinator of the Left, prime objective of which was the working out of an interparty electoral agreement. With the Coordinator's dismantling several years later, most independents endorsed José Vicente Rangel, who was more closely identified with the banner of unity than was Petkoff. Furthermore, some of the independents who had supported MAS in the 1973 and 1978 elections, on the basis of the fact that Rangel was the only unaffiliated leftist candidate, switched over to MAS's leftist rivals in the 1983 contests for the same reason.

Conclusions Regarding MAS's Position in the Venezuelan Party System

At the time of its founding MAS stood to the left of the Communist Party, especially in its view of socialism as a medium-term possibility. After the 1973 elections MAS modified its positions and made a conscious attempt to copy aspects of AD's style. MAS's new center-left location on the political spectrum was evident in its conciliatory stand toward the government, the moderation of its rhetoric, and its efforts to disassociate itself from the traditional left and the socialist bloc. Most MASistas assumed that the main obstacle to defining MAS as left-of-center would be the Communist background of its most important leaders. MAS's sharp attacks against the rest of the left and its adamant refusal to accept leftist unity were designed to overcome this credibility gap by creating a distance between MAS and the traditional left.

The main difficulty that MAS encountered, however, in reserving for itself a space in the center-left camp came from an unexpected source, namely, AD. AD's claim to be a "party of the people" and representative of the democratic left was greatly aided by the windfall of oil revenue, which allowed the Pérez administration to carry out far-reaching socioeconomic reforms. Furthermore, AD's flexibility enabled it to reenlist ex-members who had participated in the various left-wing splits that shook the party in the 1960s. Discontented voters who supported popular reforms while rejecting radical solutions tended to choose AD's tested solutions over MAS's untested ones.

MAS's internal reorganization and its advocacy of structural democratic reforms embodied in the "Declaration-80" were designed to differentiate MAS from AD. Ever since its founding, AD had arrogated to itself the mantle of guardian of the nation's democracy. AD leaders constantly harped on their party's role in implementing universal suffrage and direct elections in the 1940s and its defense of the democratic system in the face of threats from both the right and the left in the 1960s. In more recent years, however, AD ceased to play a significant role in deepening the nation's democracy. The party maintained, at best, a lukewarm attitude toward the political reforms MAS proposed. Furthermore, its refusal to allow its members to publicly question party policy, even in the most mild and indirect fashion, contrasted with MAS's more open and flexible approach.

MAS's rejection of leftist unity and the modification of its positions convinced AD and COPEI that it was part of the "loyal opposition" and that, unlike the rest of the left, it was not seeking to undermine the democratic system. That the largest party on the left avoided the intransigent stands of other leftist parties served the interests of AD and COPEI. Both parties feared that their own images as representatives of the "establishment" and the agreements they had reached between themselves (in 1958 and 1970)[37] would set in motion a polarization that would pit the two of them against a united left. This was naturally viewed as disadvantageous in that it would have minimized the differences between AD and COPEI and convinced voters that their principal choice was between AD-COPEI, on the one hand, and the left, on the other. The possibility of such a scenario was reduced by MAS's rejection of unity of the left and its willingness to identify itself with mainstream politics.

MAS's stabilizing role in the political party system helped prevent the extreme apathy and alienation that characterized the electorate in neighboring Colombia. Leftist insurgency and abstention in Colombia reflected and reinforced the polarization between those who identified with the nation's democracy and those who did not. In Venezuela, MAS from its outset adamantly criticized abstentionism as an ultra-leftist tactic that had been discredited in the 1960s. MAS's participation in student and national elections and in the nation's major labor organizations was at first attacked by other leftists but subsequently became widely accepted by them. This policy drew a large number of Venezuelans who had previously sympathized with the clandestine left into mainstream politics.

AD and COPEI leaders hinted at in public and expressed more explicitly in private their gratitude toward MAS for its part in fortifying the democratic system. Both in the government and the opposition, AD and COPEI were anxious that their positions be seconded by MAS in order to enhance their credibility. Thus, for instance, during the early months of the presidency of Carlos Andrés Pérez, AD attempted to convince MAS to go beyond its critical praise of the government by extending it unqualified support.[38]

One instance in which AD and COPEI were disposed to collaborate with MAS and reward it for its moderation was in the establishment of a philanthropic cultural organization shortly after the 1983 elections. At this time AD and COPEI had set up their own foundations, which they feared would be criticized as an undue intrusion of the "establishment" parties on the cultural life of the nation. In order to detract from the credibility of this charge, they encouraged MAS to found a third foundation, which was called the Gual y España Foundation. Representatives of AD and COPEI on the Supreme Electoral Council and other bodies voted to allocate funds to the Gual y España. Headed by Pompeyo Márquez, the foundation sponsored conferences on diverse themes related to politics, economics, and history. Both leftist and nonleftist experts were invited to deliver lectures, which enhanced the party's claim to being truly pluralistic. In short, MAS's modest growth and its status as the largest party on the Venezuelan left was compatible with the interests of AD and COPEI. Both parties hoped that MAS's relative success would dispel the notion that they monopolized power at all levels and that the democratic system was closed to political competitors.

9 MAS's Participation in Organized Labor and University Politics

The Venezuelan Labor Movement: Political and Structural Overview

The Venezuelan labor movement throughout most of its history has been characterized by parallel unionism, a problem that is an outgrowth of excessive political party interference and control. Worker members of political parties, rather than accept minority status within unions dominated by their rivals, have frequently preferred to work within their own labor organizations. In addition, they have founded skeleton unions in order to give themselves additional representation at higher levels within organized labor, or for the purpose of inflating statistics regarding their party's labor backing. These practices are generally sanctioned, if not promoted, by their respective parties, which thus place their own interests ahead of the workers'.

Historical factors explain the tight linkage between parties and unions. In European and some Latin American countries, such as Chile, the labor movement emerged prior to and independent of the first prolabor leftist parties, but in Venezuela the process was different. The first Venezuelan leftist parties were formed by the future leaders of AD and the PCV in 1936 concurrently with the founding of the first unions. Later, the leftist parties nurtured and protected the union movement when times became difficult and repression set in. Actually, the labor movement is just the most extreme case of Venezuelan institutions in general—the universities, the judiciary and, to a certain extent, the armed forces: institutional autonomy is limited by party intervention.

Parallel unionism has been the subject of heated debate on the left in Venezuela, as in other Latin American countries. Neither the orthodox Communists nor other leftist movements have succeeded in reaching a formula or have followed a consistent policy. Thus in some countries, such as Colombia and Peru, Communists have established their own confederations; in Argentina, Chile, and elsewhere they have worked within confederations they themselves do not control.

MAS's decision to withdraw from and dissolve separate labor organizations in 1974 in order to form part of the AD-controlled CTV represented a turning point in MAS's labor policy and set off internal discussion regarding the new situation faced by the party in the labor movement. What to do in cases in which MAS-controlled unions representing large numbers of workers were not accepted in the CTV, and whether or not MAS labor leaders should openly criticize CTV policies were two questions that provoked fervid discussion. In addition, a breach developed between MAS labor leaders and party heads. The former accused the latter of neglecting trade union work and were in turn criticized for failing to challenge the trade union bureaucracy from within. This chapter deals with these issues first by tracing the polemics within the PCV regarding the CTV prior to 1971, then by discussing MAS's early labor policy and its decision to join the CTV, and subsequently by analyzing MAS's experiences in the labor movement since 1975.

A final section on labor is designed to correct the impression that the Venezuelan labor movement is monolithic and lacking input from the rank and file. This mistaken view is derived from the overwhelming control AD has exercised over the CTV almost uninterruptedly since the confederation's founding in 1947. AD's dominant position in the CTV stems from the party's strength in the peasant movement, among state employees, and in sparsely populated areas. In contrast, in the capital and in other industrial regions, as well as in certain industries, AD's control is less absolute. The final section on labor deals with these strategic sectors, specifically the steel and textile workers' movements, where rank-and-file upsurges have confronted the CTV bureaucracy; the discussion examines MAS's role in these movements, as well as the challenge that they posed to MAS's labor strategy.

Debate over Parallel Unionism prior to the Founding of MAS

Dual unionism emerged in 1944 as a result of the sharp rivalry between the nation's two leftist parties, the PCV and AD. Debate within the PCV gave rise to a schism during the *trienio* period of AD rule (1945–48), when the labor movement was completely dominated by the government party. On the one hand, the PRP(C) set up its own unions and federations in protest to the allegedly undemocratic conduct of AD labor leaders. On the other hand, the PCV worked within pro-AD labor organizations even though Communists were generally excluded from leadership posts. The major exception was in the powerful Petroleum Workers Federation (Fedepetrol), where the PCV enjoyed considerable support. In early 1948 the two Communists on Fedepetrol's executive committee were expelled as a result of their opposition to the ratification of an industrywide contract. The PCV trade unionists promptly withdrew from Fedepetrol and formed their own oil workers' federation. This move was criticized by two young Communist labor leaders, Eloy Torres and Francisco J. Arrieti, at the party's Second National Congress a few months later. They argued that by leaving Fedepetrol, Communist oil worker leaders had isolated themselves from the majority of workers in the industry and would thus be unable to mount an offensive against either the companies or the government.[1]

Unity in the labor movement was achieved in the struggle against the Pérez Jiménez dictatorship (particularly during the oil workers' strike of May 1950) and the initial years of the post-1958 democratic period. However, the violent confrontation between the left and the Betancourt government in the early 1960s was reflected in the expulsion of leftist labor leaders from top positions in the CTV at its fourth congress in 1961 and the subsequent decision to set up the rival Central Unitario de Trabajadores de Venezuela (CUTV). The establishment of the CUTV was unanimously supported by leftists at the time, though some PCV labor leaders, including one prominent orthodox member of the party,[2] subsequently criticized the move. By the late 1960s Communist trade unionists proposed different strategies for reunifying the labor movement into one confederation.

One position was upheld by Eloy Torres, a former metallurgical workers' leader and a long-time opponent of dual unionism. Upon his release in 1967 from jail, where he spent five years for his participation in the military uprising in Carúpano, Torres assumed a critical stand toward the PCV's labor policy. Torres reproached the CUTV for failing to act energetically in favor of unity. The CUTV, according to Torres, had ignored the resolution of the Ninth Plenum of the PCV's Central Committee in 1968, which called for the dissolution of parallel unions. He stated that although conditions were not ripe for an immediate merger of the CUTV and the CTV, an eventual fusion should take place, since otherwise Communist trade unionists would be doomed to isolation from the overwhelming majority of organized workers, who belonged to the CTV. Torres also noted that unity would facilitate the PCV's trade union activity since the Labor Ministry discriminated against the CUTV unions for being pro-Communist.[3]

Torres called on the PCV to emphasize work in individual unions regardless of affiliation, rather than making a special effort to strengthen the CUTV. In a report to the PCV's Central Committee in September 1970 Torres characterized the lengthy internal discussions about the role of the nation's labor confederations as "sterile" and proposed "concentrating on the most important unions . . . in order to penetrate companies and sectors."[4] Such a strategy implied attaching special significance to CTV unions, since those of the CUTV grouped few workers and were almost totally absent in the critically important oil industry.

In the same report Torres applauded the consolidation of a leftist current within the CTV in the form of MEP, which included the confederation's president, José González Navarro, and other top labor leaders. Although the PCV had harshly attacked González Navarro and other future MEPistas in the early 1960s for their support of Betancourt's policy of austerity and the expulsion of leftists from the CTV, their participation in MEP was considered a promising development. Torres also noted that AD-MEP tension in the CTV had opened the possibility of a division in the confederation. These circumstances pointed to the need for Communists to work within CTV unions in order to try to influence the course of events.[5]

In his report to the Central Committee, Torres euphemistically described the CUTV as suffering from a "poor distribution of cadre," which in effect meant that it was a top-heavy bureaucracy.[6] Germán Lairet, another Communist critic of the CUTV, noted that the "bureaucratic traits" of the organization had been evident in the steel workers' conflict of 1969 when the confederation was unable to reach the workers, much less wrest control from the CTV.[7] Informally, Torres and others facetiously called the CUTV a "travel agency" whose main function was arranging trips to socialist countries for its members.[8] The anti-CUTV Communists appealed to the PCV heads to exercise greater control over the party's trade union work. Torres even called for the establishment of "industrial commissions" that would be directly responsible to the Central Committee and in this way bypass the CUTV.[9]

A group of Communist Youth members in the Caracas area, including Jesús Urbieta, Carlos Rodríguez, and Alfredo Padilla, went further than Torres by calling for immediate incorporation into the CTV. In 1966 some of them attended a meeting of the CTV's regional federation in Caracas and were denounced in the press for attempting to "infiltrate" the CTV. These younger Communists hoped that the PCV's support for MEP's presidential candidate in the 1968 elections would signal a new party policy of working with organizations to its right that would spill over to the labor movement.[10]

Torres, Lairet, Urbieta, Rodríguez, Padilla, and other critics of the CUTV became leading members of MAS. During MAS's early years the policy of making a concerted effort to join the CTV and its affiliate organizations, which Torres urged, was not shared by Carlos Arturo Pardo, MAS's National Trade Union secretary, nor by top party leaders, who argued against entering the CTV. Thus two diametrically opposed viewpoints regarding the CTV coexisted in the early MAS. Nevertheless, the PCV labor leaders who joined MAS shared a disparaging attitude toward the CUTV and favored a thorough revision of the PCV's labor policy. In addition, they were drawn to MAS because they accepted Petkoff's call to propagandize for socialism and insert the ideological message into political work. Torres expressed this viewpoint in his report to the PCV's Central Committee; he deplored "the Communist Party's virtual abandonment of the ideological struggle against alien ideas in the heart [of the working class]." He added that a dogmatic style based on abstract formulas was especially ill-suited for reaching younger workers.[11]

From Parallel Unionism to Integration: MAS's Early Labor Policy

Several weeks after the founding of MAS in January 1971, MAS and MIR labor leaders withdrew from the CUTV and set up the CUTV-Clasista. The MASistas accused their former comrades of high-handedness in relying on the votes of old-time Communist labor leaders on the executive committee, who had long retired from trade union activity, in order to maintain control of the confederation.[12] The CUTV-Clasista was led mostly by labor leaders associated with MIR, including the confederation's president, José Marcano, though MASistas Carlos Arturo Pardo and Carlos Rodríguez also occupied leadership positions. Eloy Torres, who favored making greater efforts to join the CTV, distanced himself from trade union activity.

The CUTV-Clasista was particularly hostile to the CTV and the pro-Copeyano CODESA, which it branded "two colossuses of bureaucratism." The CUTV-Clasista even criticized the PCV-dominated CUTV for its joint participation with the CTV in May Day parades, which were described as examples of "false unity." Furthermore, the PCV leaders were accused of "liquidationist tendencies" because of their support, at least in theory, of an eventual fusion of existing labor confederations.[13] In many workplaces MAS set up parallel labor organizations alongside already existing ones, which affiliated with the CUTV-Clasista.

MAS's intransigent positions during its early years were reflected in its labor policy. Just as MAS attempted to expose the unscrupulousness and duplicity of individual capitalists, the party attacked CTV bureaucrats in personal terms and even published accounts of their extravagant life styles. MAS labor leaders coined the slogan "Movement to the Rescue" to refer to their efforts to challenge the CTV for control of the labor movement.[14] This hostility toward the CTV was manifested in mid-1971 when MAS urged MEP to abandon the confederation in protest of its intervention in a steel workers' strike in Ciudad Guayana led by a MEPista.

MAS's labor leaders have generally rejected participation with other leftist parties in joint slates in trade union elections. After showing initial interest in uniting with the parties of the New Force in the elections for the Colegio de Profesores and elsewhere, MAS decided to launch its own candidates. According to the MASistas it was imperative for MAS, as a newly founded party, to project its own image in organized labor by avoiding association with other parties.

With the exception of Pardo and Torres, MAS failed to draw top PCV labor leaders at the time of its founding and was equally unsuccessful at the middle and lower levels. In spite of its initial weakness in organized labor, MAS was confident that its novel approach of appealing to the rank and file on the basis of commitment to socialism and struggle against trade union bureaucracy would rally large numbers of workers. This optimism was reinforced by the favorable results of the elections of the state steel company SIDOR in June 1971. Because of its strategic importance and its recent history of intense worker conflict, SIDOR was selected as a prime target of organizing activity. MASistas thus viewed their impressive showing as their party's first important victory and an indication of what could be expected from workers in other industries. Nevertheless, these hopes were quickly dashed by an abortive strike following the elections and MAS's concomitant loss of support in SIDOR. The experience of the elections, the strike, and its aftermath are worth examining in detail since they bore heavily on the party's subsequent revisions and the labor policy it has followed ever since.

The PCV retained the loyalty of its worker cadre at SIDOR at the time of the 1971 division. Nevertheless, a group of MAS leaders from Caracas traveled to the Guayana region and succeeded in attracting a number of young steel workers, who were impressed by MAS's militant style.[15] In the campaign for elections in the steel workers' union ATISS, MAS emphasized its commitment to trade union democracy and rejection of bureaucracy. MAS invented the cartoon character "Rufi," who was typically shown being kicked in the buttocks by the workers along with the caption: "As Rufi smiles, he is transformed from a worker into a phony labor leader." Rufi represented the ex-worker turned union bureaucrat in the person of Andrés Marcano, a MEPista whose integrity had been widely questioned and who aspired to reelection as president of the steel workers. MAS, along with the PCV, attacked Marcano for having formed "a small personal empire" in ATISS and for having squandered union funds.[16]

As part of its support for worker participation, MAS selected its slate at an open assembly of workers. In their campaign propaganda on the radio and elsewhere, MAS trade unionists stressed their commitment to socialism. The PCVistas berated MAS for its insistence on raising the issue of socialism in a union election, a practice they denounced as irresponsible and "demagogic." For its part, MAS mocked the idea, defended by PCV secretary general Jesús Faría, that the labor movement should recognize SIDOR's character as a state company by moderating its demands.[17] MAS came in second place with 596 votes, behind the moderate leftist parties of the New Force, which supported Marcano and whose slate received 1,040 votes. The PCV tied COPEI for third place, in spite of having entered the contest with a sizable group of veteran trade unionists. The fledgling MAS thus became the largest party in ATISS, at the same time that the left established itself in firm control of the union.

MAS's militant rhetoric at SIDOR was put to test a few weeks after the elections when the union, following the lead of iron workers in the nearby mines in the state of Bolívar, went on strike. The walkout was considered a major challenge to the government, which jailed union leaders and ordered the National Guard to take over Ciudad Guayana. The CTV withdrew its initial support and urged conciliation, while the MEPistas vacillated. The MASistas held out until it became apparent that the strike was lost. The union reached a gentleman's agreement with SIDOR, which promised to refrain from reprisals. The company, however, ignored the understanding and fired a large number of union militants, including 300 MASistas.

Leftists drew different lessons from the experience of the strike. For the miniscule guerrilla movement that had engaged in clandestine actions in support of the workers, the conflict confirmed the validity of extralegal activity since the union heads, who were mostly in jail or in hiding, were in no position to lead the struggle.[18] Many MEPistas, embittered by the behavior of the CTV, seriously considered withdrawing from the confederation. The MASistas, for their part, went to great pains to analyze the event, as the defeat of the strike and MAS's subsequent loss of support at SIDOR were heavy blows. They reached the conclusion that they had been strike-happy and had failed to carefully measure the consequences of their actions or to consider alternative courses. Not only was an indefinite strike called, but the union failed to engage in serious negotiations with the company. An additional mistake was committed following the strike when MASistas, chafed by the willingness of certain labor leaders to capitulate without receiving sufficient guarantees, temporarily withdrew from ATISS; they even drew up their own labor contract for the purpose of collective bargaining.[19]

In addition to the experience of the abortive steel workers' strike, the New Mode of Being Socialist document of February 1974, which sought to modify MAS's style to bring it more in tune with the consciousness of the general populace, influenced the party to abandon its intransigent positions in organized labor. To avoid the problem of "essentialism" whereby socialism is viewed as a panacea for all problems—which the "New Mode" thesis warned against—MAS trade unionists decided to stress workers' management and comanagement of the workplace, systems that, unlike socialism, were realizable in the immediate future. In addition, at their First National Assembly in July 1974, MAS labor leaders reached the conclusion that their failure to make substantial inroads was due to the mechanical application of the party's political slogans to worker struggles and the "absence of specific messages for the workers."[20]

The New Mode thesis—with its emphasis on the need to break out of the leftist "ghetto" and enter the nation's mainstream—encouraged MAS to disband its separate labor organizations and work within the CTV. Several positions emerged in MAS in 1974 at the time of the debate over the issue. On the one hand, ex-guerrilla commander Tirso Pinto, Carlos Arturo Pardo, and others argued against formal participation in the CTV. Pinto upheld an extreme position that favored the founding of a new labor confederation, whereas Pardo called for a more flexible policy of working in the "majority unions"—those which grouped the largest number of workers—regardless of which confederation they were affiliated with. These viewpoints were defeated, and instead MAS chose to work exclusively in the CTV. Jesús Urbieta expressed another opinion, in direct opposition to Pinto's, which was also rejected by the party in 1974. According to Urbieta, MAS had to obtain positions in the CTV leadership greater than that which the party's meager labor following warranted, in order to occupy a "space" in the confederation. For the time being, MAS should refrain from criticizing CTV leaders and instead reach an agreement with them in order to secure posts. MAS's official position was to reject this conciliatory line and instead call for taking up the struggle against corruption in the CTV and establishing a "socialist reference" within the confederation.[21]

MAS's decision to participate in the CTV was scornfully greeted by some CTVistas as representing "the return of extremism." AD, COPEI, and even MEP labor leaders refused to accept MAS-led unions in some statewide and industrial federations, thus limiting MAS's representation at the CTV's Seventh Congress in 1975. Merely nine MAS trade unionists attended the convention out of a total of 1,000 delegates. Nevertheless, CTV president Francisco Olivo and Ismario González, president of the federation of health workers, favored a generous policy toward smaller parties whose representation at the congress was insignificant, over the resistance of some fellow AD labor leaders. As a result, Jesús Urbieta was incorporated into the official slate as substitute member of the CTV's executive committee.

MAS's decision to join the CTV was denounced by other leftist parties as "treasonous."[22] This reaction reflected the bitterness leftists still harbored toward the CTV for having defended, and in some cases participated in, the repression against the left in the 1960s. Nevertheless, MAS's new policy of working within the CTV was dictated by the obvious necessity of reaching the mass of organized workers. Indeed, the arguments in favor of the move were so compelling that some of MAS's critics, specifically MIR and the Vanguardia Comunista (which had split off from the PCV in 1974), soon followed the party's lead by seeking entrance into the confederation.

MAS's Labor Policy since 1975

Over the last decade and a half the success of the left and MAS in particular in the labor movement has been extremely limited. The most important labor gains were handed down by executive decree rather than won through militant struggle. These benefits were made possible by the oil price hikes and the resultant windfall in government revenue. President Carlos Andrés Pérez, during his first year in office in 1974, implemented a price freeze on articles of basic necessity, salary increases, a program of free milk for school children, double severance pay for unjustified layoffs, and regulation of employment of apprentices. The left applauded Pérez's popular reforms but, with the exception of MAS, voted against the authorization of emergency executive powers.

During this period leftist labor leaders distinguished themselves from those of AD and COPEI in their support for certain far-reaching demands. The most important were a cost-of-living "escalator" mechanism for salaries to be implemented on a national scale, a reduction in the three-year duration of industrywide labor contracts, and a "Law of Labor Stability," which would impede or prohibit layoffs. All three demands had first been raised as far back as the 1940s in the oil industry and elsewhere, and had been the source of several major labor conflicts.[23] During the 1970–85 period, however, the left failed to put up a common front in Congress or rally workers on behalf of these reforms.

Since 1970 AD has maintained firm control of the CTV. Grass-roots movements, some of which were only tenuously tied to political parties, seemed at different moments to command sufficient worker loyalty to make outside intervention unlikely. Nevertheless, the CTV often displaced the natural leaders, who assumed control of these struggles, and imposed its own pliant ones in an effort to avoid labor unrest.

Throughout this period MAS's main leftist rival in the CTV was MEP, which, in spite of its loss of influence, remained by far the largest leftist party in organized labor (see table 9-1). At the 1970 CTV Congress MEP labor leaders objected to AD's pact with COPEI whereby a Copeyano was appointed to the number-two position of secretary general in spite of MEP's superior delegate strength. In the following year MEPistas denounced the CTV's conciliatory role in the steel workers' strike in Guayana. On both occasions the MEPistas considered withdrawing from the CTV to set up a truly *clasista* (pro-worker) confederation whose authorities would be elected directly by the workers.[24]

Since 1971, however, MEP labor leaders have played down conflict and have failed to adopt a militant stance in accordance with their party's leftward drift. MEP, in spite of erosion of strength, succeeded in retaining control of several important federations by following a policy it called "tactical flexibility," whereby it allied itself in some instances with AD and others with COPEI. As a result of support from COPEI, MEPistas managed to control Fedepetrol and Fetrazulia, the state federation in Zulia, throughout most of the 1970s. They also formed an alliance with discontented AD trade unionists in various states as well as with URD in an unsuccessful bid to challenge the reelection of the AD president of the communication workers' federation in 1975.[25]

Just as MEP softened its stands in the CTV after 1971 and adopted a strategy of interparty alliances, MAS entered the CTV in 1975 intent on exposing the corruption and heavy-handedness from within the confederation, only shortly thereafter to tone down its rhetoric and accept AD hegemony. Jesús Urbieta, who represented MAS in the CTV after 1975 (first as substitute and then as regular member of the confederation's executive committee), allied himself with AD in such trade union matters as its opposition to the government's closing of the CTV-owned Banco de los Trabajadores (BTV) in 1982. Urbieta argued that the rivalry between AD and MAS on the political front should not be automatically transferred to trade union affairs, and he even called for a formal alliance between the two for the 1985 CTV congress. He expressed faith that AD's widespread influence in the working class and its history of trade union militance dating back to its radical populist period made the party a worthy ally and opened the possibility that it would move to the left.[26]

In 1984, following the election of AD's Jaime Lusinchi as the nation's president, MAS refused to participate in worker protests organized by trade unionists of the opposition parties grouped in the CUTV, the CTV, and two pro-Copeyano confederations. The willingness of Copeyano trade unionists to throw in their lot with the left in a united effort against the AD government was an encouraging sign for the opposition. MAS, however, reasoned that without endorsement from AD labor leaders, with their dominant position in organized labor, the protests would be doomed to failure. Furthermore, MAS labor leaders were reluctant to ally with COPEI against AD because of the former's reputation as the party of the oligarchy.[27] This preference for AD over COPEI was not shared by most leftists, who viewed the two parties as equally representative of the interests of the ruling class.

In some states the MASistas received support from AD in their effort to enter CTV federations. In Aragua, for instance, MAS faced opposition in Fetra-Aragua, which refused to accept several unions controlled by MAS (the largest of which was TEXFIN) and the Single Textile Workers Union (SUT) in which MAS shared control with several ultra-left groups. These organizations were refused admission on grounds that they were "parallel" to other unions affiliated with the CTV. MEP, even though it enjoyed little support among textile workers in the state, was especially insistent that the pro-MAS unions be excluded, undoubtedly because it feared competition from MAS as the second-largest leftist party in the CTV.

After having made impressive inroads in the labor movement in its early years, especially in the textile industry in Aragua and the metallurgical industry in Guayana, the party's subsequent gains were modest, if not at times imperceptible. The growth of MAS's delegations at the CTV congresses over the five years from 1975 to 1980 was reflected in the configuration of the official slates, which were unanimously elected. In 1980 MAS received a regular and a substitute seat on the confederation's executive committee in place of the substitute position it had occupied since 1975. MAS's increased number of delegates in 1980 over 1975, however, was due not so much to its increased support in organized labor as to the fact that in the interim MAS-

Table 9-1 Party Representation in CTV Congresses, 1975–1985

Political party	1975 Delegates		1980 Delegates		1985 Delegates	
	N	%	N	%	N	%
AD	508	58.8	719	56.3	935	61.4
COPEI	215	21.5	268	20.9	313	20.6
MAS	9	0.9	40	3.2	51	3.3
MEP	167	16.7	157	12.3	135	8.9
MIR	2	0.2	8	0.6	6	0.4
PCV	5	0.5	6	0.5	6	0.4
URD	81	8.1	36	2.8	58	3.8
Others	13	1.3	44	3.4	19	1.2

controlled unions had gained entrance into CTV federations. Furthermore, MAS's delegate strength at the 1985 congress did not vary substantially from that of 1980 (see table 9-1), and as a result its representation on the CTV's executive committee went unchanged.

MAS trade unionists failed to develop a stronghold in any one industry, and a substantial part of its support came from small firms with an unstable work force. Most significant, MAS nearly totally lacked influence among the all-important petroleum workers. During the guerrilla period in the 1960s the government had made a concerted and successful effort to rid the industry of leftists, and thus MAS, at its outset, had no support in that sector. MAS has rejected the traditional left's emphasis on oil and other strategic industries and instead has maintained that its goal of winning over a large majority of the population to socialism obviates a strategy of concentrating efforts in certain areas.

The dispersed nature of MAS's labor influence explains the difficulty faced by party trade union leaders in developing a uniform and coherent style. Had the party established a base in certain key industries, the slogans and rhetoric utilized there would have naturally spilled over to other sectors where MAS's support was less pronounced.[28]

MAS's inconsistencies are also related to the failure of party labor leaders to develop an alternative strategy to the ultra-leftism that MAS followed in its early years (as typified by its precipitation of the strike at SIDOR in 1971 and its presence in the CUTV-Clasista) and the policy of tactical alliances with AD and COPEI, which is closely associated with the MEPistas. The MASistas have been particularly critical of MEP labor leaders, who are viewed as opportunistic bureaucrats who have not changed since their days in AD. MAS trade unionists, confident that the freshness of their message would have greater appeal than MEP's time-worn slogans, were optimistic about replacing MEP as the leading leftist party in the CTV, and thus saw that party as a competitor rather than an ally in organized labor.[29]

Internal Debate over Labor Policy

The increasingly uncritical attitude of MAS labor leaders toward the CTV and their failure to make substantial inroads in organized labor has led party leaders to question their performance. Freddy Muñoz was most vocal in insisting that MAS's trade union heads had failed to put into practice the party's original strategy of entering the CTV in order to struggle against the confederation's bureaucracy from within. Muñoz also pointed out that MAS trade unionists had neglected the socialist education of the workers, as the party had originally set out to do. This disparity between objectives and practice, according to Muñoz, explained why MAS's trade union gains were not commensurate with the party's overall growth. Had MAS been able to create a "socialist pole in the workers' movement that was the center of attraction and the motor force of a dynamic renovating current," the party's performance in organized labor would have been distinctly better.[30]

In internal documents written by Carlos Arturo Pardo and other MAS trade unionists, the party's political heads were accused of neglecting or "underestimating the importance" of trade union work.[31] Petkoff and other top MASistas recognized the validity of this criticism and suggested that the disillusionment among MASistas over the passivity of the Venezuelan working class and MAS's failure to repeat its initial successes at SIDOR and elsewhere accounted for their attitude.[32]

Mutual distrust between labor and political leaders has manifested itself in discussion over internal norms and the relationship between MAS's labor bureau and the rest of the party. Trade union leaders have denounced the excessive control of the party's political heads in labor matters as a reversion to the obsolete Leninist principle (spelled out in *What Is to Be Done*) that trade unionists left to their own are incapable of arriving at socialist solutions and thus need to be guided by political cadre.[33] Party leaders, for their part, have insisted that MAS's policy of rotation in office be extended to trade union posts. This idea has been resisted by the party's labor leaders in large part because it represents an especially heavy personal sacrifice for them. Political leaders, who are for the most part professionals, can derive a living in their respective fields and in many cases have the option of going into private practice. The trade union leader, on the other hand, faces greater difficulty in finding employment and inevitably takes a sharp cut in income.

The tension between political and labor leaders was put in evidence as a result of the party's attempt to decentralize its structure. At MAS's congress in May 1980 six commissions were created, each one for a specific activity. MAS trade unionists objected to the fact that labor was not assigned its own commission and instead fell under a broadly defined "Commission of Masses." Worse still, a political leader, Victor Hugo D'Paola, rather than a trade unionist was selected to head the commission. Previously, the appointment of Carlos Arturo Pardo to the same position had received unanimous acceptance because of his popularity and long record of dedication and personal sacrifice. Pardo, however, unexpectedly passed away, and distrust toward other important labor leaders, who it was felt strove to establish a trade union fiefdom within the party, led to the appointment of D'Paola. This nomination was unacceptable to the trade unionists, and the ensuing fray was resolved only when the commission was scrapped altogether.[34]

After the 1983 national elections MAS was run by a provisional structure that included a national trade union secretary; at the same time the party made plans to carry out a permanent reorganization at its 1985 congress. In the months preceding the congress MAS's trade union leaders decided to act as a group in order to press for greater autonomy within MAS and other objectives. In a communique signed by over a hundred MAS labor leaders, the party was criticized for its "disassociation from the social struggle in general and a notable indifference toward trade union activity." The signers of the document accused the nation's political parties, MAS included, of attempting to convert social movements into "transmission belts" (a term originally employed by Lenin) in order to promote their own interests. The subscribers pledged themselves to act together in order to elect labor leaders to party positions at the upcoming congress. They also argued that MAS trade unionists alone should select the party's representatives to the CTV executive committee. Those who put their names to the document belonged to the factions headed by Pompeyo Márquez and Bayardo Sardi, which took in a large majority of MAS's labor heads.[35]

The Metal and Textile Workers' Movements

This discussion of MAS's participation in the trade union movement would be incomplete, not to say misleading, if it left the impression that Venezuelan labor is docile and easily controlled by a trade union bureaucracy. Such a characterization, which of course accurately describes some sectors, would absolve MAS of having committed serious errors in its efforts to direct the labor movement in a more militant course. Organized labor's more combative fringe, especially the textile and metal workers' unions, has provided MAS with opportunities to establish a strong foothold in the labor movement. That neither MAS nor the other more important leftist parties have been successful over a period of time in these two sectors is an implicit criticism of the labor policies of the "established left" (the PCV, MAS, MEP, and MIR). A brief review of the two areas is thus needed to complete the discussion of MAS's position in the Venezuelan labor movement and to place in sharper focus the alternative leftist strategies MAS has had to choose between.

The militance of workers in the highly industrialized Guayana region is a reflection of the extremely harsh living and working conditions to which they are subjected. Guayana became a priority area of industrial development after 1958 with such megaprojects as SIDOR, two state-run aluminum companies (Venalum and Alcasa), the Guri Dam, and the exploitation of iron mines. This rapid growth was not accompanied by effective urban planning—notwithstanding the services rendered by a team connected with the Joint Center of Harvard and MIT—which would have lessened the impact of the influx of large numbers of workers. Chaotic urban growth was coupled with other problems such as the nation's highest rate of inflation and the insecurity faced by migrants who lack the traditional support of the extended family.

In spite of the government's attempt to neutralize discontent by contracting foreigners to work in the region, Guayana's labor movement has been the most militant in the nation. The newness of Guayana's industries and the large numbers of recently arrived workers from different regions of the country influence the average age of the work force. An inordinately large number of workers and union leaders are young and therefore more inclined to be rebellious and to lack loyalty and firm commitment to political parties. Thus, for instance, MEP, MAS, AD, COPEI, MIR, and the Causa R replaced each other in rapid succession as the ascendant party among the workers at SIDOR. Furthermore, labor leaders belonging to parties such as MEP, MAS, COPEI, and the PCV switched party affiliation, in some cases several times. The quickly changing fortunes of political parties were also evident in the iron industry (though AD managed to retain control partly because of the special privileges the iron workers enjoyed), the aluminum industry, and other sectors.

This behavior is a reflection of the deep-seated resentment toward political parties of all ideological tendencies. By the late 1970s a systematic critique of Venezuelan parties was formulated by various miniscule leftist groups (which we will refer to as the "marginal left"), several of which were based mainly in the Guayana region. These parties openly attacked the larger ones for converting worker organizations into electoral arenas and for overestimating the importance of political leaders from Caracas and union legal advisors. The term *parachutist* was derogatorily employed to refer to party spokesmen such as Petkoff, Jesús Faría, and Américo Martín, who traveled to the area in order to rally support for their candidates in union elections. The parties of the marginal left also questioned MIR's conduct in the elections at SUTISS (the successor to ATISS at SIDOR) in which that party's worker candidates took back seats to a labor lawyer, MIR's outstanding leader in the area, who also formed part of the slate. For their part, the small leftist parties at SIDOR formed a coalition headed by Andrés Velásquez of the Causa R that succeeded in winning seven of the ten seats on the executive committee of the union in the elections of 1979. One of the slogans coined by the Causa R was: "In SUTISS the political parties have always governed; now it's time for the workers."[36]

The Causa R's founding leaders, including its *jefe maximo* Alfredo Maneiro, had formed part of the dissident group in the PCV headed by Petkoff in the late 1960s that left the party to found MAS. Maneiro, however, immediately withdrew from MAS because of its failure to break with orthodox practice in which the party places more emphasis on its own growth and projection than on building the mass movement. At first the antiparty attitude of Maneiro and his followers led them to discard the possibility of forming yet another political party, and instead they decided to work exclusively in grass-roots movements. Maneiro, in calling for the founding of a political "bottom-up organization," wrote in mid-1971: "Far from starting with a pre-established party structure and working on behalf of it and its interests, we are confident that the movement of masses can take in its hands the task of producing within its own fold a new leadership."[37]

The failure of the larger parties to maintain a substantial following at SIDOR and elsewhere in Guayana over a period of time and the successes of the Causa R and other small parties of the marginal left can be interpreted as an implicit criticism of the left's failure to unite. In denouncing political parties for placing their organizational interests ahead of those of the workers, the Causa R articulated the widespread disillusionment over the refusal of the established left to place greater emphasis on the struggle for concrete demands at the workplace. Had such a priority been set, the leftist parties, which were basically in agreement on bread-and-butter issues, inevitably would have cast their ideological differences aside and united. The MASistas were particularly prone to pursue a go-it-alone policy, though this practice was shared by other leftists in Guayana who paid lip-service to the idea of unity.

In criticizing the political parties for their vertical line of command, which originated in Caracas, the Causa R expressed the sense of powerlessness that was widely felt in the region. Even the area planning agency, the Venezuelan Corporation of Guayana, unlike its counterparts in other regions, had its headquarters in Caracas. The Causa R and its leftist allies articulated this frustration regarding the remoteness of decision making. As a corrective, they established a system of elected shop stewards, which up until then had existed on paper only. In the iron workers' union the marginal parties mobilized workers in an effort to oblige the union leaders to inform them of the progress in collective bargaining discussions. In SIDOR they insisted that negotiations take place in Ciudad Guayana rather than Caracas (though Causa R would later give in on this point, provoking criticism from its coalition partners).[38]

During its early years at SIDOR following the abortive 1971 strike, the Causa R, unlike other parties, did not attempt to promote its own image or to act mainly in an electoral capacity. Instead, it worked patiently to build a base and to raise concrete issues. In time, much of its efforts revolved around two demands: the rehiring of Andrés Velásquez, who was fired because of his trade union activism, and the forty-hour work week. The Causa R's spectacular triumph in the 1979 elections, after Velásquez had been reinstated, was viewed as a mandate to push the demand for a forty-hour work week. Nevertheless, SIDOR and the government behind it refused to budge on the issue, in large part because reduction of the work week at SIDOR would have inevitably spilled over to other important industries in the area. In the face of government inflexibility, the achievement of this demand would have required a nationwide campaign supported by political parties, which would have been difficult to organize given the disunity on the left. The union slightly modified its position by accepting that the forty-hour work week be initiated only in certain high-stress departments (which took in about 15 percent of the workers), to be extended progressively to the rest of the work force.[39] An agreement based on the forty-hour work week for a more limited number of workers and its postponement for the rest of the industry—as other leftists proposed—perhaps would have been more acceptable.

By late 1981 a showdown between company and union appeared to be inevitable as the union announced its intentions of introducing a petition to go on strike. Actually, the Causa R, unlike its coalition partners, was wary of the type of confrontation that had been so disastrous in 1971 but seemed to be trapped in its own rhetoric, which revolved around the forty-hour work week. At this point the CTV took over the union and replaced its executive committee. The imposed directorate immediately reached an agreement with SIDOR, which offered the workers substantial economic concessions and in doing so helped avoid worker mobilization in opposition to the intervention.[40] Nevertheless, the vast majority of the workers refused to ratify the contract in a referendum sponsored by the CTV.

Both the experience in 1981 and the abortive strike ten years earlier are typical of the acute labor unrest that characterizes heavy industry in the Guayana region. The volatility of the situation, however, can be misleading. There are several factors that weigh against a militant course. The state, often with the backing of the CTV, has assumed a rigid stance in these conflicts because of the industries' strategic importance. In addition, leftist disunity undermines the effort to garner political support, which is especially important for unions in state-run industries such as steel, iron, and aluminum. For these reasons, union leaders have to carefully prepare both the workers and public opinion before launching a strike. The situation also requires flexibility in the formulation of demands and tactics so that concessions to management will not result in loss of face among the workers.

The success of the Causa R and other marginal groups in Guayana has been achieved in large part at the expense of MAS, MEP, and MIR, the three main leftist parties that work within the CTV. The Causa R was particularly critical of MAS for having precipitated a showdown with management in 1971 at SIDOR that the party was not willing to see through to the end.[41] In addition to that conflict, MAS received another fatal blow in the union elections of 1977. In the months prior to that race, the MASistas at SIDOR were sharply divided over the selection of a candidate to head their slate. One of the aspirants was José Barrios, an ex-Copeyano with considerable influence but whose image was tarnished by charges of corruption in union affairs. In addition, the recentness of his conversion to MAS raised doubts about his commitment to the party and its ideology. Petkoff, who participated actively in the process in Guayana, favored the selection of Barrios over his rival, a young unskilled worker who was more closely identified with MAS's radical ideas. Petkoff argued that Barrios's selection was in keeping with MAS's new policy of reaching out to Adecos and

Copeyanos in order to attract them to the party. Barrios's detractors argued that the selection of an individual who was identified with COPEI and whose integrity was open to question went counter to MAS's efforts to project an image of freshness and change as well as firmness in the struggle against union corruption. Barrios was nominated at an open meeting called by MAS, which he stacked with his followers, not all of whom were SIDOR workers. In the union election, however, the MAS slate headed by Barrios went from fourth to sixth place with respect to the previous contests at SIDOR in 1974, while receiving only one seat on the union's executive committee.

In the aftermath of the election Barrios publicly denounced Petkoff and left MAS to join AD. MAS's setbacks at SIDOR during these years set off an extensive discussion within the party. Some MASistas attributed the fiasco at SIDOR to the opportunism of Barrios and the inexperience of other MAS steel workers' leaders, many of whom promptly left the party.[42] Freddy Muñoz and other members of MAS's hardline faction maintained that the experience with Barrios pointed to the inherent danger of allowing ex-Adecos and ex-Copeyanos to rise too quickly in MAS, without first assimilating the party's ideology and proving their reliability. Labor leaders such as Carlos Arturo Pardo blamed MAS's political leadership for failing to provide them with decisive support in the struggle in SIDOR. Pardo wrote that the Trade Union Directorate's responsibility for the party's disappointing showing at SIDOR in 1977 "never reached the level that corresponds to MAS's National Directorate which failed to come through [for the workers] due to the internal situation in MAS." Specifically, Pardo attributed the ineffectiveness of the party's leadership to the sharp internal rivalry set off by the primaries for the 1978 presidential elections.[43]

The textile industry has also been characterized by labor unrest since the early 1970s. In contrast to SIDOR, however, the marginal left has failed to displace the larger parties. Because of the large number of textile companies, the industry is characterized by a hodgepodge of competing federations and unions. The labor movement at SIDOR is in a stronger position, for the workers belong to only one union, which at a given moment has always been controlled by one party, or a few of them in alliance with one another. The main problem faced by the steel workers' union is the power of the government and its determination to maintain labor peace in the region at all costs. But in the textile industry, which was highly depressed up until the mid-1980s, the adversary has lacked political and economic power.

In the latter half of the 1970s the Unión de Trabajadores de la Industria Textil (UTIT) won a number of elections in important companies in the Caracas area over AD-controlled unions that belonged to the CTV. The UTIT was controlled by a loose group of workers and intellectuals from the Central University of Caracas known as the Proceso Político that pursued the same type of bottom-up unionism associated with the marginal left in Guayana. UTIT leaders denounced the political parties for attempting to impose policies on the workers' movement and lashed out at the CTV for its role as handmaiden of AD. During negotiations for the 1977 collective contract, the UTIT held dozens of assemblies in the factories it controlled and attempted to translate the worker feedback into proposals to be introduced in the bargaining sessions. The Proceso Político team wrote that this process of rank-and-file input did not represent a "stable organizational arrangement in the union, nor a situation of steady ongoing [worker] participation. Nevertheless, it is important because it points to the advances that are possible in the exercise of democracy when the masses are mobilized."[44]

The success of Proceso Político was typical of the inroads of other political groups of the marginal left, some of which precipitated strikes without taking into consideration the economic conditions in the industry. The marginal left, unlike the established left, refused to comply with the labor law, which it considered to be specially designed to retard militant action. In 1977 mini-strikes and slowdowns occurred during the sixty-day period of collective bargaining, which is supposed to be free of all forms of labor conflict. The marginal left broke the rules in the belief that, should the government attempt to impose a solution through compulsory arbitration as it was empowered to do, the workers would not be demoralized nor constrained from going on strike.[45]

The greatest challenge to the textile workers was the sheer number of parties with an important representation in the United Trade Union Front of Textile Workers, which brought together the unions during the two most important recent strikes in the industry, in 1977 and 1980. In both events the marginal left played an important leadership role but clashed with the parties of the established left, which favored a more cautious approach once the strike lost its impetus. In both cases MAS was singled out by the marginal left for special attack because of its failure to maintain a militant stance. In 1977 the MAS-controlled union at TEXFIN suspended a strike that it had called with the Single Union of Textile Workers (SUT), controlled by the marginal left, to protest layoffs that were reprisals for a recent twenty-four-hour industrywide shutdown. A similar situation occurred in the six-week strike in 1980 when, after a settlement was reached on terms favorable to the companies, the ultra-left trade unionists decided to continue the walkout. This action was criticized by the established left on grounds that the strike's main accomplishment—an agreed-upon moratorium on layoffs—was put in danger by the failure of the unions to coordinate their actions and order their members to return to work in unison.[46] Carlos Arturo Pardo echoed statements made by the PCV and MEP when he wrote in the aftermath of the conflict:

> The collective bargaining, in spite of a situation of incoherence, inter-party friction, incomprehension, and inflexibility in the heart of the United Trade Union Front of the Textile Workers, could have been brought through patience to a point that would have permitted us to defend ourselves adequately in the face of the class enemy. . . . Nevertheless, internal [rivalry] slowly led us . . . to the point that we lost the initiative in the confrontation with management . . . and were thus placed on the defensive due to the lack of coherence, agreements and opportune definitions.[47]

Conclusions Regarding MAS's Behavior in Organized Labor

Various explanations can be offered for the success of the marginal left in the Guayana region and the textile industry. In the first place, groups like the Causa R and Proceso Político have concentrated their work in specific sectors and locations. It may be argued that any political organization regardless of size can score impressive gains and even eclipse larger parties by focusing their efforts in particular conflict-ridden areas.

A second explanation is that the severe economic problems facing heavy industry in Guayana and the near collapse of the textile industry before the mid-1980s created a volatile situation that was easy for the ultra-left to exploit during peak moments of the crisis. Nevertheless, these small parties have been as unsuccessful as the larger ones in devising a viable strategy that would allow them to establish a permanent presence among the workers. SUTISS members failed to actively protest the removal of their elected leaders from office in 1981 and have remained surprisingly passive ever since (though the Causa R's 17-percent vote in the 1984 municipal elections in the state of Bolivar, where Ciudad Guayana is located, indicates that it has not lost its popularity in the region). In the case of the textile industry, the failure of the 1980 strike and the subsequent layoffs of militant workers cut into the strength of some of the marginal left groups. Not only did AD reemerge as the largest force in the industry but Proceso Político lost control of UTIT. These setbacks indicate that the gains of individual parties of the marginal left have been short term and are more a reflection of worker alienation than an acceptance of any particular ideological tendency.

A third explanation is that the marginal left's criticism of the larger parties for attempting to control and manipulate the labor movement has struck a responsive chord among the workers. Political parties in Venezuela play a dominant role in the institutional life of the nation. This overextension has been frequently denounced by intellectuals, among others, but it was natural that highly discontented workers who face awesome challenges both on and off the job should strike the biggest blow against the system in their daily struggle. These workers were attracted to the marginal left not only because of its verbal attacks against party intervention in organized labor but because it emphasized direct worker participation in the formulation of union policy as a corrective to party control. The attitude of the marginal left recalls the anarcho-syndicalist movements of the early part of the century, which viewed parties as inherently middle class and thus extraneous to organized labor and unrepresentative of the interests of the workers.

The antiparty thrust of such groups as the Causa R is an indictment against the left—and MAS in particular—for its failure to unite. Undoubtedly, had the parties of the established left not been so disunited, they would have been in a stronger position vis-à-vis the marginal left. MAS rejected the strategy of interparty leftist alliances, both in national elections and in organized labor, and carried out propaganda more in favor of MAS as an organization than around specific bread-and-butter issues. Although the larger socialist parties—MEP, MIR, and the PCV—committed themselves to unity, they also failed to support united leftist slates in elections in the steel and textile workers' unions.

In spite of differences in style, MAS's labor policy did not differ substantially from that of MEP. The about-faces of MEP and MAS in the labor movement in the 1970s obeyed similar motives. Both parties pursued an initial policy of rejecting unity with AD and COPEI. MEP refused to join AD-COPEI slates for the executive committees of the CTV and its affiliate federations, while the MASistas set up dual unions. Trade unionists of both parties toned down their stands as they realized that in the face of AD's formidable control of the labor movement, a policy of confrontation and outright opposition was doomed to failure. After reaching an accommodation, MAS and MEP secured positions in the CTV bureaucracy that were disproportionate to their modest following among organized workers. Thus, for instance, AD's preponderance in the CTV entitled it to the two top posts in the organization, but at the CTV Congress in 1985 it granted the number-two position of secretary general to a MEPista.

AD, however, more than MEP and MAS, benefited from these concessions. By soliciting the support of and striking up deals with other parties and independents, AD attempted to dispel the notion that it pursued sectarian policies. Before 1983, for instance, two ex-URDistas (José Beltrán Vallejo and Rafael Castañeda), who belonged to a miniscule party, received seats on the CTV's executive committee in return for their consistent endorsement of AD positions. MEP's and MAS's backing of the CTV on such controversial issues as the closing of the BTV and the referendum in SUTISS was especially welcomed. As leftist parties, MAS and MEP had a special claim to representing working-class and popular viewpoints. Their willingness to close ranks with other trade unionists within the CTV lent credibility to the confederation's assertion that it defended the general interests of all the workers and not the partisan ones of AD.

MAS and The Student Movement

The founding of MAS coincided with a period of disturbances on the nation's campuses that was the product of the movement known as the Academic Renovation. Patterned after the French student movement of 1968, the Renovation proposed to examine all facets of university education, from course programs and pedagogic techniques to the philosophy of education. The suspension of classes and takeover of buildings that characterized the Renovation met an energetic government response in the form of military intervention on campuses. This reaction was partly due to the fact that the Renovation was directed against the status quo which, while vaguely defined in reference to society as a whole, was clearly represented in the student movement by the government party COPEI, whose strength far surpassed that of AD.

The most protracted occupation was carried out under the name Operation Kangaroo at the UCV in 1970. One of the government's objectives was to gain control of, or at least neutralize, the nation's largest university, which had been a hotbed of subversive activity and protest throughout the 1960s. The left accused the Caldera administration of removing leftist faculty members in order to place Copeyanos in their positions. University authorities were also forced out, including the rector, Jesús María Bianco, a popular academician who had been twice elected with leftist support. His replacement, Rafael Clemente Arraiz, formulated conciliatory statements toward the opposition and called for a rapid withdrawal of troops and return to normalcy, but he faced opposition from other provisional authorities who favored a hard line. As a result, in March 1971 after just three months in the post, Arraiz resigned. His successor defended the continued presence of troops on campus.

The harshness and long duration of the occupation evoked a strong response from diverse sectors of the university community. Student leaders denounced the imposition of university authorities by the government as a flagrant violation of the principle of university autonomy. Much of the left called for a boycott of the student elections that were sponsored by the rectorate. These leftists argued that the UCV officials lacked the moral integrity to be entrusted with the task of organizing elections.[48] Furthermore, participation in them would represent a tacit acceptance of the occupation as well as the 1970 Reform of the Law of Universities drafted by the Caldera administration. By regulating campus elections and intruding in the institution's life in other respects, this law infringed upon university autonomy.

In contrast, MAS called on UCV students to exercise their right to vote. Although they recognized the cogency of the arguments in favor of abstention, MASistas argued that the rationale for participation was far more compelling. Most important, the policy of abstention represented a continuation of the ultra-leftism of the previous decade, which had been so thoroughly discredited by the guerrilla fiasco. In order to gain credibility, the student movement needed to assume a responsible stand in the face of pressing events. The alternative—open confrontation between the government and the university community—endangered the UCV's status as an autonomous institution.[49]

MAS's position on the organization of the student movement was also more moderate than that of the rest of the left. MIRistas and other leftists called for dismantling the FCU, which they believed to have been bureaucratized beyond repair, in order to search for radically new forms of organization and struggle. MAS, on the other hand, maintained that the FCU, which during the renovation period had lost much of its influence, should be rebuilt and strengthened. To abandon it in favor of an ill-defined, loose structure would be to open the student movement up to anarchism.

MAS's policy on campus was surprising for a party that was characterized by intransigent stands and confrontational tactics in the labor movement and elsewhere. MAS trade unionists, for instance, not only called for strikes in such companies as SIDOR but refused to work within the CTV, which they considered highly bureaucratic. The party's policy on campus demonstrated that the early MAS, in spite of Petkoff's claim of constituting a "leftist" alternative to the PCV, also represented a sharp reaction to ultra-leftism, which was especially pronounced in the student movement.

MAS's policy of accepting the existing structure of the student movement and cooperating with authorities whose legitimacy was under question was risky in that it laid the newly founded party open to accusations of being collaborationist. Nevertheless, MAS's decision to participate in student elections proved to be a master stroke. Within six months of its existence MAS established itself as the largest party in the student movement, not only at the UCV but in the nation as a whole. MAS's victory in the UCV elections (along with its equally impressive triumph at SIDOR) boosted morale within the fledgling party. Furthermore, it was interpreted as a repudiation of the government for its intervention at the UCV and a vote in favor of university autonomy. Equally significant for MAS was the fact that the boycott supported by the rest of the left (with the exception of the PCV) failed to prosper.

MAS's dominant position in the student movement went unchallenged until 1976 and 1977 when MIR won a series of electoral victories on campuses throughout the nation. The FCUs of three of the nation's five autonomous universities—the UCV, the University of Carabobo, and the University of the Andes—as well as the Pedagogical Institute of Caracas and the Technological Institute of Coro fell into the hands of MIRistas. MAS's setback was explained in large part by the party's failure to carry through on its promise to rebuild the student movement. The FCUs ceased to play the vital role either in the universities or in national politics that they had played in the 1960s. Furthermore, MAS failed to take advantage of its widespread support in institutions of higher learning by establishing a nationwide student organization. The MIRistas reacted to this inertness by calling for the FCU's rejuvenation and committing themselves to asserting the FCU's presence in university faculties and departments.[50]

MAS's responsibility for the lethargy of the student movement was recognized by Freddy Muñoz and other top MASistas. According to Muñoz, MAS's youth leaders, in attempting to avoid the extremism of the previous decade and to differentiate themselves from the ultraleft, had committed the opposite error of soft-pedaling student demands. In the early 1970s, Muñoz stated, the MASistas had played a key role in reactivating the student movement, only to end up, in many cases, "reestablishing the same vertical structures and bureaucratic methods of leadership [that existed before] so that massive numbers of students distanced themselves from their organizations and lost faith in those who led them."[51]

MIR's success on campus also reflected the widespread support for the party's efforts to achieve leftist unity in the 1978 presidential elections and general disapproval of MAS's resistance to the idea. MAS's defeats on campus induced the party to modify its behavior by calling for roundtable discussions in 1978 with other leftist organizations to iron out differences. Though MAS's earnestness in formulating this proposal was questionable, it demonstrated the importance the party attached to the outcome of elections on campus. In short, national political developments influenced the results of the student elections in 1976 and 1977, which in turn exerted an influence on MAS, thus demonstrating the close interaction between student and national politics.

During the presidential period of 1979 to 1984 national politics again had a direct impact on MAS's behavior and performance on campus. As a part of the agreement in which MIR endorsed the presidential candidacy of Teodoro Petkoff, MAS supported MIRistas to head the FCU at the UCV and the University of the Andes. The tension that arose between MIR and MAS at the national level during the 1983 presidential campaign was reflected at the UCV, where the MIRista candidate was elected FCU president. The faction in MAS headed by Luis Bayardo Sardi, which was highly critical of the alliance with MIR, opposed the UCV pact, which also took in the PCV.

MAS's positions on education policy in the early 1980s differed from those of the rest of the left. MASistas were generally unwilling to defend university autonomy and open admissions as absolute principles. This attitude reflects changes in the nation's university environment since the founding of MAS. The demand for autonomy had been a logical response to government intrusion in the universities during the military dictatorship of the 1950s and the guerrilla period of the 1960s. The relative calm that prevailed on campus after the withdrawal of troops from the UCV in 1971 reduced the emotional impact of the call for autonomy.[52]

Leading members of the university community now turned their attention to the inefficiency, waste, and even corruption in institutions of higher learning; some of them affirmed the right of the government to intervene in cases of misuse of public funds. Though not explicitly conditioning autonomy on the sound management of the institution, MAS leaders maintained that the principle of autonomy did not give university officials carte blanche to dispose of school money as they pleased. At the same time the MASistas pointed out that the major part of the blame for university misgovernment lay with AD and COPEI, which throughout the 1970s ran the nation's five autonomous universities[53] (only in the first half of the 1980s were José Mendoza Angulo—a MASista—and Edmundo Chirinos—an independent leftist—

elected rectors of the University of the Andes and the UCV, respectively).

Leading MASistas also questioned the principle of free and open admissions, though the party was reluctant to uphold an official position on such an emotionally charged issue. As a result of the rising expectations set off by the prosperity of the 1970s, the demand for a university education skyrocketed at a rate that budgetary increases could not keep pace with. Proposals to ameliorate this critical problem included charging tuition fees, requiring admission exams, and putting limits on course repetition known as the "regulation on repetition."

Because the demand for a university education in the 1970s was so acute the "regulation on repetition" seemed less objectionable than in the previous decade. Petkoff, in an interview published under the title *Teodoro Petkoff: Viaje al fondo de si mismo,* expressed repulsion at the possibility "that a person can remain at the university year after year, repeating course after course, without ever graduating, constituting a type of plug for those who wish to enter . . . and at the same time being transformed into a financial burden for the university and the State."[54]

Some top MAS leaders in the early 1980s were receptive to proposals to establish tuition fees which, while theoretically designed to charge only those who could afford to pay, would have undoubtedly been applied to all but the very poor. Before being elected rector of the University of the Andes (ULA), José Mendoza Angulo, along with Carlos Raúl Hernández, MAS's national secretary for universities, drew up a student program that included the charging of tuition and a "regulation on repetition." The program was supported by top MAS leaders but was vetoed by the party's student leadership (and also vehemently criticized by the renowned MAS sociologist and UCV professor José Agustín Silva Michelena).[55] Mendoza set off a storm of controversy at the ULA when, upon being elected rector, he advocated the implementation of these reforms.

Student leaders of other leftist parties harped on the defense of autonomy and opposed admission exams while calling for open admissions regardless of the university's capacity to absorb existing demand.[56] MAS, for its part, was reluctant to support confrontations on campus. In the mid-1980s in such conflicts as a strike of UCV employees and a nationwide strike of professors, both in pursuit of economic benefits, and a hunger strike of students at the University of the Orient in opposition to the "regulation of repetition," MAS university leaders either openly opposed the conflict or assumed an ambivalent position.[57] In their eagerness to disassociate themselves from the student leftism of the 1960s, MAS youth activists coined the slogan "Struggle and Study" (later copied by MIR and other leftist parties), which implied that students should not immerse themselves in political struggle at the expense of their academic responsibilities.

Until 1985 MAS's national youth leadership was dominated by the followers of Pompeyo Márquez. The *teodoristas* and later the orthodox wing of the party headed by Freddy Muñoz sharply criticized MAS's student leaders for their lack of firmness in waging campaigns on behalf of their constituency. Thus, for instance, the *teodoristas* attacked Pastor Heydra, the FCU president at the UCV in the mid-1970s, for negotiating directly with the municipal authorities of Caracas in favor of such services as pay telephones on campus, without first rallying student support behind the demands.[58] After the *teodoristas* gained control of the party in 1977, the National Youth Directorate was accused of being unrepresentative of the party's rank-and-file youth and was temporarily dissolved. Márquez's followers denounced the move as a reprisal for the Youth Directorate's overwhelming support for the nomination of José Vicente Rangel in opposition to Petkoff's presidential aspirations.[59]

At MAS's fifth national youth convention in 1985, the followers of Freddy Muñoz wrested control of the National Youth Directorate from Márquez's supporters and elected Gonzalo González (a former FCU president at the UCV) secretary general. During his campaign for the position González criticized the directorate for failing to reach out beyond the university student population. He called for a broadening of the directorate's concerns to take in such activities as high school education, sports, and the ecological movement. González proposed assigning a specific sphere of activity to each of the twenty-one members of the directorate, thus ensuring sufficient attention to nonuniversity objectives.[60]

González committed himself to reasserting MAS's influence at the high school level. In the 1960s high schools in the nation's main urban areas were highly politicized, to the extent that parties, particularly those of the left, established chapters in individual schools. Within a few months of its founding MAS emerged as the largest political party among high school students nationwide. In succeeding years, however, high school authorities succeeded in depoliticizing their institutions, and as a result MAS's organized presence was nearly eliminated.

Although MAS lost influence in the student movement during the first decade and a half of its existence, other parties did not fare much better. MIR, for instance, momentarily displaced MAS in many schools prior to the 1978 elections, but its subsequent division (when ex-presidential candidate Américo Martín left the party) seriously cut into its student support. Furthermore, the organizational activities of all parties, not just those of MAS, were reduced to a bare minimum in the high schools. A steady increase in the abstention rate in student elections put in evidence the state of apathy at the university level. For the first time since 1958, a slate of independents (known as "Movement 80"), which attacked the ineffectiveness of political parties on campus, won student elections at the UCV in 1985 and again two years later (and made impressive inroads elsewhere). MAS staunchly denied that the outcome of the contests "reflects a rejection of political parties" since the members of the "Slate 80," far from being apolitical, belonged to or were identified with individual parties on the left.[61] Nevertheless, the fact that the Movement 80 decided to label itself "independent"—rather than a coalition of specific parties—demonstrated the extent to which political parties had been discredited on campus. In short, MAS's greatest challenge in the universities did not stem so much from rivalry from other political organizations either on the left or center as from student apathy and skepticism toward the highly politicized student movement. These attitudes are attributable to the failure of student organizations to play a decisive role in the academic and political life of the nation as they had in the 1950s and 1960s.

The revisions in MAS's ideology and policies throughout its short history have been accompanied by modifications in its internal structure. MASistas have readily accepted these changes, for they openly rejected what several important party leaders called a priori truths in politics[1] and were thus in constant search for appropriate models to accord with changing situations. This flexible view in favor of revision and change was expressed in a party document in 1974 that stated, "there is no reason why the [organizational] scheme that is formulated for a given moment should take on the value of a principle. On the contrary, it should be subject to modifications on the basis of its performance in practice."[2] MAS's tendency to constantly question the effectiveness of its structure was also manifested at all five national conventions, where the party's reorganization was discussed and approved. The clearest demonstration of this attitude came on the heels of the 1983 electoral fiasco when MAS's immediate impulse was to replace its entire structure with a provisional one as the first step in a protracted reexamination of everything the party stood for.

MAS's initial structure was a response to the perceived lack of internal democracy in the PCV, which had led to the division in 1970. The early MASistas payed lip-service to the Leninist concept of the party but emphasized the democratic side of democratic centralism and attempted to create regular channels of rank-and-file participation in party decision making. A second stimulus to MAS's organizational design was the overhaul in the party's doctrine following the 1973 national elections. At that time, MAS began to base its claim to being a unique party, not on the preeminence it assigned to the struggle for socialism, as it had up until then, but on the firmness of its commitment to democracy. Although on this score it was easy for

MAS to set itself off from other parties on the left, especially those that defended the "dictatorship of the proletariat," MAS could not easily challenge AD and COPEI, which had long boasted of their role as pillars of the nation's democratic system. Their Achilles' heel was their internal organization and practices, which were highly vertical and suppressed challenges to decisions emanating from upper leadership levels. The MASistas branded AD's and COPEI's structure as "Leninist" in order to underscore the originality of their own reforms. Indeed, several of MAS's statutory modifications that were first discussed in the late 1970s were unique, at least for Venezuela. These provisions included the "legalization" of internal factions and their proportional representation in the party's leadership, internal elections for important party positions, and rotation in office.

Early Reforms

At their party's founding convention in January 1971 the MASistas attempted to correct certain traditional Communist practices they had denounced in previous years as undemocratic. Unlike orthodox Communist Party congresses, which are generally highly staged,[3] MAS's convention was open and participation was encouraged. There were sixty-three nominations from the floor for the thirty-three regular and ten substitute positions on the party's first Central Committee. Furthermore, provisions were made to guarantee the autonomy of the Central Committee in its relations with the party's executive council (known as the Political Commission). The committee was kept small, thus permitting it to meet as frequently as once every month or two during the party's early years. It was decided that all listings of members of the Central Committee would be alphabetical without special reference to those who belonged to the Political Commission (with the exception of the secretary general). The Political Commission was made responsible for the transfer of all information to the Central Committee. These and other procedures were designed to avoid the type of rigid control exercised by the PCV's Politburo over the Central Committee, which had been a major grievance of the dissident Communists. Another source of contention had been the nonrepresentation of the members of the Communist Youth at party congresses, a problem to which the founding MASistas also addressed themselves.

The early MAS's rejection of orthodox Communist practice was reflected in its effort to create a loosely structured "movement of movements" within the nation's institutions, specifically in trade unions and professional and student organizations. In the movement of movements (briefly discussed in chapter 7), MASistas attempted to achieve unity around specific objectives within the institution, but not in the name of MAS or any other political party. According to this concept, MASistas were to make compromises in the formulation of a program and the configuration of slates in order to accommodate diverse currents of opinion within the institution. The absence of close or formal ties between MASistas at the institutional level and the MAS organization implied that the movement of movements was to maintain a relative autonomy vis-à-vis political parties. This freedom of action contrasted with the organic link between orthodox Communist parties and their "cells," which were the instruments of party control of "mass organizations."

MAS was most successful in establishing "movements" under different names at the Universidad Simón Bolívar (where it was known as Fórmate y Lucha), the Universidad Simón Rodríguez (the Movimiento Simón Rodríguez), the Universidad de Oriente (Frente de Transformación Universitaria), the Colegio Nacional de Periodistas (Movimiento Prensa Libre), the Colegio de Ingenieros de Venezuela (Movimiento Profesional Antonio José de Sucre), the Colegio Nacional de Médicos (Movimiento José María Vargas), and in women's organizations (the Movimiento de Mujeres Socialistas). These movements generally issued newsletters and newspapers that made little mention, if any, of MAS and the other parties that supported them. The most successful movement was Prensa Libre, which for a long time maintained control over the journalists' professional association (the Colegio de Periodistas) and their labor organization (known as the Sindicato Nacional de Trabajadores de la Prensa). MAS leader Eleazar Díaz Rangel was elected president of the Colegio Nacional and was later named head of the continental organization the Federación Latinoamericana de Periodistas (FLAP).

MAS did not implement the movement-of-movements strategy on all fronts during its early years. Where MAS's influence was most felt, such as at the Central University and other large autonomous universities, MAS acted in its own name. This policy left the impression that once MAS developed a significant following in any particular movement, it would pull out and establish its own front.[4] In addition, the movement-of-movements idea was never significantly put into practice in the labor movement.

By the late 1970s MAS quietly abandoned the movement-of-movements approach. This move was related to MAS's effort to break out of the leftist "ghetto" and reach out to the majority of Venezuelans. In the first place, the "movements" which MAS helped found failed to develop into truly autonomous structures disassociated from political parties. In practice, they often took on the form of leftist "fronts" whose leaders responded to the directives of their respective parties. The MASistas feared that formal ties with the rest of the left would blur the party's democratic image.

Moreover, MASistas began to emulate certain features of AD, which they credited with having captured the essence of Venezuelan political culture. In particular, MAS theorists emphasized the importance of political party loyalty, which AD had been so skillful in instilling in its followers. The movement of movements, it was felt, was too loose a grouping to allow MAS to stimulate this sense of allegiance among its members and potential recruits.

In subsequent years MASistas tended to work openly in the name of their party in organizations they had originally helped build as part of the movement of movements. As a result of MAS's shift, relations with members of other leftist parties in those groups became strained.[5] Thus, for instance, MIRistas withdrew from the Movimiento Simón Rodríguez, which became transformed into a virtual university fraction of MAS. Similarly, a group of leftist communications workers left the Movimiento Prensa Libre to found the rival Cuartilla, which endorsed PCVista Héctor Mujica as president of the Colegio de Periodistas in the elections in 1984. Cuartilla attacked Prensa Libre for being the vehicle of a closed and exclusive group of mainly MASista journalists and for having struck up an agreement with COPEI within the college. Prensa Libre responded by claiming that its concerns were professional and not political. Mujica drew enough votes from Prensa Libre to provide the pro-AD slate with a plurality, which thus wrested control of the organization from Prensa Libre.

MAS's 1980 National Convention and the "Legalization of Factions"

MAS's radical structural modifications after 1973 were designed primarily to foster internal democracy, which became a major party goal. These revisions were a response to changing conditions in Venezuela and on the left. The early MASistas had been influenced by their experiences in the 1960s, when the illegal status of the leftist parties and their guerrilla strategy had imposed on them a vertical line of command. Thus, for instance, during MAS's early years, great efforts were made to circumscribe internal rivalry and guard against factionalism, in accordance with orthodox Marxist practice. The 1970s, however, were characterized by the absence of mass movements or subversive threats that would have invited government repression. This liberalization encouraged MAS—and, to a lesser extent, other leftist parties—to open up and democratize its internal structure.

The internal situation in MAS also induced the party to modify its structure. The party primaries for the 1978 presidential elections intensified the rivalry between the followers of Teodoro Petkoff and Pompeyo Márquez (who supported the candidacy of José Vicente Rangel), leading to suspensions and other disciplinary measures against members of the minority faction in several states. The statutory modifications in the late 1970s and early 1980s in favor of the rights of minority groupings in MAS were designed to avoid the breakup of the party as a result of these reprisals.

Undoubtedly, the most far-reaching statutory reform was the legalization of internal factions, which was introduced at MAS's fourth national convention in 1977 and approved at the next one in 1980. This concept was spelled out in Article 15 of the party's statutes:

> As an expression of internal democracy, the opportunity to search and gain support for positions will be recognized. When in the course of debate, the maintenance of common opinion leads to the formation of currents of opinion, these will be recognized as legitimate, as long as they do not signify the employment of factional mechanisms which weaken the free exercise of the rights of members and undermine the unity and coherence of the Movement.[6]

The same article went on to recognize the right of minority factions to be represented at all levels of party leadership in proportion to their relative strength. The acceptance and even encouragement of internal diversity which this measure contemplated was far-reaching if not unique for any party worldwide. MASistas justified the new arrangement by arguing that internal currents of opinion were inevitable in all organizations and that it was better to recognize than to attempt to suppress them.

The practical application of the legalization of factions was difficult to work out. Few parties would object to the practice of publishing minority opinions in internal party bulletins. As it turned out, however, MAS went beyond this modest measure. Since MAS's publications for internal diffusion were never considered secret, factional differences easily spilled over to the public arena. The step from criticizing official party policy in a semi-internal document to issuing a public declaration critical of the party's line was easily taken. Another hazy area involved the proselytizing activity of factions within the party. Theoretically, national leaders who traveled to the interior to carry out party business could not engage in work on behalf of their factions. Naturally, this stipulation was difficult if not impossible to enforce. Furthermore, the three major factions that emerged convoked strategy meetings and printed their own publications, activities not contemplated in party statutes. In a particularly blatant violation of party discipline, members of a given faction sometimes supported candidates in institutional elections in opposition to the MAS-endorsed slate. In addition, some MASistas devoted an inordinate amount of time and energy to working on behalf of their faction at the expense of their party obligations.

During these years MAS implemented various measures related to internal elections as part of its effort to promote party democracy. In the statutes ratified in 1980, the percentage of nonelected delegates to party conventions, who automatically attended by virtue of the positions they held, was limited to 20 percent (a draft drawn up several years earlier had set it at 30 percent). In a particularly interesting innovation, the commissions that supervised internal elections were made free of interference from the party's executive authorities.[7] A resolution unanimously approved at MAS's 1985 convention enhanced the autonomous status of the party's National Electoral Commission by stipulating that its members would be elected at the party's national convention. This system was designed to avoid the type of discord that arose in the Communist Party in 1970 when Petkoff and other Communist dissidents accused the party's Politburo of manipulating the selection of delegates to the PCV's upcoming congress.

MAS's statutes departed from the Leninist notion that all party members should be veritable professional revolutionaries. The statutes, in addition to spelling out the obligations of party members, specified their rights. The 1980 statutes listed as many as fifteen clauses in the section under "rights of members." Among the statutes' new clauses were the right of MASistas to "solicit exemption from those tasks and responsibilities which they believe to clash with their conscience," and "the right to a respite" from party work.[8] MAS also guaranteed its members the right to withdraw from the organization without being reprimanded or humiliated in any way. This practice contrasted with orthodox communism, which assumes that party membership entails a life-long commitment. According to some MASistas, these provisions regarding the rights of members were inspired by the U.S. Constitution—more accurately, the Bill of Rights.[9] Although the claim may have been exaggerated, it demonstrated the willingness of the MASistas to copy and praise the positive features of democracy in nonsocialist nations.

MAS's statutes also distinguished between MAS's "militants" and "partisans," both of whom were considered to be party members, and "sympathizers," who were allowed to participate in internal party meetings in a nonvoting capacity. Partisans were defined as members with a modest level of political participation who were not subject to work assignments. The statutes provided partisans with the same rights as militants with the exception of the right to vote in internal elections and run for office. (Members of the faction in MAS headed by Bayardo Sardi forcefully argued that partisans should enjoy these two rights as well.) The purpose of the provision was to encourage the "friends of MAS" (or sympathizers), whose political commitment was of a limited nature, to join the party as partisans and to take on a steady share of responsibility. The measure, however, failed to achieve its desired results, since most partisans were, in effect, MAS-istas who engaged in political activity only during national elections every five years.[10]

Another set of reforms incorporated into MAS's statutes in 1980 was the limitation on reelection to party office and the delegation of authority to a sizable group of MASistas at the highest leadership level. The new statutes stipulated that the party's secretary general could be reelected only to one two-year term, after which he had to wait two more terms to be eligible for the same office. In a related move, the statutes prohibited members of the party's National Directorate (which was equivalent to the Central Committee in the Communist Party) from holding two important positions simultaneously.

At the same time MAS divested the secretary generalship of some of its power by creating new positions at the top executive level, the most important of which was that of president. The secretary general presided over the meetings of the National Directorate; the president directed those of the National Council (which was in charge of reforming party statutes and disciplining party members). Both secretary general and president were to represent the party at important public gatherings and direct the party's international relations. The 1980 statutes created an adjunct secretary general, which also cut into the authority of the secretary general, as well as a first and second vice president. MAS's 1985 national convention stripped the regional secretary generals of some of their power by ruling that, although they would automatically belong to the party's National Directorate, they would not necessarily have the right to vote.

These provisions were designed to eliminate the tendency, especially characteristic of Communist parties including Eurocommunist ones, to confer excessive authority on the secretary general, whose term of office was considered life-long. Although many of MAS's new practices and policies were first advocated by the party's renovation faction headed by Bayardo Sardi, the reforms regarding the secretary generalship were pushed by the orthodox Freddy

Muñoz. In *Más allá de las palabras* Muñoz argued that rotation in office, including the secretary generalship, should be a normal procedure that in no way reflects negatively on the performance of the party's leadership. Muñoz criticized orthodox mentality and practice whereby the replacement of the secretary general throws the party into a crisis (as indeed subsequently occurred in the Spanish Communist Party) and implies a veritable coup d'etat within the organization. In *Más allá* Muñoz wrote:

> In the leadership of MAS and especially at the highest level, a reduced circle that is not easily penetrable and possesses inordinate power and influence . . . has been created. It could be maintained that this circle had a natural origin in the leadership which various outstanding figures assumed in MAS when it was founded. But the prolongation of this situation . . . when the leadership capacity [in the party] has multiplied . . . represents an obstacle to the exploitation of such talent and an impediment to its cultivation.[11]

MAS's long-time secretary general Pompeyo Márquez (who, ironically, was Muñoz's father-in-law) regarded Muñoz's statements as a personal affront. Márquez claimed that Muñoz had been "inconsiderate" and indiscreet and that he should have limited his remarks to political parties in general rather than speaking specifically of MAS.[12] Nevertheless, the dispute reflected more than mere differences in style. By 1980 Márquez's influence in the party had waned somewhat, at the same time that the crystallization of factions had undermined Márquez's image as the party's undisputed leader who was above internal rivalry. Muñoz, who headed his own faction, was eager to occupy the position of secretary general. In spite of this personal dimension of the issue, the measures related to the secretary generalship and rotation in office were unanimously approved at the 1980 convention.

Statutory reforms were also designed to facilitate participation in the National Convention and broaden its powers, at the expense of the Secretariat. The National Convention was defined as the "supreme authority" of the party. Petkoff and other MASistas were inspired by the example of the national conventions of the Spanish Communist Party, in which participation from the floor was encouraged and resolutions proposed by the Politburo were often voted down by a majority of delegates.[13] As dissidents in the Venezuelan Communist Party, Petkoff and others had called for secret elections to select members of the Central Committee, and thus it was not surprising that MAS's statutes guaranteed the secrecy of all internal elections. Another grievance of the dissident PCVistas in the late 1960s had been the infrequency with which national conventions were held, as only one had been convoked since 1948. The dissidents had proposed that the party commit itself to one every three years. Although MAS's statutes stipulated that conventions would be held every two years, it has in practice averaged one every three.

MAS's main governing bodies at the national level, specifically the convention, council, and directorate, were reproduced at the state, district (Venezuela's equivalent to county), and municipal levels (see figure 10-1). The smallest unit was the base committee, which was established in barrios, workplaces, and institutions. According to the 1980 statutes, the municipal, district, and regional conventions were to select at least 80 percent of the delegates to the convention of the immediately superior level, as well as the members of the administrative committee (including the secretary general and other positions) of the same level.

MAS's intricate multitiered system undoubtedly overestimated MAS's size. In most parts of the country (the major exception being Caracas) the party's municipal organization was nonexistent. Furthermore, the stipulation that 80 percent of all convention delegates at all levels had to be elected meant that much of the time and energy of party members was absorbed in internal elections.

Nevertheless, the structure reflected MAS's priorities in two respects. In the first place, MAS's geographically based system in which the party's national leaders were elected by delegates who were nominated at city, county, and finally state conventions was designed to spread out MAS's territorial presence as much as possible. By assigning an important role to the municipal and county organizations in the overall configuration of the party, MAS attempted to encourage its members to set up chapters in remote areas. This strategy obeyed a definite electoral function. The Venezuelan left had traditionally forfeited the votes of sparsely populated regions because it lacked an organizational base in those parts of the country. The left tended to concentrate its efforts in strategic sectors, which did not include the peasantry. MAS, on the other hand, attempted to pattern itself after AD, which in its early years extended itself throughout the nation and was determined to leave, in the words of Rómulo Betancourt, "not a single county nor a single municipality without a party chapter."[14] This organizational drive paid handsome electoral dividends for AD in the long run.

In the second place, MAS's structure of five levels linked to each other by elected delegates from one level to the next produced inordinate electoral activity in the party. The intense competition for virtually all elected positions in MAS resembled the situation in AD and COPEI, unlike other smaller parties in which the rivalry that occasionally flared was limited to nominations at the highest levels. The MAS-istas viewed the frequency of electoral contests in MAS as the outcome of its pathbreaking efforts in favor of internal democracy. They also pointed out that the participation of a large number of party members as candidates in internal elections channeled rather than suppressed their personal ambitions. According to this viewpoint, the orthodox left had promoted the myth of the "professional revolutionary" who was thought to be indifferent to the possibility of personal advancement and, in doing so, it failed to recognize human nature.[15]

Decentralization of Authority

After abandoning the movement-of-movements strategy in the mid-1970s, MAS made its basic working unit within organizations and institutions (trade unions, universities, etc.) the party fraction, which consisted exclusively of MAS members. This trend was evidenced in the party's 1980 statutes, which assigned greater power to the fraction by omitting the clause in which it was assigned merely "advisory and consultative [tasks] with respect to their sector or association" and was excluded from having decision-making power ("executive functions"). In addition, the 1980 statutes dropped all reference to the amorphous movement of movements, previously referred to as "specific movements," whose members were not clearly identified with any party in particular.[16]

Nevertheless, the MASistas rejected Leninist practice whereby party leaders dictate policy to cells that operate at the institutional level. They were in general agreement that MAS should provide its lower-level organizational units a degree of autonomy, even if it meant that occasionally they would assume positions that diverged from those of the national leadership. Thus the 1980 statutes stipulated that any party organism with the approval of two-thirds of its members could request exemption from having to enforce or implement a party decision. The statutes also contributed to the semi-autonomous status of MAS's fractions by stipulating that conventions would be held in each sector (health, engineering, etc.) to elect a national directorate, thus depriving MAS's national leadership of a direct role in the selection.

MAS's reorganization in favor of decentralization created a veritable tug-of-war between the party's national apparatus and lower-level units, and became the source of considerable internal debate. Local MAS organizations occasionally became involved in an emotionally charged struggle in the region, in which they found themselves taking positions that contradicted MAS's general philosophy. MAS in the state of Aragua, for example, called for suppression of certain lines or scenes from a Venezuelan film that were considered insulting to the residents of the region; MAS's national leaders objected to this stand on grounds that it was at odds with MAS's opposition to all forms of censorship. Elsewhere, local MASistas supported land invasions and in doing so clashed with the party's explicitly stated position of respect for private property.

One important step toward the decentralization of MAS's organization was the new system for constituting electoral slates. In 1973 and 1978 MAS's candidates were selected by the party's national leadership, a policy that began to change in the 1979 municipal elections. Although MAS's 1980 statutes authorized the National Directorate to choose the party's congressional candidates, this norm was later modified. The party's congressional slates for the 1983 contests were formed by the party's state organizations and were revised by MAS's National Directorate, which had the right to lower candidates from one slot to the next one below, in order of selection. As MAS expected to elect two national deputies in various states, this arrangement conferred considerable power on the party's regional leadership.

Tension between MASistas in the eastern state of Anzoátegui and the party's national leadership over the selection of regional authorities and candidates was typical of the difficulties that arose in other states. A brief discussion of MAS's organization in Anzoátegui will illustrate the type of problems the party's commitment to decentralization created. Ever since the naming of Alexis Adam as the party's first secretary general of Anzoátegui, Caracas has played the determining role in the selection of the party's top figures. The influence of MAS's national leadership did not diminish in the late 1970s, when the regional convention began to choose the party's regional secretary generals. Some of MAS's leading members in Anzoátegui were from outside of the state, such as Adam and Alexis Ortiz (both former presidents of the FCU of the UCV). With the development of a regional consciousness in the party, these outsiders or "parachutists," as they were disdainfully referred to, were resented, at least upon their arrival.

Ortiz first went to Anzoátegui after being placed on the party's congressional slate there at the urging of Teodoro Petkoff. In spite of his condition as a "parachutist," Ortiz closely identified himself with the interests of Anzoátegui in the national congress, for which he was widely praised in the state both in and out of the party. This role in favor of the region accorded with MAS's rhetoric, which emphasized the need to limit the decision-making power of the nation's executive branch and to bolster that of the provinces.

Nevertheless, it was generally felt that Ortiz went overboard in his activities on behalf of Anzoátegui. Thus, for instance, he actively participated in a campaign in favor of the construction of a coastal turnpike from Caracas to Barcelona. This stand was criticized in MAS for being more in tune with the interests of local construction firms and the automobile industry than those of the people, who would have been better served by a railroad connecting the two metropolises. He was also widely censured in MAS for endorsing Fucho Tovar, a powerful local businessman, in his bid for the presidency of Fedecamaras, the nation's main business organization. Ortiz claimed that since Tovar represented the regional economic elite he was ipso facto more progressive than his rivals for the position, who were backed by the larger interests of the nation's center.

MAS's organization in Anzoátegui, like its counterparts in other states, refused to accept the National Directorate's priorities in the formation of the party's slate for the 1983 national elections. The national leadership favored selecting a large number of independents and MASistas who were prominent at the national level to run for Congress, at the same time that it attempted to honor a deal with MIR that obliged MAS to accept MIRistas on its slates. Difficulties arose in choosing a state for Teodoro Petkoff to represent in which he would be sure of being elected national deputy. Originally he was to run in Aragua, but resistance from MASistas there who insisted that their slate include only leaders from that state forced the national organization to look elsewhere. Its decision to lower Alexis Ortiz to the number-two position in Anzoátegui in favor of Petkoff also generated discontent among local MASistas. Previously, MASistas from Anzoátegui had blocked the placement of Felipe Mujica (head of MAS's National Youth Directorate) in the leading position on the slate on grounds that he was an "outsider" and had even threatened to carry the issue to the local press. MASistas also strongly resisted the attempt to include a MIRista in the second position for the state assembly as part of the pact between the two parties.

The national leaders criticized this uncooperative attitude, which they pejoratively called a "localist vision," and on several occasions they sent Freddy Muñoz, Pompeyo Márquez, and Bayardo Sardi to the state to work out a solution. The MASistas from Anzoátegui argued that Ortiz's activist role in favor of the state would not be continued by an outsider whose interests were broader in scope. Although belonging to the faction in MAS headed by Bayardo Sardi in a state controlled by Muñoz's followers, Ortiz received ample support in Anzoátegui in favor of his bid to head the slate. Ortiz resigned from MAS shortly after the elections, in part to protest the party's decision on the matter.[17]

The conflict in Anzoátegui was indicative of the degree to which MAS's support for decentralization was reflected in the internal life of the party. No other party in Venezuela would have had to face a similar predicament in placing its standard-bearer in a prominent position on the party's congressional slate. Furthermore, the regional sentiments of MASistas from Anzoátegui transcended their factional loyalties, thus explaining the extensiveness of the backing Ortiz received.

MASistas who participated in women's organizations and organized labor also faced challenges in defining their role in MAS and working out their relations with the party's national organization. In the mid-1970s MAS women formed the Movement of Socialist Women, which was patterned after the movement-of-movements concept. In order to assert their independence from MAS's national leaders, who had distinct priorities regarding women's issues, the women decided to achieve financial self-sufficiency in paying for their locale and staff. Toward the end of the 1970s the Movement was replaced by the Feminist Front, which, being organically linked to MAS, had a greater commitment to work within the party to achieve women's objectives. The Front called for enforcement of a minimum representation for women at all levels of party decision making. MAS's National Council stipulated that at least 15 percent of the members of MAS's slate for the 1983 elections would be women. Furthermore, it was decided that women would be represented in all campaign acts. The following year Argelia Laya (who had participated in the guerrilla movement in the 1960s and was MAS's leading woman figure) ran as secretary general of MAS. Laya characterized her candidacy as symbolic, designed to raise issues and to encourage other women to step forward and run for positions in MAS.[18]

The success of MAS women in their campaign to raise consciousness and gain representation within the party has been extremely limited. MAS failed to fulfill its commitment to maintain a minimum percentage of women in decision-making positions. At the 1985 convention only two women were elected permanent members of the National Directorate (until 1980 Laya had been the only one). Furthermore, pressure from the national leadership forced women to make major concessions. Thus the Front's call to include legalization of abortion on the platform for the 1983 presidential elections was rejected in favor of support for therapeutic abortion. Finally, pressure from the national leadership led MAS women to change their name from Feminist Front to Women's Work Front. It was argued that the word *feminist* had been largely discredited and that the party would be more effective if it appealed to women in their condition as members of a household and as workers rather than feminists. Laya strongly objected to the change in name on grounds that it resembled the approach followed by AD and COPEI women.[19]

A similar conflict over decision-making authority pitted MAS labor leaders against the party's political leadership. The trade unionists objected to the National Directorate's efforts to shape labor policy. Following the 1980 convention they refused to participate in the "Front of the Masses," which included professionals and other non-manual workers and was to be headed by a nontrade unionist. The party's orthodox wing led by Freddy Muñoz was the most vocal in rejecting the special prerogative of labor leaders in the area of labor policy, while the renovation faction, headed by Bayardo Sardi, was more receptive to labor's claim to autonomy.

The debate in MAS that was set off by the delegation of considerable authority to lower levels of leadership, particularly labor, is not without precedent in the history of socialism. Invariably, the reformist currents within socialist parties have favored greater organizational flexibility and autonomy for lower-level decision makers than have orthodox Marxists. The issue was raised as far back as 1906 when the German Social Democratic Party granted its labor bureau a veto in matters related to trade unions. This measure was sharply criticized by Lenin and Rosa Luxemburg. The latter wrote that the party's acceptance of the "theory of the 'equal authority of unions and party'" was not only the result of pressure from social democratic trade unionists but was also defended by the party's "opportunistic-wing," which "strives to transform Social Democracy from a revolutionary proletarian party into a petty-bourgeois reformist party."[20] Thus both in the German Social Democratic Party as in MAS, those labor leaders who strove to achieve an autonomous status within the party were backed by politicians who defended an evolutionary path to socialism (such as Bayardo Sardi) at the same time that they were criticized by other leaders (such as Rosa Luxemburg and Freddy Muñoz), who belonged to their party's leftist and orthodox wings.

Recent Reforms

The extensive self-examination that followed MAS's disappointing showing in the 1983 elections centered on the power granted to lower-level decision makers in the party. A consensus emerged that the legalization of factions had created serious organizational problems that explained the party's poor electoral results. A document submitted to the 1985 convention by a group headed by Freddy Muñoz pointed out that when the legalization of factions was adopted, MAS had been unaware of the "complex implications of the matter" and failed to specify the scope of acceptable activity of the new system.[21]

Most MASistas agreed that factions in MAS impaired internal democracy in that each one created lines of command that detracted from the liberty of party members to make decisions on the basis of personal criteria.[22] Despite this general agreement, different opinions emerged regarding the source of the problem. Followers of Bayardo Sardi and Pompeyo Márquez argued that the faction in MAS was tantamount to a political machine that promoted the personal interests of its leaders. Furthermore, the factional struggle lacked ideological content, as demonstrated by the frequent alliances of two factions against a third during internal party elections. Freddy Muñoz, on the other hand, maintained that the ideological differences among factions, far from being ill defined, were too great to be contained in one party.[23]

The factionalism and lack of coherence that afflicted the party amounted to three basic problems:

1. Public statements by lower-level leadership often contradicted the official party position.

2. Public statements by members of minority factions often contradicted the official party position.

3. Factional discord in the party was widespread.

After the 1983 elections MASistas took great interest in searching for ways to resolve the first and second problems, which concerned public displays of disunity. The MASistas unanimously agreed that the party had to define its positions with greater precision in order to overcome these divergences. In an attempt to achieve this objective, MAS decided to divide its next national convention into two sets of sessions, the first devoted to programmatic and ideological resolutions and the second to elections for leadership positions in the party.

Not all MASistas viewed the public disagreements among party members as a major problem. In an interview with this author Teodoro Petkoff pointed out that expression of opinions that differed from the official party line demonstrated that MASistas at least thought for themselves. He stated that the sanctions taken by AD's National Executive Committee in 1984 against a leading party figure (Cristóbal Hernández) for having mildly criticized AD was the type of practice

MAS was trying to avoid.[24] At MAS's 1985 convention discussion over this issue centered on article 13 of the party's statutes, which guaranteed members "the right to formulate opinions" with "sufficient possibilities to express and disseminate viewpoints" of any sort.[25] The followers of Muñoz and Márquez interpreted this provision as referring to internal party discussion, but the faction led by Bayardo Sardi viewed it as sanctioning the right of MASistas to express personal opinions publicly. The triumph of the orthodox wing headed by Muñoz at the convention and the election of Márquez as MAS president spelled a return to the traditional practice of prohibiting party members from contradicting official positions in public.

The convention in 1985 failed to clarify MAS's policy with respect to the third problem. Over the preceding several years MASistas had concurred that excessive factionalism had inflicted great harm on the party. Indeed, immediately following the 1983 national elections Pompeyo Márquez declared that he would no longer meet in closed gatherings with members of his faction. Nevertheless, not only did his group fail to dissolve itself but it actually divided into two. The announced intentions of Muñoz's group to "suppress factionalism"[26] was not accompanied by any formula regarding what practices in particular were to be eliminated. The fact that of the principal factions in MAS, Muñoz's was the most well organized and disciplined made it unlikely that it would take the initiative in dismantling its own machine.

Although MASistas were resolved to curb certain liberties in the organization, they in no way reconsidered their commitment to internal democracy. Indeed, MAS's National Council in 1984 implemented a new system for selection of the party's National Directorate that was more democratic and far-reaching than any plan considered by other Venezuelan parties until then. The system of indirect elections in which delegates were elected for the local, state, and then national conventions—the latter of which chose the party's National Directorate—was scrapped in favor of primaries in which delegates to the national convention were chosen directly by the voters.

The National Council also ruled that factions could organize their own slates while voting would be based on nominal selection, thus permitting MASistas either to split their vote or select an entire slate. Each slate was to receive proportional representation in the National Directorate. The system naturally placed those MASistas who were not affiliated with any faction at a disadvantage. Such nationally prominent figures as Petkoff, Argelia Laya, and Carlos Tablante, who ran as independents, were elected substitute rather than regular members of the National Directorate. Various formulas were considered at the convention to enhance the possibilities of those MASistas who aspired to be elected to the National Directorate but did not form part of any slate.[27]

In adopting the system whereby the national convention selects the party's highest authorities on the basis of proportional representation, the National Council considered an alternative method that was viewed as even more far-reaching and democratic. According to this proposal, the primaries for selection of MAS's president and secretary general would be based on direct elections, thus bypassing the national convention. The risks which this plan posed to MAS's established leaders were considerable since it would mean that a MASista with the support of the rank and file but without any influence at the leadership level could be elected party head. Under the convention system such a possibility was unlikely because the party's national leadership was elected by delegates who tended to be top or middle-level party leaders. At the 1984 National Council, Petkoff and others argued that MAS was not ready for such a radical organizational arrangement. Nevertheless, at the national convention in 1985 the system was ratified for the following internal elections, which were due to take place in 1988. In taking this measure, the MASistas congratulated themselves for having gone one step further in perfecting the party's internal democracy.[28]

MAS's recent reforms are illustrated in figure 10-1, which shows that the party's vertical lines of command are partly counterbalanced by horizontal flows. Most important, the nominating power of the primary no longer rises through various geographically based levels (municipal, county, state, etc.), as in the system of indirect elections of most political parties in Venezuela and elsewhere. Furthermore, the vertical-horizontal organizational structure is more intricate than the structures in other parties. Organizational complexity (partly the result of countervailing powers—as against a simplistic top-to-bottom vertical line of command) has been a stated goal of the MASistas, who view it as a guarantee against abuse of authority.

MAS's Organizational Reforms in Comparative Perspective

In recent years political scientists have emphasized the vertical structure of political parties in Venezuela. David Myers, for instance, in the revised edition of *Venezuela: The Democratic Experience,* described the methods used by the national executive committees of the major parties to control lower-level leaderships. Not only are local leaders easily sanctioned and removed by the national secretary general, but

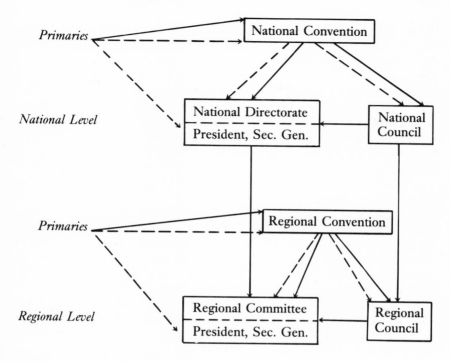

Key: Flow of authority: ————
Selection of leadership positions:— — —

Figure 10-1 MAS Organization after 1985 (National and Regional Levels). SOURCE: Lucas Leal (MAS's National Secretary of Organization), interview with the author, Caracas, April 30, 1987.

local and state secretariat respond directly to their counterparts at the national level.[29]

During the period under study, from 1971 to the mid-1980s, Venezuelan parties implemented organizational reforms that loosened internal controls and promoted rank-and-file input in decision making. Indeed, party renovation was a natural complement to the democratic liberties and stability that prevailed in the nation at the time. MAS was in the vanguard of this process, both on the left and in the nation as a whole.

In the mid-1980s, for instance, AD considered a series of measures to enhance popular participation, including proportional representation of slates in the national convention and primaries for the selection of the party's national authorities and presidential candidate. Those who advocated these reforms (including the head of AD's parliamentary representation, Carlos Canache Mata) argued that AD should not be left behind MAS, which had pioneered in these areas.[30] Nevertheless, in spite of considerable debate, the party retained its former structure, which it labeled "democratic centralist." AD decided against the system of primaries for the presidential nomination partly because of its bitter experience in 1967 when that method, which was employed for the first time in the nation's history, sparked a division that resulted in the formation of MEP. Proportional representation was also ruled out on grounds that it was conducive to factional struggle. Internal elections—which were themselves indirect—were adopted for the selection of the party's national authorities, but not its presidential candidate.

MAS's originality was no less outstanding when considered in a worldwide context. Perhaps the greatest resistance to change in the Eurocommunist parties was in the area of organizational reform. Modest steps were taken, such as the recognition of different levels of commitment among party members and the opening up of debate on the floor of party congresses. Nevertheless, the Eurocommunists shied away from the radical innovations that MAS carried out, such as the legalization of factions and their proportional representation (the PCI's reforms in this area were not nearly as far-reaching).[31] They also rejected rotation in office, which was perhaps the most telling indication of the willingness of a party's leadership to accept internal reform; thus the secretary generalship remained in effect a life-long position, except (as in the case of the PCE) when internal political conflict led to removal. The case of Petkoff, who went from party president to substitute member of the national directorate without falling into disgrace, had no parallel in the Eurocommunist parties, or most others for that matter.

MAS's record was equally impressive when compared with European social democratic parties, in spite of their much-acclaimed commitment to internal democracy. Among the reforms that Jordi Borja, in the prologue to Maurice Duverger's *Open Letter to Socialists,* called on the social democrats to implement were the recognition of internal factions, representation of diverse opinions in the party's press, the establishment of a federal structure, decentralization, the granting of autonomy to committees in the base of the party, rotation in office, nomination of candidates for parliament in party primaries, enumeration of the rights of party members, and secret voting procedures at party meetings.[32] MAS, of course, had made pathbreaking efforts to carry out all of these reforms, though with varying degrees of success. Its claim to uniqueness on the basis of its commitment to democracy could not be dismissed or scoffed at as mere party propaganda.

Overview

The origins of MAS's organized factions date back to the 1960s when dissident Communists led by Petkoff formed a group within the PCV that challenged the party's leadership both publicly and internally on a wide range of political, organizational, and philosophical issues. The opposition of the PCV leadership to the factional methods employed by Petkoff was consistent with a long-standing Communist tradition. Ever since the early years of international communism, Communist parties have adamantly opposed the existence of solidified groups within their organization that assume separate ideological and programmatic positions. The issue was debated at the Soviet Communist Party's Tenth Congress in 1921, when it was agreed upon to temporarily suppress factions (the most important being the Workers' Opposition), a decision that was never reconsidered. A key difference that emerged in later years between orthodox communism and Trotskyism was the latters' defense—at least in theory—of organized internal groups as an acceptable "Bolshevik method."[1]

Petkoff concurred with Trotsky's position on this issue in his *Socialismo para Venezuela?* (1970),[2] for which he was denounced as a "Trotskyist" by his orthodox Communist detractors. Nevertheless, upon the founding of MAS, the notion of the free play of factions was scrapped in favor of the maintenance of party unity. To avoid factional tensions, Petkoff and his followers accepted the more orthodox Pompeyo Márquez as MAS's secretary general and refrained for the time being from pushing far-reaching policy and organizational revisions that would have jeopardized unity.

The primaries for the presidential elections of 1978, in which Márquez supported the candidacy of José Vicente Rangel against that of Petkoff, produced the first major internal clash. Although defeated in these contests, Petkoff used the opportunity to build a veritable machine within the party, which succeeded in gaining control of the national leadership. Subsequently, the *teodoristas'* status as an organized faction—as well as that of the followers of Márquez—was formally recognized by the party. The proliferation of currents of opinion in MAS culminated in the 1985 internal elections for secretary general in which as many as six important MAS leaders, each one with organized backing, launched their candidacies. One important grouping led by Bayardo Sardi (which perhaps most nearly expressed Petkoff's own opinions) viewed themselves as a vanguard while disdainfully characterizing their internal rivals as "orthodox" and "retrogressive." This mentality was reminiscent of the attitude of Petkoff's followers toward the old-time PCvistas before the division in the party in 1970.

From the outset, Márquez and his supporters harbored great reservations regarding the "legalization of factions" in 1980. They resented the *teodorista* claim of representing a vanguard within the party and reproached them for having organized a veritable faction prior to 1980. Indeed, all MASistas acknowledged that factional rivalry had intensified and was a major factor in the party's poor showing in the 1983 national elections.

The legalization of factions, however, should not be written off as an effort to legitimize an acute or unprincipled struggle for power within MAS. In many ways it was a laudable experiment designed to formalize internal democracy. Marxists have always defended the abstract right of free expression within the party but have generally failed to face the task of providing structural means to guarantee that this right be respected in practice. The case in favor of the legalization of factions has as its premise the need to ensure that dissenting party members will have the opportunity to present their viewpoints to the rest of the organization. By allowing groups of dissidents to act collectively, MAS facilitated the diffusion of ideas within the party, and in the process the right to hold opinions became transformed into the right to be heard. An optimistic view of MAS would maintain that the legalization of factions is a feasible ongoing arrangement and that the modifications that were signaled by the 1985 convention represented an effort to deal with the rough spots of a system still in its experimental stage. With certain built-in constraints, the legalization of factions may prove to be an attractive corrective to the inordinate centralism that characterizes political parties in third-world countries, and Venezuela in particular. In light of the novelty of the system, a detailed examination of the factional struggle in MAS throughout its history is warranted.

From the Founding of MAS to the 1978 Elections

The popular reforms implemented by Carlos Andrés Pérez in the first year of his presidency in 1974 set off an internal debate in MAS. The party's official position of support for most government policies contrasted with the more critical posture of other sectors of the left. Germán Lairet and Antonio José Urbina called on MAS to reach a formal agreement with AD and to offer the government systematic support. Lairet argued that AD and COPEI would probably continue to monopolize the Venezuelan electorate for some time. In the face of this continuous "bipolarization," MAS was forced to come to terms with the more progressive of the two parties in order to open up for itself its own "political space."[3]

This position evoked an unexpectedly harsh response from Petkoff. Not only did he pejoratively label Lairet a "social democrat" but he accused him of subordinating principle to the objective of securing bureaucratic posts in the government in return for the party's support. In lashing out at Lairet, Petkoff made a plea for MAS to assert itself as a truly socialist party and to avoid any policies that would compromise its radical platform. Petkoff warned that social democracy manifested itself in MAS in the tendency to exaggerate the importance of elections at the expense of mass mobilizations and other forms of social struggle. The "social democrats" in MAS, according to Petkoff, called for political moderation as a corrective to the left's intransigence which dated back to the guerrilla period. By writing off everything the left did and stood for in the 1960s, these MASistas failed to analyze the events of that decade in all their complexities in order to pinpoint the left's errors and acknowledge the correctness of some of its stands.[4] In warning against the danger of electoralism in MAS and defending the guerrilla experience of the 1960s as something less than an unmitigated disaster, Petkoff implicitly identified his internal position as the "left-wing" of MAS. (In similar fashion, Petkoff had lashed out at the Communist Party's leadership in the 1960s, by claiming to represent the PCV's "leftist" faction.)

The severity of Petkoff's attacks on Lairet and Urbina was far out of proportion to their relative influence in MAS. In fact, his broadside against social democracy was a smoke screen for his opposition to the candidacy of José Vicente Rangel for the 1978 presidential elections. Among the arguments in favor of Petkoff's nomination over that of

Rangel was the need for MAS to avoid adulteration of its radical socialist message in any way—thus the importance of selecting a MASista rather than an independent whose ideas did not completely coincide with those of MAS.

Although a number of upper- and middle-level leaders accepted Petkoff's arguments and identified with his faction in the party, many of them backed the candidacy of José Vicente Rangel. They felt that not enough time had transpired since the 1960s to allow Petkoff to disassociate himself from his guerrilla past. Whereas the *teodoristas* were divided, Márquez's followers were unanimous in their support for Rangel, thus ensuring his easy triumph in the party's internal elections. Márquez's supporters, who were more inclined to accept unity of the left under certain conditions than were the *teodoristas*, hoped that the nomination of an independent would facilitate a leftist electoral agreement. Nevertheless, Márquez won a pyrrhic victory in that at the 1977 party convention, where Rangel was officially proclaimed MAS's presidential candidate, the *teodoristas* became a majority in the National Directorate. Once in firm control of the party, the *teodoristas* pursued policies that disrupted relations with other leftist parties and thus blocked the possibility of achieving unity.

The *teodoristas* assured for themselves leading positions in the direction of the presidential campaign. Petkoff's closest ally at the time, Freddy Muñoz, was named campaign manager, while another *teodorista*, artist Jacobo Borges, became the head of the propaganda section. Upon accepting his appointment, Muñoz announced his intention of unifying the "direction of the campaign" and the "direction of the party," which meant in effect that MAS, rather than a group of independents who supported Rangel, would be in full charge.[5] This policy reflected the *teodorista* concern that Rangel, the independent, would conduct the campaign in accordance with his own criteria, which were more in line with other sectors of the organized left, without taking into due account MAS's positions and interests. In addition, most of the best positions on MAS's slates were assigned to *teodoristas*, while those accused of being "social democrats," Lairet and Urbina in particular, received particularly low designations.[6] In one concession to Márquez's followers, the *teodoristas* dropped their insistence that José Vicente Rangel not be included in the party's congressional slate and instead accepted his placement in a leading position, which assured his election.[7]

The rivalry between the two factions during these years took on the form of an internecine struggle, producing scars that did not easily heal. The *teodoristas* were particularly inclined to resort to sanctions in states where they were in control, though Márquez's followers responded in kind in Mérida (against *teodorista* José Mendoza Angulo) and other states where they were dominant. In the way of justifying harsh measures against some of his MASista rivals, Petkoff insisted that social democracy could not coexist in MAS with the revolutionary tendency, which he purportedly represented.[8]

Márquez and most of his followers disagreed with the way MAS distanced itself from the rest of the left, creating obstacles to the type of unity Rangel was tactfully trying to achieve. Nevertheless, they were reluctant to openly or forcefully criticize MAS's conduct in the presidential campaign for fear of undermining the party's electoral effort. Only the small group headed by Lairet and Urbina, both of whom had been excluded from the party's National Directorate, acridly lashed out at MAS's management of the campaign. According to them, MAS should have taken advantage of its position as the largest leftist party by unifying the rest of the left on its own terms. In a series of strongly worded internal documents, Lairet characterized MAS's attitude as "sectarian and arrogant" and blamed the party for contributing to the proliferation of leftist presidential candidates.[9]

As a result of his role in leaking one of the documents to the press, MAS trade unionist Jesús Urbieta was prohibited from holding office in the party for two years. The response of Márquez and his followers to the incident was telling of their behavior in internal matters, specifically, their reluctance to face up to and resolutely challenge the *teodoristas* and their methods. Márquez agreed with much of the document's content; most of his followers on MAS's governing council voted against the sanctions against Urbieta. Nevertheless, they did not believe that internal disputes should be publicly aired, especially in the midst of a presidential campaign. Not only did Márquez's group fail to close ranks and defend Urbieta and Lairet, but Márquez issued a public statement denying Lairet's claim that MAS was responsible for disunity on the left.[10]

One casualty of MAS's internal struggle during this period was Joaquín Marta Sosa, one of the few leading party figures who had not formerly belonged to the PCV. In the 1960s Marta Sosa had been a leader of the left wing of the Copeyano youth movement. His switch in party allegiance was hailed by the MASistas as the beginning of a massive defection of Adecos and Copeyanos to MAS. Marta Sosa criticized MAS leaders and Petkoff in particular for maintaining sectarian positions that prevented the party from attracting a significant number of nonleftists, specifically, Catholics. He supported Rangel in MAS's internal primaries in the hope that the nomination of an independent would enable the party to reach out to the rest of the country. At the same time he clashed with the *teodoristas*, who accused him of "conspiring" against Petkoff's candidacy, for which he resigned from the party's national leadership in protest.[11]

During this period the followers of Petkoff and Márquez were commonly referred to as *patria* and *perros,* respectively. As the name implies, the *patria* favored symbols and slogans that affirmed MAS's patriotic commitment to Venezuela, while they rejected positions on international issues that would have aligned MAS with the Soviet bloc. In order to lend credibility to MAS's posture of neutrality, the *patria* urged the party to avoid scathing criticisms of the United States. *Patria* leaders spurned Marxist orthodoxy and favored radical revisions in the Leninist concept of the party. They also placed a high value on maintaining MAS's ideological purity. Alliances with other parties on the left were rejected out of fear that such associations, regardless of how circumstantial or tenuous, would blur the type of democratic socialism that MAS championed.

The *perros,* for their part, were committed to a nondogmatic Marxism but made an incomplete break with traditional Communist practices and conceptions. Márquez openly criticized socialist bloc nations, although he recognized that they had "not lost their attractiveness for the Third World."[12] He stressed the need to come to the defense of these governments and pointed to their positive achievements, not so much in the construction of socialism as in their successful defiance of U.S. imperialism. In one statement (subsequently criticized by fellow MASistas) Márquez praised Cuba for its intervention in Angola and denied that it acted at the behest of the Soviet Union. This combination of praise and criticism was expressed in an interview with Alfredo Peña, a prominent Venezuelan journalist:

> I am in disagreement in the Cuban case as in all cases of existing socialism. But I sympathize with the Cuban revolution in its search for autonomy in the sense that the United States has no right to impose on the people of Latin America the regime which Washington wants. . . . The Cuban Revolution has served to place the struggle for new forms of social organization in our hemisphere on a superior level.[13]

At the time that Petkoff's followers gained the upper hand in MAS at the party's fourth national convention in 1977, the *patria* group split in two. A left wing, headed by Freddy Muñoz, became known as the *halcones* (hawks) because of its hard line toward government policy. The other wing, headed by Luis Bayardo Sardi, favored radical innovations on a number of fronts, such as the "New Mode of Being Socialist" concept (the document itself had been drafted by Bayardo) and the "legalization of factions" (which had first been proposed by

Bayardo's ally, Anselmo Natale). Bayardo's faction was called the *tucán* (a multicolored tropical bird) because its eclecticism covered a wide range of ideological positions.

It would be simplistic to reduce the differences between *halcones*, *tucanes*, and *perros* to locations on a left-right spectrum. It is true that the positions of the *tucanes* coincided to a large degree with social democracy with its evolutionary approach and could thus be considered "rightist," whereas the *halcones* with their hardened opposition to the government represented a leftist tendency. It could be further argued, though somewhat less convincingly, that the *perros* occupied a "centrist" position in that they attempted to reconcile extremes for the sake of maintaining party unity. These categories, in any case, tell only part of the story. The self-identification of each faction and their perceptions regarding MAS's role in Venezuelan society and their own role within MAS transcends left-right categories. To a large extent the internal polemic in MAS has no equivalent in any other political party, and thus an analysis of the debate reveals the uniqueness of MAS as a party. First it is necessary to discuss the two new factions that developed out of the *teodorista* grouping in the late 1970s.

The *Tucanes*

At the time of their emergence as a faction, the *tucanes* viewed the revisions in MAS's original positions as incomplete. They urged modifications on a number of fronts, including interparty relations, foreign policy, class analysis, and Marxist-Leninist ideology, in order to carry the process of renovation to its logical conclusion.

Thus, for instance, upon its founding, MAS assumed a critical attitude toward other parties on the left, which in the course of time was translated into reluctance to enter into alliances with them. The *tucanes* favored going one step further. They called on MAS to issue a public statement formally renouncing any affinity with the rest of the left and ruling out the possibility of entering into an alliance with the PCV under any circumstance. In the 1983 elections the *tucanes* reluctantly accepted MAS's pact with MIR but viewed the agreement as purely tactical. Diego Bautista Urbaneja expressed the thinking of the *tucanes* in an internal party document in which selective alliances with parties such as MIR were described as convenient in order to "cushion the aggressions and maneuvers against MAS perpetuated by a left which MAS has increasingly less to do with."[14] The *tucanes* attributed MAS's poor showing in the 1983 elections in large part to its pact with MIR.[15]

The *tucanes* also viewed MAS's evolution away from Marxist dogma as incomplete. Although MAS had abandoned the Marxist and Leninist labels in quick succession, the party's position on Marxism was still under discussion. The orthodox MASistas, though willing to accept non-Marxists in the party and to cease calling itself a Marxist organization, insisted that its leaders should be committed to Marxism. The *tucanes*, on the other hand, opposed this requirement and discarded the validity of Marxism as a doctrine while maintaining that its chief value lay in its use as an instrument of social analysis.[16] The *tucanes*, unlike their two rival factions, questioned two pillars of Marxist dogma: the primacy of the working class in the struggle for socialism, and the revolutionary path to socialism.

The *tucanes* saw themselves as a vanguard within MAS that favored extending the modest reforms and policy changes the party had already undertaken. More than their rival factions, the *tucanes* put a premium on introspection and self-criticism, and felt that renovation should be an ongoing process in the party. They complained that MAS had lost its original innovative spirit, whose two major achievements had been the New Mode of Being Socialist thesis and the movement-of-movements strategy.[17]

By the late 1970s the New Mode document became a source of internal party debate. Freddy Muñoz and other orthodox MASistas felt that the party had gone too far in the application of the thesis. The *tucanes*, for their part, maintained just the opposite, namely, that MAS had not yet fully "assimilated" the concept. The *tucán* critique was expressed by a commission headed by national deputy Anselmo Natale, which stated that "the New Mode of Being Socialist has to be implemented on a higher level than ever before in order to promote a more accurate perception of our identity and policies."[18]

The *tucanes*' ardent defense of the movement of movements and their minimization of the role of the political party were indicative of the importance they assigned to the "vanguard." The *tucanes* defended the primacy of the vanguard both in the society as a whole (in the form of the movement of movements) and within the party (in the form of their own faction). In the *tucanes*' version of the movement of movements, the movement displaces the party as the motor force—or the *vanguard*—in the revolutionary process. The *tucanes*' opposition to proposals to strengthen party discipline and to limit the radius of action of the individual factions was also evidence of the importance they attached to the vanguard within the party.

The movement of movements was originally conceived of as autonomous organizations that united students, trade unionists, and mem-

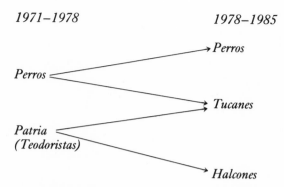

Figure 11-1 Transformation of MAS's Two Principal Factions at the Time of National Elections of 1978

bers of other groups regardless of their party affiliation. In practice, however, they became closely associated and linked with parties of the left. The *tucanes* called on MAS to correct this defect by making greater efforts to reach out to nonleftists, rather than scrap the concept altogether. The *tucán* strategy implied that MASistas at the organizational level would be free to form pacts with Adecos or Copeyanos and thus disassociate themselves from the rest of the left. According to the *tucanes*, such agreements would have been desirable as long as the alliance partners were not being controlled or manipulated in any way by their respective parties. The *tucanes* deplored that, party rhetoric notwithstanding, MAS had never fully committed itself to the movement of movements, and that, in the words of Urbaneja, the concept was "neither well thought out nor thoroughly practiced."[19] They pointed out that, although the organizations considered part of the movement of movements were independent of one another, most of them were controlled by MAS and were not allowed to develop autonomous status.

The *tucán* grouping represented a fusion of members of the *teodorista* and *perro* factions of the party (see figure 11-1). Bayardo Sardi and Anselmo Natale had been leading *teodoristas*, but others such as Diego Urbaneja and those who had been accused of being "social democrats" (Lairet, Urbina, and Urbieta) had belonged to the *perros*. This realignment reflected the new sources of internal debate in MAS. The *tucanes* combined the *teodoristas'* stress on innovation and heterodoxy with the *perros'* concern for reaching out to large numbers of Venezuelans who identified with or belonged to other parties.[20]

The *Halcones*

Those *teodoristas* who supported MAS's early revisions but by the mid-1970s felt that the party had gone too far in its reformist impulse formed the *halcón* faction headed by Freddy Muñoz. Muñoz and his followers criticized what they considered to be a rightward drift in MAS, which not only distorted its original socialist objectives but transformed it from a party of combat and social struggle to a purely electoral organization. The *halcones* argued that MAS had gone overboard in its efforts to disassociate itself from socialist bloc nations and the traditional left. In this area the *halcones* occupied a middle ground between the *tucanes,* who favored a complete and explicit break with both existing socialist regimes and the rest of the left, and the *perros.* Muñoz maintained that MAS overreacted to the traditional left by harping on the fallacies of its positions and engaging it in unnecessary polemics, in the process resorting to the anticommunism generally practiced by the right. He also pointed out that once having joined the Coordinator of the Left in 1978 (which was first proposed by Pompeyo Márquez, head of the *perro* faction), MAS spent several years vacillating between attempting to achieve leftist unity and feuding with other parties of the left.[21] Though he deplored the indecisiveness of MAS's behavior in the Coordinator, it was unclear whether Muñoz favored making greater efforts on behalf of unity or preferred that MAS not have committed itself to negotiations in the first place.

Muñoz also cautioned against a radical deviation from MAS's original stands as a result of an overreliance on or "erroneous comprehension" of the New Mode of Being Socialist thesis.[22] According to Muñoz, the New Mode document, when it was first put into practice, served to rectify the tendency in MAS to simplistically hold out socialism as a panacea while failing to deal with concrete problems confronting the nation. Influenced by the New Mode thesis, however, the party veered in the opposite direction whereby it refrained from challenging the power structure and downplayed socialism. At the rally in which he was proclaimed candidate for the position of secretary general in 1985, Muñoz stated: "MAS has to raise its voice, as we have in effect done here and now, to hold out to the Venezuelan people our socialist aspirations."[23]

In still another respect, the *halcones* upheld the positions that the *teodoristas* and Petkoff in particular had maintained during MAS's early years. Both as a dissident Communist and a member of the fledgling MAS, Petkoff had lashed out at the labor leaders of his own party for failing to raise the socialist banner and engage in militant struggle. In later years, however, Petkoff altered his viewpoint and argued that the passivity of the labor movement was indicative of the absence of sharp social struggle in Venezuelan society as a whole. He drew the conclusion that MAS should direct its energy along electoral lines rather than attempt to activate mass struggle. The *halcones* represented Petkoff's earlier thinking with regard to the need to follow a combative course. Muñoz and his close associates criticized MAS labor leaders for failing to challenge the labor bureaucracy from within the CTV, as had been MAS's original motive for joining the organization in 1975. They also called on MAS trade unionists to educate the workers about socialism.[24]

These criticisms drew a united response from the *perro* and *tucán* trade unionists, who represented the large majority of MAS's labor leaders. They pointed to MAS's inroads in organized labor as evidence that the party's labor policy had not been a total disaster, as the *halcones* insinuated.[25] Furthermore, they viewed the critique formulated by Muñoz as part of a power play designed to replace them with trade unionists who were identified with the *halcón* faction.[26]

The *halcones* warned that MAS's transformation from a Leninist organization to a loosely structured one was undermining party discipline and opening it up to ideological currents that were incompatible with its socialist commitment. Muñoz pointed to the special risks MAS faced in fulfilling its goal of recruiting large numbers of Adecos and Copeyanos. According to him, the former members of clientelistic parties whose idealism was combined with a drive for personal gain had to be well prepared and educated in what MAS was all about before being admitted into the party. Otherwise, their opportunism and lack of discipline would rub off on the party's rank and file. As an antidote, Muñoz, in *Más allá de las palabras,* called for "fortifying the commitment . . . , sense of responsibility [and] discipline of party members."[27]

At the insistence of the *halcones* MAS established the "System of Admission and Readmission" (SIR) following the 1983 elections, which laid down norms for the acceptance of new members and collected basic data on the party's membership. The cautious and distrustful attitude of the *halcones* toward recruits contrasted with that of the *tucanes,* who favored opening MAS up to discontented Adecos and Copeyanos and promoting them within the party in order eventually to fuse the party's historical leadership with "new blood." The *tucanes* protested that the SIR was too restrictive and created obstacles to increasing membership.[28] Whereas for the *tucanes* the SIR's main function should have been to draw those who were on MAS's periphery to the party, the *halcones* were mainly interested in gathering information about the party's rank and file in order to facilitate tighter control at the organization's base.[29] This difference is characteristic of heterodox and orthodox currents in other leftist parties throughout the world: the former generally proposes recruitment campaigns and an open-admissions policy in contrast to the latter, which favors defining criteria for accepting new members.

MAS's Three Factions: A Comparative Overview

Political scientists generally recognize the different roles and ideological preferences of distinct prototypes of Communist and Socialist party members. Two such categories are especially fitting for leading MASistas: the *intellectual* and the *organizational person*. The intellectual (or ideologue), in the words of the author of one study on the Brazilian Communist Party, "resents the status quo, desires social change, and is an articulate spokesman of Marxist and Leninist philosophies."[30] Such a person is especially concerned with promoting democracy and thus favors pluralistic policies and a loose and open party structure. The organizational person is concerned mostly with party affairs and views the popular movement mainly as a vehicle for strengthening the party.

These categories are useful for describing the *tucanes* and *halcones*, respectively. The intellectualness of the *tucanes* was demonstrated by their tendency to dwell on the type of socialist utopia that MAS was trying to achieve. The speculative nature of such thinking is telling of the concerns of intellectuals, who are generally highly motivated by utopian visions. Like left-wing intellectuals elsewhere, the *tucanes* favored renovation and displayed a special interest in searching for new formulas to strengthen internal democracy. As may have been expected from leftist intellectuals who lack a vocation for power, the *tucanes* were inept at building an organizational base within the party. Though attracting top party leaders and intellectuals, the *tucanes* failed to establish an important presence in more than a handful of states. They were not even able to control the party's two sections in Caracas (the Federal District and the state of Miranda), even though a large number of important *tucán* leaders were from the nation's capital. The loss of influence at the highest leadership level following the 1983 national elections induced a large number of *tucanes* to leave the party. These defections, however, were piecemeal and were not accompanied by a move to regroup in a new party. Had the *tucanes* had greater organizational interests and skills, they would have thought in terms of forming a splinter group rather than withdrawing from party politics altogether.

The leadership traits of the *halcones* contrasted sharply with those of their two main rivals, the *tucanes* and the *perros*. Bayardo Sardi was a poet and visionary thinker and thus a likely candidate to head the intellectually oriented *tucán* faction. Neither he nor Pompeyo Márquez were particularly dedicated to organizational work. Freddy Muñoz, on the other hand, was continually traveling to the nation's interior on behalf of party business and, of course, his own faction. As a result of their organizational skills, the *halcones* were able to firmly establish themselves in important positions in the party's bureaucracy. They were often accused of manipulating the party's apparatus in favor of their own faction, for which their staunchest detractors in MAS called them "Stalinists." The *halcones'* organizational mentality was also reflected in Muñoz's writings, in which he stressed the need for MAS to instill in its members a greater sense of discipline and to clearly define lines of command.

Each of the three factions had distinct perceptions regarding its role in MAS and of its rivals. The *tucanes* viewed themselves as a vanguard and as such were conscious of the need to put off the struggle for certain changes in MAS for which the party was not yet ready. They were convinced that just as in the past MAS had accepted ideas that had previously been considered unthinkable, the party would undertake radical revisions in the future that would vindicate their own advanced notions. They also saw themselves as the ideological rivals of the *halcones*, whom they considered to be imbued with a traditional Marxist mentality that was a carry-over from their days as Communists. They viewed the *perros*, on the other hand, as pragmatists who lacked any ideological frame of reference and thus had no reason to exist as an organized faction. While Muñoz, Bayardo Sardi, and Petkoff elaborated on political theories and prescriptions for MAS in their writings and remarks destined for internal party consumption, Márquez was mainly concerned with national and international issues.

The *halcones* attempted to restore the party's initial banners of socialism and anticapitalism and to recapture the idealism and zeal that had characterized the early MASistas. The *halcones* viewed the *tucanes* as social democrats who, in imitating AD and COPEI, accepted and even fostered clientelistic practices that undermined party discipline. At the same time they attacked the *perros* for favoring close relations with the rest of the left, even at the risk of diluting the party's ideological message. Thus both the *tucanes* and *halcones* were greatly concerned with the party's ideology, but whereas the *tucanes* applauded the evolution of MAS's positions, the *halcones* championed the party's original stands.

The *perros*, for their part, held the *teodoristas* and subsequently the *halcones* responsible for the discord and anarchy that reigned within MAS. According to them, the *teodoristas* had resorted to unfair tactics against their internal rivals and had constituted a veritable faction, even before the legalization of factions, in order to gain control of the party apparatus. The sanctions against leading *perros* in 1976 and 1977 were seen as reprisals for having supported the candidacy of José Vicente Rangel in MAS's presidential primaries. Rather than correct these abuses, the legalization of factions after 1980 only accentuated party fragmentation. The *perros* felt that the corrective to inordinate factionalism was defining and limiting the scope of permissible activity of party dissenters, unlike the *tucanes* who were avid defenders of the rights of minority factions.

In internal elections for party office two of the factions frequently allied with each other against the candidate of the third. Most commonly the *tucanes* and *perros* reached electoral understandings in opposition to the *halcón* grouping, which was the largest of the three. The *tucán-perro* alliance originated with the *tucán* support for the reelection of *perro* chief Pompeyo Márquez as secretary general of MAS at the national convention in 1980. The same agreement enabled the *perros* to retain control of the party's Youth Directorate. The critics of the system of organized factions in MAS denounced these agreements as "bureaucratic" and "opportunistic" on grounds that they were designed to secure positions in the party and were devoid of programmatic or ideological considerations.

Before MAS's 1985 convention the *tucanes'* weight at the national level was disproportionately greater than its support at the base of the party. This influence was due to the positions the *tucanes* had occupied as congressmen and members of the National Directorate before the division in the *teodorista* camp, as well as to their ability to project themselves in the communications media. It was also a result of the tacit support extended to the *tucanes* by Teodoro Petkoff.

Because of his aspirations to represent MAS in the 1983 and 1988 presidential elections, Petkoff decided to remain aloof from the party's factional struggle. Nevertheless, his stands on important national and international issues approximated those of the *tucanes*. Furthermore, Petkoff occasionally encouraged *tucán* leaders and promoted them within the party. Thus, whereas Pompeyo Márquez and other MASistas sharply attacked *tucanes* Carlos Raúl Hernández and Jean Maninat for publishing *Cuba-Nicaragua:expectativas y frustaciones* portraying Nicaragua as a tool of Soviet policy, Petkoff attended the book's "baptism." Perhaps the most visible evidence of a special relationship between Petkoff and the *tucanes* was his selection of Bayardo Sardi as campaign manager in the 1983 presidential elections. In private, some of the *tucanes* tried to prevail upon Petkoff to openly join their faction, even though such a move would have meant going against the majority in the party. They drew a comparison with Felipe González, who refused to submerge his differences with orthodox leaders who controlled the Spanish Socialist party and even threatened to resign, only to emerge later in full control of the organization.[31] The analogy, however, had one fatal flaw: whereas González enjoyed widespread popularity outside of his party that bolstered his position within it, Petkoff lacked such support in the nation as a whole.

The Intraparty Struggle After 1980

Before the 1978 national elections the majority of MASistas did not belong to any of the party's original factions. Only in the populated central region did the struggle between factions filter down to the party's lower ranks. This situation changed partly as a result of the 1978 elections, when many MASistas who were unaffiliated with any faction were overlooked in their attempt to run for office because of lack of support at the national level. Those party members, on the other hand, who belonged to either the *teodorista* or *perro* groupings generally fared better.

At the time of the 1978 elections members of a miniscule Caracas-based faction in MAS known as the Third Way passed out pamphlets in public that put forth their viewpoints.[32] Later, the principal factions agreed to publish all literature in their own name, as against that of MAS, and to refrain from distributing it outside of the party. Another important agreement took place at the party's fifth national convention in 1980 when Freddy Muñoz dropped his opposition to the reelection of Pompeyo Márquez as secretary general in return for the creation of the position of party president, which was to be occupied by Teodoro Petkoff.

As a result of the triumph of the *teodoristas* over the *perros*, José Vicente Rangel distanced himself from MAS, as did a small group of *perros* headed by Subsecretary General Tirso Pinto. During the 1978 presidential campaign Rangel had committed himself in internal MAS meetings to join the party following the elections. Nevertheless, Rangel subsequently reconsidered his decision. He feared that with his adversaries, the *teodoristas*, in full control of MAS, he would be constrained from pursuing interparty leftist unity and would not receive the treatment in the party that a leader of his stature merited.[33]

The *teodoristas* reacted strongly to the rapprochement between Rangel and the other leftist parties. They harshly criticized Rangel for having broken ranks with MAS in Congress, to which he had been elected on the MAS ticket. They claimed that, having been MAS's presidential nominee on two occasions, Rangel was morally obliged to support MAS's choice for the 1983 elections and thus should have refrained from launching his own candidacy. At MAS's 1980 national convention the *teodoristas* sharply denounced Rangel, though in spite of enjoying a superiority of 54 percent in delegate strength, they were unable to pass a resolution formally censuring him.[34]

MAS's subsecretary general, Tirso Pinto, supported the candidacy of José Vicente Rangel even after Petkoff's nomination at the 1980 convention. As far back as 1974, when MAS extended qualified support to the government of Carlos Andrés Pérez and decided to enter the CTV, Pinto had criticized the party for moving in a rightist direction and for adopting blatantly anticommunist positions. In early 1983 Pinto was suspended from his position in MAS. As a result he left the party altogether and campaigned on behalf of Rangel as well as his own candidacy for the national congress on the ticket of the "New Alternative."[35]

MAS's treatment of Rangel and Pinto was telling of the failure of the *perros* to assert themselves forcefully in the party. Obviously, the condemnation of Rangel and Pinto reflected the sentiments of the *teodoristas* alone, who at the time of the 1980 convention represented just slightly over 50 percent of the party. The sanctions against Pinto seemed particularly unjust in light of the party's failure to censure those *teodoristas* (such as Carlos Raúl Hernández and Manuel Caballero) who also made public statements diverging sharply from MAS's official policy. Had the *perros*, as a sizable minority in MAS, insisted on a more cordial treatment for Rangel (by virtue of having been twice MAS's presidential runner) and Pinto (who had belonged to the *perro* faction), the *teodoristas* undoubtedly would have been impelled to modify their behavior.

Following the 1980 national convention MAS incorporated positions of all three factions into its platform. For the 1983 elections each faction worked within a commission in which it was dominant, thus placing its mark on MAS's campaign. While *tucán* Bayardo Sardi was Petkoff's campaign chief, the *perros* controlled the commission in charge of elaborating the party platform and the *halcones* were a majority in the Electoral Strategy Commission. Following the elections most MASistas concurred that this arrangement had produced political incoherence, which was in large part responsible for the party's disappointing showing.

A sharp and prolonged struggle between the party's three main factions developed over the constitution of slates for the 1983 elections. MAS's National Council set up a Consensus Commission in order to work out a compromise arrangement. These efforts failed, however, when the *perros* protested that an alliance between the *tucán* and *halcón* factions had been formed in order to push them out of key slots on the slates. In addition, National Deputy Anselmo Natale and other leading *tucán* congressmen actually went to the press to express dissatisfaction at their low placements. They maintained that MASistas who had performed well in office should be given a second chance, regardless of the relative strength of their faction.[36]

The *tucanes*, who were the foremost exponents of opening up to sectors unidentified with the left, were largely responsible for MAS's inclusion of Reinaldo Cervini, the president of the liberal business organization Association Pro-Venezuela, on the party's slate, over the objections of various *halcones*.[37] They were less successful, however, in getting MAS to accept an electoral agreement with the New Generation, a small political organization that frequently placed advertisements in the press expressing a neoconservative philosophy.

MAS's poor showing in the 1983 elections undermined the position of the *tucanes*. Not only had Petkoff's campaign chief been Bayardo Sardi, but MAS's democratic commitment was stressed over its belief in socialism, in accordance with the *tucanes'* approach. The resignations of a significant number of *tucanes*, demoralized by the electoral results and by the advance of their rivals in the party, further cut into the *tucanes'* strength. A revised correlation of internal forces emerged at MAS's 1985 national convention, where the *tucanes* placed only six of its followers on the party's forty-five-member National Directorate. Several resolutions sponsored by the *tucanes* and their allies failed to receive more than a handful of votes at the convention. These motions called on MAS to change its name to the Democratic Party for Change, and to "abandon the socialist label" for all practical purposes.[38] In his defense of these proposals at the convention Carlos Raúl Hernández invoked the examples of Nicaragua and Cuba, where revolutionaries did not commit themselves to socialism and did not move openly to the left until after they were firmly in power. Thus MAS, it was argued, would be better off dropping the socialist label now and taking up socialist objectives only after coming to power.

The *perro* faction suffered a division when two of its members ran for the position of secretary general at the time of the 1985 convention. One of them, Juvencio Pulgar, adopted stands that were strikingly similar to those of the *tucanes*. Stressing the need for MAS to renovate itself, Pulgar called for decentralization of the party's structure and the input of nonparty members in decision making. On foreign policy, Pulgar's moderation in his critique of the United

States coincided with the *tucanes'* and seemed unlikely, coming from a MASista long identified with Pompeyo Márquez. His political strategy also resembled that of the *tucanes* in placing the accent on the struggle to vitalize the nation's democracy.[39]

The other *perro* candidate, Rafael Thielen, stressed the need to emphasize socialism, engage actively in social struggle, and "defend a revolutionary profile." This strategy was as similar to that of the *halcones* as Pulgar's was to the *tucanes*. Thielen also lashed out at sectarian behavior both within MAS and in the party's relations with other political organizations. One of the planks of Thielen's program left open the possibility of unity on the left: "We will attempt to achieve a national convergence of all those receptive and disposed to commit themselves to transformation and social change."[40]

The candidacies of Pulgar and Thielen with their radically different positions demonstrated that the *perro* faction had all along been based on the personality of Pompeyo Márquez and lacked a commonly accepted program. Although Márquez had supposedly spoken for his faction on national and international issues, what held the *perros* together was not these stands but rather a common rejection of the high-handed tactics employed by the *teodoristas*.

Conclusion

The New Mode of Being Socialist and other innovations promoted by MAS's renovation wing (the *patria* and later the *tucanes*) coincided with the boom in oil prices in the 1970s when the standard of living of most Venezuelans improved substantially and general confidence in the nation and its future set in. This novel situation influenced most Venezuelan leftists to shift their attention from armed struggle and mass mobilization to such types of political activity as electoral politics and the diffusion of propaganda. In addition, leftists reexamined their attitudes toward democracy and discarded the notion that the existing democratic system was a mere adjunct of the capitalist structure and thus irrelevant to the socialist society they were striving to create. This backdrop helps explain the receptivity that the reforms to democratize MAS's internal structure and to open the party up to the nation's mainstream encountered in MAS.

The exchange controls implemented in February 1983 signaled a downward swing in the nation's economy, which in turn generated widespread discontent. This deterioration fortified the position of the orthodox hardliners in MAS at the expense of the renovators. At the 1985 national convention MAS's left-wing groups headed by Freddy Muñoz and Rafael Thielen elected twenty-four and five members, respectively, to the party's National Directorate. The remaining six-teen positions were shared between the factions headed by Bayardo Sardi and Juvencio Pulgar. With Freddy Muñoz at the helm of the party, MAS hardened its opposition to the AD government and prom-ised to put greater emphasis on the party's socialist message. MAS thus came full circle in its political strategy, at a time when the economic and social conditions in the nation resembled those that prevailed during the party's early years.

Conclusion

The Communist dissidents who founded MAS in 1971 considered themselves to be to the "left" of the PCV leadership. They criticized the PCV for subordinating the party's socialist message to reformist objectives and for failing to denounce thoroughly the enemy, which included capitalists, CTV bureaucrats, and AD and COPEI politicians. By the early 1980s MAS shifted to the right, so much so that it hardly resembled its original self. MAS's mild criticism of U.S. foreign policy, its acceptance of private property, and its willingness to cooperate with AD and COPEI governments were now far to the right of PCV policies.

Indeed, the number of positions upheld by MAS fifteen years after its founding that were diametrically contrary to its original stands was striking. It could be argued that these turnabouts confirmed the principle frequently cited by leftists: ultra-leftism tends in time to lead to its contrary, namely, rightist deviation.

MAS's shifts may also be explained by the economic and political conditions that prevailed in Venezuela during the period under study. The windfall in government revenue following the oil price hikes in 1973 and 1974 filtered down to the middle, working, and even lower classes and conditioned their political behavior. An improved standard of living produced widespread optimism with regard to the nation's future, which discouraged participation in movements of protest and social disorder. The significance of this transformation was captured by Petkoff and other MASistas, who wrote off the strategy of worker mobilization as doomed to failure in the Venezuelan setting of the 1970s.

Nevertheless, in spite of the thoroughness of the modifications in MAS's positions, the premises behind them remained the same. Most important, MASistas upheld a voluntaristic notion of revolutionary change and relegated objective conditions to secondary importance. In emphasizing the role of the subjective factor, MASistas considered the attempt by Venezuelan revolutionaries in the 1960s to seize state power to be of paramount importance. They maintained that even though serious mistakes were committed in the armed struggle, for which a high price was paid, the left's view that power could be attained in the short run was basically correct. Thus the subjective factor, namely, the decision of the vanguard to seek state power, was emphasized over objective factors, that is, socioeconomic conditions.

The MASistas inherited the left's optimism of the 1960s and saw socialism as a short- or medium-term goal in Venezuela. Although MAS's rhetoric was toned down in later years, the party continued to believe that gaining power in the not-too-distant future was within the realm of possibilities. For this reason MAS's failure to substantially improve its electoral showing shook up the organization. MAS's stagnation in the 1983 elections produced a large number of defections, and the party itself turned inward and debated intensely the causes of what was considered a veritable fiasco. Whereas other leftist parties attributed their difficulties largely to objective conditions, specifically, the prosperity brought on by oil price hikes and the resultant social tranquility, the MASistas believed that the subjective factor, namely, the errors committed, were responsible for their failure to advance.

MAS's basic strategy of stressing ideological issues over agitation over concrete demands was another constant throughout the period. The Communist dissidents who formed MAS in 1971 accused the PCV of following an "economist" approach whereby the party over-emphasized nonstructural reforms and failed to clearly identify itself with socialist objectives. In later years MAS was less emphatic in its call for socialism. Nevertheless, the MASistas continued to stress the importance of ideology over agitation, as demonstrated by the intensity of the examination of the type of society they were trying to create. The MASistas thus contrast with most socialists throughout history—including Marx himself—who have felt that providing a blueprint of the new socialist society and the utopia that lies beyond is a futile exercise.

MAS, in its zeal to achieve ideological clarity, has always been reluctant to accept unity of the left. Agreements with other leftist parties with distinct socialist visions, it is felt, would only blur the type of democratic socialism MAS is committed to. Had MAS assigned greater importance to concrete demands, it would have accepted unity based on those immediate objectives that all leftist parties hold in common. In universities, labor organizations, and national and local elections unity would have been a logical strategy to facilitate the struggle for short-term demands. MAS's rejection of unity was a reflection of the importance the party assigned to ideological differentiation.

The rationale behind MAS's policy of opposing leftist unity on grounds that it would dilute the party's ideological purity was open to question. In the first place, interparty alliances do not necessarily detract from the effort of each member party to define its positions. Coalition partners usually tone down mutual criticism and refrain from harping on issues that are the source of profound differences among them. Nevertheless, alliances do not necessarily have to be governed by such discretion. MAS, being the largest party on the Venezuelan left, could have dictated its own terms of unity, which could have included the liberty of each party to assume publicly its own positions.

In the second place, it was unclear whether MAS's motive for rejecting unity was to *maintain* its ideological clarity or provide itself with time to *develop* ideological clarity. If the latter was the case, MAS's anti-unity policy was clearly a failure, since after fifteen years of existence in which the party spurned unity of the left in three presidential elections, it still admittedly suffered from ideological vagueness. Indeed, in a special effort to define its positions, the party divided its 1985 national convention into two groups of sessions, one to elect party authorities and the other to discuss ideology and arrive at definitions. Furthermore, although MASistas hailed certain programmatic and ideological revisions formulated by MIR, MEP, and other leftist parties that approximated those of MAS, such modifications did not prompt MAS to reconsider its anti-unity stand in the 1978 and 1983 elections.

In addition to MAS's voluntaristic outlook and its emphasis on ideology over agitation, a third common strain can be detected in its thinking throughout its history. The MASistas staunchly opposed dogmatism, which mystified basic truths, and attached prime value to openness and frankness. Most top MAS leaders came of political age in the 1960s when young people rebelled against societal inhibitions and taboos and encouraged free and open expression without restrictions (as was the case in the hippie and "free speech" movements). This orientation was evident before the founding of MAS, when Petkoff and other dissident Communists criticized the PCV for failing to discuss and propagandize on the basis of the party's true socialist goals. Petkoff maintained that for the Communist Party, socialism was a veritable taboo.

In another manifestation of straightforwardness, the MASistas called for an open debate on the role of the military in politics, a topic that, as the MASistas pointed out, was taboo in Venezuela. The MASistas called for recognition of a self-evident truth, namely, that military personnel had a great interest in political issues and played an active role in the organization of civilian society and its decision-making process.

In addition, MAS's legalization of organized factions in 1980 was designed to accept a reality of all political organizations, which most of them had chosen to suppress: the existence of internal currents of opinion. This move was defended on grounds that providing the opportunity to articulate internal differences was preferable to fostering illusions regarding the uniformity of criteria within the party.

The virtues of candidness and sincerity that Petkoff and other MASistas extolled was to a certain extent contradicted in practice. The MASistas have always disdained political purism and strict adherence to principles that obstruct their ultimate goal of achieving power. This pragmatism has often led them to defend positions that do not truly represent the course they are pursuing. Examples of this divergence between overt and hidden policies abound. Petkoff, as a dissident Communist, swore allegiance to the PCV and spoke in the name of Communist unity at the same time that he consciously pursued a strategy of splitting the party. At MAS's founding convention in 1971, Petkoff, Bayardo Sardi, and other top MASistas decided to conceal their innovative plans for MAS until the party was ready to accept them. In this vein they proclaimed MAS's allegiance to the international Communist movement in spite of their conviction that MAS needed to break away entirely from the Soviet camp. In the mid-1970s Petkoff attacked some of the followers of José Vicente Rangel in MAS as "social democrats," only to move in a similar direction once Rangel's influence in the party was eliminated. After 1977 Petkoff refused to openly take sides in the party's internal disputes in order to promote his presidential aspirations. Thus, pragmatic politics, which led Petkoff to conceal his preferences, took precedence over the straightforward approach he purported to favor.

The hiatus between professed and unstated objectives was also manifested in MAS's proposal to establish the Coordinator of the Left in early 1978. The MASistas participated in protracted talks sponsored by the Coordinator even though their interest in leftist unity was, at best, lukewarm. In fact, their real aim was to avoid being branded "anti-unity." Such an accusation had wrested a considerable number of votes from MAS in elections on campus and elsewhere in previous years, when its rejection of leftist unity was a publicly stated policy.

An additional pillar of MAS's thinking was opposition to all forms of bureaucracy. This stand was another legacy of the youth movement of the 1960s, with its espousal of participatory democracy. MAS avidly supported decentralization and offered concrete and well-publicized plans for the transfer of decision-making power from the national executive to state and municipal governments. Similarly, MAS promoted decentralization within the party in forms that had few parallels in other parties throughout the world.

One last salient feature of MAS as a party was its constant effort to arrive at new and untested formulas in order to make the "Venezuelan Road to Socialism" a reality. MAS's perception of itself as a unique party (which in many ways it was) was another throwback to the 1960s. The New Left of that decade, which so thoroughly influenced MAS, viewed itself as cut off from the past and unrelated to previous movements and struggles. This ahistorical notion has permeated MAS's thinking. Not only did MAS not identify itself with the old Communist Party from which it emerged, but it was reluctant to associate closely with other parties throughout the world. In spite of the manifest influence that European Communist parties exercised over the early MAS, the MASistas denied that they were indebted to Eurocommunism. Furthermore, MASistas have always profusely congratulated themselves for the uniqueness of their reforms, including the New Mode of Being Socialist, the movement of movements, the legalization of factions, and the system of primaries for selecting party authorities and candidates.

In attempting to avoid following in the footsteps of other parties, MASistas see themselves as occupying a political space between the traditional left and social democracy. Thus MAS has made great efforts to distinguish itself from the far left at the same time that most party leaders rule out evolutionary socialism in the absence of class struggle, as put forward by social democrats.

A principal objective of this study has been to measure the degree to which MAS's claim to uniqueness has been borne out in fact. Chapter 1 described the outstanding features of Eurocommunism in order to place MAS's birth in an international context and specify areas of influence. Eurocommunism served as an inspiration to the MASistas. Their political formation had been based on orthodox Communist notions of "internationalism," with its emphasis on the interconnection and mutual dependence of socialist movements throughout the world. For this reason, the questioning of established Communist dogma by leading prestigious European Communists did much to legitimize ideological renovation in the eyes of the dissident Venezuelan Communists and encouraged them to strike out in similar directions. Specific areas of convergence were noted. Both MAS and the Eurocommunists demonstrated a high degree of commitment to pluralism and democracy and argued for the autonomous status of each constituent party in the international Communist movement. In addition, the very political slogans coined by the Eurocommunists were utilized by the early MASistas.

Nevertheless, key differences were also noted. In the first place, MAS's voluntarist philosophy, as evidenced by its view that socialism was an immediate possibility, was not shared in its entirety by the Eurocommunists. In addition, the sectarianism of the early MAS, in which alliances with parties to its right were spurned, contrasted with the attitude of the Eurocommunists. Indeed, the policy of the PCI and other European Communist parties of opening up toward organizations to their right was broader in scope and more far-reaching than in the popular frontism of the 1930s and 1940s.

MAS's case for being a unique party is much more convincing during its later years. The New Mode of Being Socialist document in 1974 signaled a conscious effort on the part of MAS to distinguish itself from the traditional left. At the same time the party retained its commitment to revolutionary change and socialism, even though it was somewhat played down. Few parties, if any, have gone so far in rejecting the policies, style, and strategy of the traditional left without completely abandoning the revolutionary camp and embracing social democracy. In addition, MAS's reforms in favor of internal democracy have no counterpart in other leftist parties throughout the world. The Eurocommunists, in spite of their professed commitment to democracy, have been extremely cautious in implementing organizational changes. Social democratic parties, which boast of their democratic internal life, have only discussed the possibility of carrying out such measures as the direct election of party authorities and candidates, recognition of internal factions, and other reforms described in chapter 10. The range of activities of MAS's organized factions and the openness in which they operate have no equivalent, even in more conservative parties that permit public criticism of the official party line.

The question may be posed, has MAS's intense and drawn-out internal debate and introspection, which was facilitated by the legalization of factions and other democratic reforms, contributed in any way to the party's potential for growth? Undoubtedly, the propensity of MASistas to engage in lengthy discussions of ideological issues appeals to a relatively small sector of the population consisting of students and intellectuals. Although the intellectual component of a leftist party is important, without a worker base its possibilities of success are extremely limited. Throughout its history MAS has not been able to recruit large numbers outside of the middle sectors. This failure demonstrates that an open and democratic organizational life will not help a leftist party much in attracting nonprivileged sectors to the party's fold.

MASistas generally maintained that absolute formulas in politics do not exist. They viewed the constant revisions in MAS's internal structure and in its programmatic and ideological formulations as a natural and healthy process rather than the result of party vacillation and uncertainty. Nevertheless, it was unclear whether MASistas felt that these revisions would conduct the party in a general direction approximating an absolute model or whether they were designed to accord with changing objective conditions in the nation and the world. If the latter was the case, then the new hard line the party embraced with the election of Freddy Muñoz as secretary general in 1985 was a logical move, given the economic crisis and growing discontent in Venezuela at the time. The *tucanes*, who were the great losers at the 1985 convention, felt otherwise. They viewed MAS's new orientation, not as a necessary adjustment to changing conditions, but rather the undoing of the reforms MAS had pioneered. The more disillusioned *tucanes*, who left the party, viewed MAS's new stance as signifying a return to the policies of the Communist Party. Undoubtedly, this claim was exaggerated, if not completely unfounded.

More accurately, the election of Muñoz signified the reapplication of MAS's original strategy. During MAS's first three years the party stressed socialism and assumed a hardened opposition to the government, while eschewing the confrontation tactics employed by the clandestine ultra-left. The MASistas also spurned the dogmatism and timeworn formulas that were associated with the PCV, thus allowing them to put into practice novel ideas. In this way, MAS's early strategy combined flexibility and firmness, along with rejection of both orthodoxy and adventurism. This approach met several spectacular successes in trade union and university elections. More important, it raised great expectations in the nation as a whole and the party in particular.

The strategy was abruptly scrapped in favor of a policy of qualified support for the government of Carlos Andrés Pérez and the New Mode thesis in 1974. The three years between 1971 and 1973 was too short a period to have permitted an empirical evaluation of the approach. A return to the line in 1985 was an attractive option for

MASistas who were frustrated by the party's nearly imperceptible growth. Unfortunately, in 1985 the strategy was lacking in what it contained when it was first taken up in 1971, namely, the element of novelty that has always fascinated the MASistas. Thus, its adoption in 1985 was not new, though, at least for Venezuela, it was still virtually untested.

Appendixes

1 Excerpt of speech by Leonid Brezhnev at the Twenty-fourth Congress of the Communist Party of the USSR, 1971, printed in *Teodoro: Candidato Presidencial del MAS*

But we cannot, comrades, close our eyes to the fact that negative phenomena have not been overcome in all places. The struggle against revisionism on the right and the "left" and against nationalism continues to be an important [task]. It is precisely in the nationalist tendencies, especially those which take on the form of anti-Sovietism, in which ideologists and bourgeois propagandists place their hopes. . . . They push the opportunistic elements in the Communist Parties to a certain ideological reconsideration. They appear to be saying to them: if you demonstrate that you are anti-Soviet, we are willing to proclaim that the true "Marxists" are you and your independent positions. The unfolding of events has shown for us that these people also light up the road in the struggle against the Communist Parties of their countries. Examples of them are the renegades like Garaudy in France, Fischer in Austria, Petkoff in Venezuela, and the group "Maniefesto" in Italy. The sister Parties consider the struggle against such elements an important prerequisite for fortifying their ranks. These examples, which could be multiplied, are sufficient to demonstrate that the struggle against revisionism and nationalism continues to be an important task for Communist Parties.

2 Article signed by "A. Mosinev," published in *Pravda,* October 20, 1970, and reprinted in *Tribuna Popular,* November 5–11, 1970

Venezuelan Communists are actively preparing for the Fourth Ordinary Congress, the inauguration of which is planned for December 4 of this year. The congress is to present conclusions regarding the activity of the Party during the ten years that have transpired since the Third Congress (March 1961), approve the Programmatic Thesis and Party Statutes, elect new members to the leadership organs, [and] establish the political line for the upcoming years.

In Venezuela the ten-year period between the Communist congresses has been characterized by great intensity in the class struggle, during which time the Party, together with other forces on the left, took up the armed struggle against the terrorist and unpopular regime of Betancourt, which enjoyed the backing of the North American oil and steel trusts. In spite of the great heroism and courage displayed by Venezuelan Communists, this five-year armed struggle ended in the defeat of the revolutionary forces . . .

In the [internal] organizations of the Party, an ample discussion has been initiated with regard to the combative experience of the Party, the question of the construction of the Party, and the tactics to be employed in the new situation. The proposals for the Programmatic Thesis and Statutes published by the Central Committee are taken as the basis for discussion . . .

At this point, when the date for the realization of the Fourth Congress is a month and a half away, the discussion has taken on an extremely sharp character. In the Party, a group that maintains anti-Leninist positions on a series of important problems related to the Venezuelan revolutionary movement as well as the international Communist movement has intensified its activities. Under the guise of "renovating" the Party this group, headed by Teodoro Petkoff, member of the CC [Central Committee], tries to revise Marxism, distort its most important theses, discredit the Party's most loyal leaders, undermine the Party from within, [and] reject Leninist principles of organization. In articles published in the bourgeois press and in two books, Petkoff, exposing his renegade creed, attacks the Soviet Union and the international Communist movement of the Communist Parties of Latin America and the socialist countries of Europe. With a special hatred that is no way dissimulated, he talks of the Soviet Union, debasing with malicious intent the process of Communist construction in the USSR.

In his book *Czechoslovakia: Socialism as a Problem*, Petkoff converges with the imperialists in his evaluation of what is happening in that country, defending the antisocialist forces [and] the counterrevolutionaries that attempted to take Czechoslovakia out of the socialist camp . . .

The writings of Petkoff manifest brazen hatred for the first socialist state in the world, the Soviet Union, and the Party of Lenin. As Ortega Díaz and García Ponce, outstanding leaders of the CP of Venezuela, accurately indicate in their pamphlet *Anti-Socialist Ideas of T. Petkoff*, "Anti-Sovietism is the thread that holds Petkoff's books together from the first to last page. It can be accurately said that the theme of Czechoslovakia is only a pretext to put forward a theory of antisovietism, in order to unleash the most absurd and calumnious attacks against the USSR [and] the most arbitrary interpretations of the [historical] process of the Russian Revolution." Lacking data to confirm his calumnious assertions, Petkoff chooses as witnesses the most rabid troubadours of antisovietism, from Trotsky to Deutscher, Garaudy, and Sik.

Passing over to positions of the enemies of socialism, Petkoff consciously lies about the process of its creation in the USSR and other socialist countries for the purpose of discrediting it. He labors eagerly to demonstrate that socialism in the Soviet Union has been developed "according to the peculiar unreproducible conditions" [in that nation] and that the Soviet Union constitutes "a particular socialist model, limited by [that nation's] unique historical circumstances."

Petkoff goes to the extreme of making the monstrous assertion that the strength of the socialist countries does not reside in their unity but rather in fragmentation. He says that the fragmentation of the socialist camp would create new points of support for the development of the revolutionary movement (?!). Motivated by his hatred of socialist countries, the calumniator goes to the absolute extreme of calling himself a "friend" of the socialist countries. Comrade Jesús Faría, secretary general of the PCV, is correct in replying to the attacks of one of Petkoff's followers [Manuel Caballero] with the question: "If these are friends, then who are the enemies?" . . .

The author of the cited libelous book defames the sister parties of Latin America and Europe. . . . Instead of [working in] the already existing parties that have demonstrated in practice their vitality and combative capacity, he suggests creating opportunistic parties to the right with their majority and minority [factions] and abandonment of the principle of democratic centralism and the Leninist theory of the dictatorship of the proletariat. Petkoff submits the principles of Marxism-Leninism to revision. He denies the historical mission of the working class and its vanguard role in the overthrow of capitalism and the construction of the new society. In the judgment of Petkoff, "the working class tends to transform itself into a conservative factor," while the true revolutionary force, the force that spreads the revolutionary spirit to the working class, is according to him the "intellectuals and their revolutionary youth."

Petkoff criticizes the slogan of the Seventh Congress of the Comintern for creating popular antifascist fronts. He definitively states that the formation of the popular fronts gave capitalism the possibility of "breathing" again (!) . . .

Facing obstacles in the Party, Petkoff appeals to the student youth. . . . With the publication of his libelous work he attempts to blackmail the leadership of the Party and the Communists at the base with the threat of a schism. As was spelled out in a declaration to the Politburo of the CC of the PCV, Petkoff has actually dared to place conditions on the unity of the Party: that it abandon the Leninist principle of organization, suppress the exercise of democratic centralism in the internal life of the Party [and] permit the existence of factions.

The efforts of the renegades face a firm response from the leaders and the organizations at the base of the Party. In the declaration of the Politburo of the CC it was said that the machinations of Petkoff have met with general repudiation. The leadership of the CP of Venezuela has called on all the organizations at the base of the Party, and on the youth to defend energetically the unity of the Party, and has made clear that Petkoff is openly confronting the [entire] structure of the Party and its political line in his effort to lay the groundwork for a new organization, and has exhorted Communists in the cells and local committees [of the Party] and on radio to provide an appropriate response to Petkoff's threatening initiatives . . .

3 "Necessity of a New Mode of Being Socialist" (Summary of "A New Mode of Being Socialist," document ratified by MAS's Central Committee in February 1974)

Shortly after the conclusion of the past electoral process, MAS initiated—especially at its upper leadership levels—an analysis of the policy that we sustained, of the activities that we realized, of the results in general and of those that we obtained [in particular], of the new situation which was created and of the prospects and challenges that we are faced with for the development of the socialist movement . . .

In the document approved by the CC in its meeting of February 1974, we evaluated the extent of the achievements obtained during the campaign. We appreciate the fact that the great [electoral] polarization which took place was not able to impede or conceal the emergence of MAS as an ascendant movement and advocate of a socialist alternative which had never before been presented to the country [and] which has gained for its alternative vision a cultural and political space which opens new possibilities for expansion. This we said had a value which goes beyond that of mere electoral statistics. But, at the same time, we recognize the grave significance of the fact that the vast majority of Venezuelans opted for AD and COPEI.

Our examination of the electoral results was designed to reach the depth of political realities. We refused, from the outset, to adopt a conformist position which would have distanced us from a thorough comprehension and have eliminated the prospects for new developments.

We emphasized the source of our relative success: the explicitly anticapitalist and socialist character of the policies which we formulated; the postulation of socialism as an alternative for our times; the search for a Venezuelan road to revolution and a Venezuelan blueprint for socialism; the rupture with the dogmas and schemes of the traditional left, a process which opens up the possibility of a theory and practice rich in socialist struggle; the rupture with the eternal "frontist" [strategy] of the left, which keeps it attached to reformist leadership and sham and outdated politics; the affirmation that we [MAS] are not—nor is the left at the present time—the only force which can intervene as a factor in favor of social change and the search for new agents in the transformation of society; the effort to speak and act for the country as a whole and for those who constitute a majority, overcoming the thinking and conduct of [political] sects. This is what made it possible for MAS to acquire the weight that it has today and the potential which even its deep-seated enemies recognize.

But the results of December 9 . . . also indicate that the socialist message did not reach or convince the vast majority of our countrymen.

Perhaps we do not have any basic responsibility for this fact?

We have reached the conclusion that we do. The analysis of our electoral activity has permitted us to establish that, notwithstanding the virtues of [our] socialist politics, we maintained ourselves in isolation from the popular sectors. And this occurred because the content of [our] socialist propositions, their insufficient tie-in with the concrete problems of the people, and shortcomings in language and style preserved the communications barrier which for so long has existed between the revolutionary forces and the great majority. This occurred because, notwithstanding our intentions, we still do not know in large part the real people: their daily lives, their aspirations for change, the perceptions which they have regarding their situation [and] the manner in which their political opinions are arrived at. This occurred because a large part of the country did not come to view the socialism which we spoke of as something essentially distinct from that which for decades the dominant ideology has spoken of, nor was MAS recognized as an alternative to the present.

There is something basic which [our campaign] generated and which will again be produced if we do not succeed in overcoming it: the residue of the cultural and political inheritance which comes to us by way of the old left, from which we still have not completely broken away. Here we find the basis of much of our erroneous behavior: essentialism . . . which tends to harp on the prompt radical solution of socialism in response to the concrete situation in the country. The primitive and simplistic conception which thinks of the consciousness of the people as a by-product of misery and directly proportional to it, for which [reason] the fundamental importance of the struggle for reforms is not comprehended. . . . The inability to understand that the destiny of all revolutionary politics is concrete people with concrete problems and with concrete levels of comprehension [and that] their consciousness and willingness to struggle cannot be substituted for by just any vanguard, nor artificially created by it.

Conceptions, tendencies, and manners of thinking such as these have made the old left a marginal force bereft of the possibility of victory. With this we have to consummate the rupture [of 1970] . . .

The "new way of being socialist" has to be a real exercise, effectuated on the basis of the social, political, and cultural conditions in the country, and, in particular, the conditions created by the elections of December 9. In an effort to concretize these aims, we have established some basic orientations related to the political practice of the Movement:

1. In order to overcome our lack of communication with a large part of the country, we should get much closer to the real world of the people . . .

We should get to know this real world (through study, direct relationships, and practical politics) and accept it as it is in order that our general politics identifies what the people are all about, reaches them at their levels of comprehension, and is connected to them in action.

2. We should assign a fundamental place to the struggle for reforms so that the concrete problems of the people and the country are converted effectively into the center of socialist politics. In the face of the general problems generated by capitalism, the permanent allusion to the goodness of the future socialist society does not have anything to do with our condition as an alternative, or of creating a new consciousness.

3. So that the idea of socialism of which we are advocates reaches the levels of

consciousness of the masses, educational activity which diffuses [our message] through diverse types of propaganda is not enough. Our mission is not completed—as we frequently think it is—when we put together a political message full of theoretical conceptions and an alternative vision and transmit it to the nation. We have to accompany the people in the living of their own experiences, and we have to tailor our actions to correspond to them. This presupposes a sustained and intense effort which combines our general propagandistic action—what the Movement [MAS] up until now has most effectively carried out—with struggle, mobilization, and propaganda work at places where the masses realize their social existence (work places, areas of residence, educational centers, etc.).

4. The growth of socialist forces requires that our rejection of the present society not be reduced to or be perceived as a cathartic [exercise] carried out from a corner, incapable of going beyond the modest limits of the world of the old left. For this reason it is necessary to act without vacillation in the political space dominated by our adversaries (legislatures, worker and popular organizations, communications media, etc.) in order to dispute with them the positions which they hold.

5. We understand that the viable existence of a socialist alternative implies our convergence with other forces capable of participating from their own angle in the struggle to transform society. This convergence nevertheless should be stimulated by us, [while] overcoming the limits of traditional "frontism" proposed so many times by diverse formations on the left.

The fundamental basis for the construction of an alternative bloc which is not exhausted at the frontier of a determined organization is in a social space that is not precisely that occupied by the left. It is not, therefore, the interior of this [that is, the left] but rather the country as a whole where we have to direct most of our efforts.

The convergence [of political forces] capable of generating a victorious movement has to be produced with the social currents that do not currently have a defined party alignment [and] which are present in diverse organizations and institutions. From that position the search for unity should be proposed, more in the plane of social forces and less in the plane of political organizations, more in the terrain of the concrete social process (joint struggle, mutual understanding, convergence of common propositions) and less in the terrain of formal organizational crystallizations. This is currently the best way to guarantee that socialism becomes truly a movement of the masses.

Notes

Introduction

1 "Genio y figura de Pompeyo Márquez" (introduction), in Pompeyo Márquez, *Socialismo en tiempo presente* (Caracas: Avilarte, 1973), pp. vii–xxxii.

2 Petkoff's family's background as Jewish immigrants may explain, albeit only partially, his determination to integrate into the nation's political mainstream. This eagerness to move away from the aloofness that immigrant status often entails is characteristic of second-generation immigrants. Petkoff, it may be added, is one of the few Venezuelan politicians who has expressed sympathy for the state of Israel.

3 Judith Ewell, *Venezuela: A Century of Change* (Stanford: Stanford Univ. Press, 1984), pp. 148–49; *Teodoro: Candidato presidencial del MAS* (1983 presidential campaign material).

4 Luigi Valsalice, *Guerrilla y política: curso de acción en Venezuela 1962/69* (Buenos Aires: Editorial Pleamar, 1975), pp. 197–210 ("notas bibliográficas"); Antonio Zamora, *Memoria de la guerrilla venezolana* (Caracas: Síntesis Dosmil, 1974), p. 140 ("personas mencionadas en el relato").

1 The International Setting

1 One of the first Latin American political leaders to criticize the tendency to look to the metropolis for an all-encompassing guide was Victor Raúl Haya de la Torre, who in 1929 wrote "we live searching for a mental overseer to free us from having to think for ourselves." See Naudy Súarez Figueroa, "El joven Betancourt (II)," *Nueva Política* 16 (April–Junio 1975): 47.

2 One leading Communist at the time of the division in the PCV, which gave rise to MAS, wrote that Petkoff, "with absolute contempt for the scientific method, divides the life of our party into *prehistory*—from Gómez until the outbreak of the guerrilla period—and *history*, from that point until the present. For Petkoff there is no coherent history of our Party. He buries the old militants of the party in the caves of prehistory . . . along with reformism and opportunism of the right. The 'prehistory' is a period without importance or value of any sort." See Radamés Larrazábal, *Socialismo bobo a socialismo para Venezuela?* (Caracas: Ediciones Cantaclaro, 1970), pp. 46–47.

3   J. Mark Ruhl, "Understanding Central American Politics," *Latin American Research Review* 19, no. 3 (1984): 145.

4   The first European Communist to employ in public the term *Eurocommunist* was Enrico Berlinguer at a meeting that took place in Paris in June 1976. G. López Raimundo and A. Gutíerrez Díaz, *El PSUC y el eurocomunismo* (Barcelona: Grijalbo, 1980), p. 39.

5   Luigi Barzini, "A Founding Father," *New York Review of Books*, Sept. 28, 1967, p. 22.

6   Donald Blackmer, *Unity in Diversity: Italian Communism and the Communist World* (Cambridge: MIT Press, 1968), pp. 25–27.

7   *Pekin Informa* 1 (special edition, 1963): 6; Winberg Chai, *The Foreign Relations of the People's Republic of China* (New York: G. P. Putnam's Sons, 1972), pp. 140–42; Harold C. Hinton, *Communist China in World Politics* (Boston: Houghton Mifflin, 1966), p. 98.

8   Santiago Carrillo, "Somos un partido obrero," in Vidal Sales, *Santiago Carrillo: Biografía* (Barcelona: A.T.E., 1977), p. 227.

9   Hinton, *Communist China in World Politics*, p. 104.

10 Giorgio Napolitan, *La alternativa eurocomunista* (Barcelona: Blume, 1977), pp. 57–61.

11 Palmiro Togliatti, *Comunistas, socialistas, católicos* (Barcelona: Editorial Laia, 1978), p. 80; Edward Crankshaw, *The New Cold War: Moscow v. Pekin* (Middlesex, England: Penguin Books, 1963), p. 17.

12 Karl-Ludwig Gunsche and Klaus Lantermann, *Historia de la Internacional Socialista* (Mexico: Editorial Nueva Imagen, 1979), pp. 171–76; Willy Brandt (interview), "La Internacional Socialista: Una fuerza político-moral de dimensión internacional," *Nueva Sociedad* 66 (May–June 1983): 35–36.

13 Maurice Duverger, *Carta abierta a los socialistas* (Barcelona: Ediciones Martínez Roca, 1976), p. 17; Alfonso S. Palomares, *El socialismo y la polémica marxista* (Bruguera: Zeta, 1979), p. 182.

14 Duverger, *Carta abierta*, p. 20.

15 Adam B. Ulam, *A History of Soviet Russia* (New York: Holt, Rinehart and Winston, 1976), p. 261.

16 Ronald H. Chilcote, *The Brazilian Communist Party: Conflict and Integration, 1922–1972* (New York: Oxford Univ. Press, 1974), pp. 66–67.

17 Donald L. Herman, "Mexico," in *1980 Yearbook on International Communist Affairs*, p. 376; James Nelson Goodsell, "Mexico," in *1982 Yearbook on International Communist Affairs*, pp. 123–24.

18 Rollie E. Poppino, *International Communism in Latin America: A History of the Movement, 1917–1963* (London: The Free Press of Glencoe, 1964), p. 166.

19 Eduardo Fioravanti, *Ni eurocomunismo ni Estado* (Barcelona: Península, 1978), pp. 140, 151–52.

20 In March 1965 the Venezuelan government detained two Italians who had connections with the PCI and confiscated $330,000 that was apparently destined for the guerrilla movement. See D. Bruce Jackson, *Castro, the Kremlin and Communism in Latin America* (Baltimore: Johns Hopkins Univ. Press, 1969), p. 45; Luigi Valsalice, *Guerrilla y política: Curso de Acción en Venezuela 1962/69* (Buenos Aires: Editorial Pleamar), p. 87.

21 Pastor Heydra, *La izquierda: una autocrítica perpetua (50 años de encuentros y desencuentros del marxismo en Venezuela)* (Caracas: UCV, 1981), p. 219.

22 Fioravanti, *Ni eurocomunismo*, p. 118.

23 Teodoro Petkoff, *Proceso a la izquierda* (Barcelona: Editorial Planeta, 1976), pp.

93–94, 121–27; Thomas Greene, "The Communist Parties of Italy and France," *World Politics* 21, no. 1 (Oct. 1968): 5.

24   *Mundo Obrero*, March 2–8, 1978, p. 13.

25   Togliatti, *Comunistas, socialistas*, p. 229.

26   Adam Przeworski, "Social Democracy as a Historical Phenomenon," *New Left Review* 122 (July–Aug. 1980); 50.

27   Berlinguer, *Gobierno de unidad democrático y compromiso histórico* (Madrid: Ayuso, 1977), p. 63.

28   Some writers, including MASistas, have maintained that PCI leaders fear that their nation's proximity to the USSR could jeopardize the position of neutrality of a Communist government in Italy and that this concern has influenced the PCI to tone down criticisms of the Soviet Union. Luis Bayardo Sardi, "Notas sobre un tema movedizo: El eurocomunismo," *Reflexiones* 9 (June 1977): 52.

29   The role of intellectuals has been less pronounced in the case of pro-Moscow parties such as the PCF. Greene, "The Communist Parties," pp. 28–31.

30   E. H. Carr, *The Bolshevik Revolution, 1917–1923* (Middlesex, England: Penguin Books, 1966), pp. 275–78.

31   V. R. Haya de la Torre, *El antiimperialismo y el APRA* (Caracas: Ediciones Centauro 76, 1976; 1st ed., 1928), pp. 146–54. Rodolfo Stavenhagen argues that members of the middle class, far from playing a revolutionary role in the struggle against imperialism, defend the system and the privileges that they derive from it. See Stavenhagen, "Seven Fallacies about Latin America," in James Petras and Maurice Zeitlin, eds., *Latin America: Reform or Revolution?* (Greenwich, Conn.: Fawcett, 1968), pp. 23–26.

32   Betancourt has denied that during these years he was influenced by Haya, but this claim has generally not been accepted by historians. Jesús Sanoja Hernández, "Prólogo," in Arturo Sosa A. and Eloi Lengrand, *Del garibaldismo estudiantil a la izquierda criolla* (Caracas: Ediciones Centauro 81, 1981), pp. x–xi.

33   *Libro Rojo del General Contreras, 1936: Documentos robados por espías de la policía política* (Caracas: Catalá Centauro Editores, 1975), pp. 201–202.

34   K. N. Brutents, *National Liberation Revolutions Today*, vol. 1 (Moscow: Progress Publishers, 1977), p. 154. Until the elections of February 1946 the Argentine Communists maintained a hostile position toward Perón, for which they were criticized by their Brazilian comrades, who pointed to the necessity of recognizing the progressive role of the national bourgeoisie, as represented by the *peronista* movement.

35   Edwardo González, "Castro's Revolution, Cuban Communist Appeals and the Soviet Response," *World Politics* 21, no. 1 (Oct. 1968): 39–68; Rodney Arismendi, "On the Role of the National Bourgeoisie in the Anti-Imperialist Struggle," *World Marxist Review* 2, no. 5 (May 1959): 29–39; Arismendi, "On the Role of the National Bourgeoisie in the Anti-Imperialist Struggle," *World Marxist Review* 2, no. 6 (June 1959): 31–39.

36   Robert Jackson Alexander, *Latin American Political Parties* (New York: Praeger, 1973). See also Donald L. Herman, "Looking Ahead," in Herman, ed., *The Communist Tide in Latin America: A Selected Treatment* (Austin: Univ. of Texas, 1973), p. 186.

37   A typical Jacobin Left (or New Left) writer who has written extensively on this topic from an historical viewpoint is Alonso Aguilar of Mexico. See Donald Hodges and Ross Gandy, *Mexico, 1910–1976: Reform or Revolution?* (London: Zed Press, 1979), pp. 104–106. The Jacobin Left was represented in Venezuela by MIR, which, before the founding of MAS, rejected the theory of revolution in

two stages. See Moisés Moleiro, *La izquierda superada* (Caracas: Editorial Ateneo de Caracas, 1983), p. 44.

38   Pedro Ortega Díaz, *Tribuna Popular*, Oct. 24, 1969, p. 2. The Mexican Communist Party abandoned the two-stage theory altogether in 1975. See Barry Carr, "Mexican Communism 1968–1981: Eurocommunism in the Americas?" *Journal of Latin American Studies* 17, pt. 1 (May 1985): 211.

39   Brutents, *National Liberation*, p. 202.

40   Not all Latin American Communist parties accepted the idea that the national bourgeoisie as an independent and revolutionary sector had ceased to exist. Both the Argentinian and Panamanian Communist parties defended the older dogma, thus justifying their support for the Peronist movement and the government of Omar Torrijos, both of which were purportedly representative of the anti-imperialist bourgeoisie. In addition, a number of ultra-leftist parties, some of which were pro-Maoist, upheld the notion of the "national bourgeois democratic revolution." See Victor Volski, "Etapa Actual de la lucha revolucionaria de liberación," *América Latina* 1 (published by the Academy of Sciences in Moscow) (1977): 20–21; Athos Fava "Condiciones indespensables para el progreso social," *Revista Internacional* 131–32 (Venezuelan ed., April 3, 1984): 122.

41   *Debate sobre debate* (Caracas: Editorial Primero de Mayo, 1975); PCV, *VI Congreso—1980: Programa* (Caracas: Cotragraf, 1980), pp. 70–71; Alcides Rodríguez, *Problemas de la revolución* (Caracas: Comisión Nacional de Educación [PCV], 1970), p. 42.

2   The National Setting

1   *Libro Rojo del General López Contreras, 1936* (Caracas: Catalá Centauro, 1975), pp. 204–205.

2   The only previous case of Communist fusion with other sectors of the left occurred during the equally moderate Second Period of international Communism of 1921–27, when the Chinese Communists entered the leadership of the Kuomintang—a type of move that Lenin had cautioned against several years before—with disastrous results. E. H. Carr, *The Bolshevik Revolution, 1917–1923* (Middlesex, England: Penguin, 1966), p. 255.

3   Steve Ellner, *Los partidos políticos y su disputa por el control del movimiento sindical en Venezuela, 1936–1948* (Caracas: Universidad Católica Andrés Bello, 1980), pp. 54–58.

4   This analysis of the events of June is put forward by, among others, Fuenmayor. See his *Historia de la Venezuela política contemporánea, 1899–1969*, vol. 2 (Caracas: Talleres Miguel Angel García e Hijo, 1976), pp. 324–25.

5   Paul Nehru Tennassee, *Venezuela: Los obreros petroleros y la lucha por la democracia* (Caracas: E.F.I. Publicaciones, 1979), pp. 186–87.

6   Vitale, *Notas sobre el movimiento obrero venezolano* (Caracas: UCV, 1978), p. 28. For another example of this viewpoint see Alberto J. Pla, Pedro Castro, Ramón Aizpurua, "Crisis política, sindicatos y movimientos sociales en Venezuela: 1936," in Pla, Castro, Aizpurua et al., eds., *Clase obrera, partidos y sindicatos en Venezuela, 1936–1950* (Caracas: Ediciones Centauro 82, 1982), pp. 25–89. The authors conclude that the political leaders who controlled the mass movement in 1936 failed to "elaborate a concept of class and revolution, and instead carried out an ideological surrender with far-reaching historical consequences" (p. 77). The authors attribute this failure to the mistaken policies of popular frontism, as defended by the international Communist movement at the time. See also

Compañero 3 (Caracas) (June 1976): 4–5; Pla, Aizpurua, and Castro, "Crisis política y movimientos sociales en Venezuela: 1936" (paper presented at the First Conference of the Taller Movimiento Obrero Latinoamericana [MOLA] at the UCV, May 1979); Castro, "Problemas de historia del movimiento obrero venezolano, 1936–1950" (mimeographed, School of History, UCV, 1984).

7   Eric Hobsbawm, *Primitive Rebels* (New York: Vintage, 1959).

8   Ellner, "The Venezuelan Left in the Era of the Popular Front, 1936–45," *Journal of Latin American Studies* 11, no. 1 (May 1979): 183–84.

9   William E. Ratliff, *Castroism and Communism in Latin America, 1959–1976: The Varieties of Marxist-Leninist Experience* (Washington: American Enterprise Institute for Public Policy Research, 1976), pp. 71–73.

10   Eduardo Gallegos Mancera (head of the PCV's international affairs department), interview with the author, Sept. 5, 1983, Caracas.

11   In a similar vein, Rómulo Betancourt (and his closest supporters) retrospectively tried to justify his active participation in the Costa Rican Communist Party in the early 1930s, on grounds that it maintained an independent line in the world Communist movement. Considering that international communism was much more monolithic in the 1930s than later, this argument regarding the uniqueness of the Costa Rican Communist Party in its early period is more convincing than that forwarded by the MASistas with respect to the PCV prior to 1971. See Robert J. Alexander, *Rómulo Betancourt and the Transformation of Venezuela* (New Brunswick, N.J.: Transaction Books, 1982), pp. 67–80. Guillermo García Ponce, who led a split in the PCV in 1974, also argued that Venezuelan Communists maintained a position of relative autonomy vis-à-vis Moscow in the 1950s and 1960s. See García Ponce, *El país, la izquierda y las elecciones de 1978* (Caracas: Miguel Angel García e Hijos, 1977), p. 162.

12   Pompeyo Márquez, "Del dogmatismo al marxismo crítico," *Libre* 3 (March–May 1972), pp. 33–34. Togliatti, in his *Il Partito Comunista Italiano* (1961), also harped on the importance of recognizing the advanced consciousness of certain thinkers who were not directly influenced by the Communist movement. See Thomas Greene, "The Communist Parties of Italy and France: A Study in Comparative Communism," *World Politics* 21, no. 1 (Oct. 1968), p. 28.

13   Márquez, *Santos Yorme o Pompeyo Márquez: Combatiente sin tregua* Caracas: Ediciones Centauro 82, (1982), p. 294; Petkoff, *Socialismo para Venezuela?*, 3rd ed. (Caracas: Editorial Fuentes, 1972), p. 35.

14   Other Communists also retrospectively denounced the exclusion of foreign delegates at that day's meeting for violating the concept, promoted by the Soviets themselves, that the international Communist movement was equivalent to one big party in which each individual member, regardless of nationality, was subject to discipline but also endowed with equal rights. Márquez, *Santos Yorme*, pp. 195–96.

15   Ramón Hernández (interviewer), *Teodoro Petkoff: Viaje al fondo de si mismo* (Caracas: Editorial Fuentes, 1983), p. 27; Petkoff, "Hacia un nuevo socialismo," *Nueva Sociedad* 56–57 (Nov.–Dec. 1981): 38; Márquez, *Santos Yorme*, pp. 293–95.

16   Márquez, "Prólogo" in Petkoff, *Socialismo para Venezuela?*, p. 8; Guillermo García Ponce and Francisco Camacho Barrios, *El diario desconocido de una dictadura* (Caracas: Publicaciones Selevén, 1980), p. 225.

17   Petkoff, "La división del Partido Comunista de Venezuela," *Libre* 1 (Sept.–Nov. 1971): 19.

18   Robert J. Alexander, *Communism in Latin America* (New Brunswick, N.J.:

Rutgers Univ. Press, 1957); Victor Alba, *Esquema histórico del comunismo en Iberoamerica*, 3rd ed. (Mexico: Ediciones Occidentales, 1954); Rollie E. Poppino, *International Communism in Latin America* (London: Free Press of Glencoe, 1964).

19 See also Alan Angell, *Politics in the Labor Movement in Chile* (London: Oxford Univ. Press, 1972), p. 90. The English Marxist Perry Anderson, in an interesting article about scholarly research on the Communist movement, has criticized "Cold War histories which tend to present each national communist party as if it were just a puppet whose limbs were manipulated mechanically by strings pulled in Moscow." Anderson argues that "we can see a complex dialectic between the international and national determinants of party policies." Anderson, "Communist Party History," in Raphael Samuel, ed., *People's History and Socialist Theory* (London: Routledge and Kegan Paul, 1981), p. 150.

20 Freddy Muñoz, *Revolución sin dogma* (Caracas: Ediciones Alcinoo, 1970); Luis Bayardo Sardi, *Versión no corregida para uso política* (mimeographed, n.d.), p. 40.

21 Petkoff, "Al MAS no le conviene un golpe militar," in Alfredo Peña (interviewer), *Corrupción y golpe de estado* (Caracas: Editorial Ateneo de Caracas, 1980?), p. 104.

22 Manuel Caballero, "Genio y figura de Pompeyo Márquez," in Márquez, *Socialismo en tiempo presente* (Caracas: Ediciones Avilarte, 1973), p. xxx.

23 Anselmo Natale, "Anselmo Natale," in Agustín Blanco Muñoz (interviewer), *La lucha armada: Hablan 6 comandantes* (Caracas: UCV, 1981), p. 244; Petkoff, "Teodoro Petkoff," in Agustín Blanco Muñoz (interviewer), *La lucha armada: Hablan 5 jefes* (Caracas: UCV, 1980), p. 286.

3 Division in the Venezuelan Communist Party

1 Steve Ellner, "Political Party Dynamics and the Outbreak of Guerrilla Warfare in Venezuela," *Inter-American Economic Affairs* 34, no. 2 (Autumn 1980): 8.

2 Alfredo Peña (interviewer), *Conversaciones con Douglas Bravo* (Caracas: Editorial Ateneo de Caracas, 1978), p. 80.

3 Pedro Duno, *Sobre aparatos, desviaciones y dogmas* (Caracas: Editorial Nueva Izquierda, 1969), p. 60.

4 An example of this contradiction in party positions was the guerrilla takeover of a passenger train at El Encanto outside Caracas, which resulted in several deaths. See Gustavo Machado, *En el camino del honor* (Caracas: Veneprint, 1966), pp. 92–93; Agustín Blanco Muñoz, *La lucha armada: Hablan 5 jefes* (Caracas: UCV, 1980), p. 312.

5 Santiago and El Tabano (pseuds.), *Teodoro Petkoff: Dos épocas del oportunismo de derecha* (Caracas: Ediciones Hombre Nuevo, 1972), p. 73; *Que pasa en Venezuela*, Oct. 7, 1966, p. 7.

6 MIRista guerrillas who later formed the Liga Socialista (LS) and the Organización de Revolucionarios (OR) formulated this accusation against their party's leaders, as did the to-be-MASistas against the PCV heads. Ironically, MIR secretary general Moisés Moleiro leveled this same charge at the PCV. Moleiro wrote, "The PCV withdrew [from the guerrilla struggle] acting as if it had never withdrawn . . . without undertaking a serious self-critical analysis of the whole period, of the causes of defeat, and of the errors committed—many of them of diverse origins." Moleiro, *La izquierda y su proceso* (Caracas: Ediciones Centauro 77, 1977), pp. 83–84; Iván Loscher (interviewer), *Escrito con la izquierda: Entrevistas* (Car-

acas: Libros Tepuy, 1977), p. 40; Eduardo Semtei, "El modo de producción política," *Rojo y Negro* 1 (Jan.–Feb. 1985): 59.

7   Blanco Muñoz, *La lucha armada: Hablan 5 jefes*, pp. 156, 220.

8   Ramón Hernández (interviewer), *Teodoro Petkoff: Viaje al fondo de si mismo* (Caracas: Editorial Fuentes, 1983), p. 166.

9   Robert J. Alexander, *The Communist Party of Venezuela* (Stanford, Calif.: Hoover Institution Press, 1969), p. 196.

10   Petkoff, "La división del Partido Comunista de Venezuela," *Libre* 1 (Sept.–Nov. 1971).

11   *Tribuna Popular*, Feb. 4–10, 1971, p. 20.

12   Jesús Faría, "A la derecha de quién estaría yo?" *Deslinde* 6 (June 1–15, 1969): 3.

13   Teodoro Petkoff, *Socialismo para Venezuela?* 3rd ed. (Caracas: Editorial Fuentes, 1972), p. 61.

14   Freddy Muñoz, *Revolución sin dogma* (Caracas: Ediciones Alcinoo, 1970), p. 115.

15   Angela Zago, *Aquí no ha pasado nada* (Caracas: Síntesis Dosmil, 1972); Daniel H. Levine, "Review Essay: Portraits of Venezuela," *Journal of Interamerican Studies and World Affairs* 23, no. 2 (May 1981): 218–21.

16   Although other Latin American Communist parties were also verbally attacked by the Cubans, they maintained a discreet silence. Only the more independent Mexican Communist Party came to the defense of the PCV and published an article by Petkoff in one of its periodicals in response to Castro. See D. Bruce Jackson, *Castro, the Kremlin, and Communism in Latin America* (Baltimore, Johns Hopkins Univ. Press, 1969), p. 118; Blanco Muñoz, *La lucha armada: Hablan 5 jefes*, pp. 225, 232.

17   Eduardo Pozo (national PCV student leader in the 1960s and founding member of MAS), interview with the author, Caracas, Sept. 9, 1984.

18   Hector Silva Michelena and Heinz Rudolf Sonntag, *Universidad, dependencia y revolución*, 8th ed. (Mexico: Siglo Veintiuno Editores, 1980), p. 174.

19   Daniel H. Levine, *Conflict and Political Change in Venezuela* (Princeton: Princeton Univ. Press, 1973), p. 189; Jesús Sanoja Hernández, *La universidad: Culpable o víctima?* (Caracas: Fondo Editorial Venezolano, 1967).

20   Juvencio Pulgar, "Obstáculos y desviaciones de la renovación universitaria," *Deslinde* 5 (May 1969): 6.

21   César O. Solórzano, *El socialismo y la democracia* (Caracas: Editorial Testimonios, n.d.), p. 64; Alonso Palacios (Communist Youth leader in 1960s; member of MAS's National Directorate in 1970s), interview with the author, Feb. 5, 1986.

22   Héctor Mujica, "La discusión y los metodos," *Deslinde Ideológico* 1 (1970?): 4–5.

23   Gustavo Machado, "Transformar la lucha de opiniones . . . ," *Deslinde* 14 (Dec. 1–15, 1969): 3.

24   Luis Bayardo Sardi, "La izquierda entre el mito y la revolución," *Joven Guardia* 7 (May 1970): 24–25.

25   Teodoro Petkoff, *Proceso a la izquierda* (Barcelona: Editorial Planeta, 1976).

26   Garaudy attempted to demonstrate that the model of "workers management" first promoted by the Yugoslavians was compatible with Lenin's view of socialism. See Roger Garaudy, *The Crisis in Communism: The Turning-Point of Socialism* (New York: Grove Press, 1970), pp. 140–87.

27   Petkoff, *Checoeslovaquia: El socialismo como problema*, 3rd ed. (Caracas: Sorocaima, 1981), p. 168.

28   Manuel Caballero, *El desarrollo desigual del socialismo y otros ensayos polémicos* (Caracas: Editorial Domingo Fuentes, 1970), p. 202.

236

29 *Nueva Voz Popular,* Sept. 5, 1968, p. 16.

30 Eduardo Pozo, interview with the author, Sept. 9, 1984, Caracas.

31 The only major PCV leader who argued against supporting Prieto was Gustavo Machado. Blanco Muñoz, *La lucha armada: Hablan 5 jefes,* p. 71; Petkoff, *Proceso a la izquierda,* p. 68.

32 Blanco Muñoz, *La lucha armada: Hablan 6 comandantes* (Caracas: UCV, 1981), p. 234. The left-wing Vanguardia Popular Nacional headed by José Herrera Oropeza supported Burelli Rivas.

33 Pompeyo Márquez, "Quién hará la revolución en Venezuela?" *Deslinde* 8 (July 1–15, 1969): 5.

34 Radamés Larrazábal, *Socialismo bobo o socialismo para Venezuela?* (Caracas: Ediciones Cantaclaro, 1970), p. 10.

35 Teodoro Petkoff, "Me parece lícito hablar de derechas e izquierdas dentro del Partido Comunista de Venezuela," *Deslinde* 8 (July 1–15, 1969): 3.

36 Larrazábal, *Socialismo bobo,* p. 133.

37 Teodoro Petkoff, interview with the author, Caracas, Sept. 4, 1984.

38 Pompeyo Márquez, *Qué discuten los Comunistas?* (Caracas: Ediciones "Deslinde," 1970), p. 58.

39 Ibid., p. 22; Pompeyo Márquez, "La unidad política en el núcleo dirigente y su influencia en la unidad del partido," *Deslinde Ideológico* 3 (April 1970?): 2–3.

40 Pompeyo Márquez, *La vigencia del PCV no está en discusión* (n.p., 1966), p. 45.

41 *Deslinde* 23 (Dec. 18, 1970): 5.

42 Pedro Ortega Díaz, "En el P.C.V. persisten tendencias desesperadas y aventureras," *Deslinde* 12 (Oct. 15–31, 1969): 3; Blanco Muñoz, *La lucha armada: Hablan 5 jefes,* p. 254.

43 Petkoff, interview, Sept. 4, 1984.

44 Caballero, *El desarrollo desigual del socialismo,* p. 209.

45 Pastor Heydra, *La izquierda: Una autocrítica perpetua* (Caracas: UCV, 1981), p. 158.

46 Blanco Muñoz, *La lucha armada: Hablan 5 jefes,* p. 266.

47 Eleazar Díaz Rangel, *Como se dividió el P.C.V.* (Caracas: Editorial Domingo Fuentes, 1971), p. 52.

48 Ramón J. Velásquez, Arístides Calvani, Allan R. Brewer-Carías et al., *Venezuela Moderna: Medio Siglo de historia, 1926–1976,* 2nd edition (Barcelona: Ariel, 1979), p. 367.

49 Eleazar Díaz Rangel, *Como se dividió el P.C.V.* (Caracas: Editorial Domingo Fuentes, 1971), pp. 49–50.

50 Ibid., p. 83.

51 *El Nacional,* Jan. 25, 1971, p. D-8.

52 Díaz Rangel, *Como se dividió el P.C.V.,* p. 80.

53 *El Nacional,* Jan. 4, 1971, p. D-6.

54 "Declaración internacional del Movimiento al Socialismo," *Deslinde* 25 (Jan. 22, 1971): 4.

55 Petkoff, *Socialismo para Venezuela?* pp. 135–36.

56 "Declaración internacional del Movimiento . . .", p. 4.

57 *Deslinde* 28 (Feb. 17, 1971): 1.

58 Díaz Rangel, *Como se dividió,* p. 106.

59 Freddy Muñoz, *Revolución sin dogma,* p. 13.

60 *Bravo Pueblo,* June 1–15, 1971, p. 15.

61 Ibid.

62 Eduardo Gallegos Mancera, interview with the author, Caracas, Sept. 3, 1984.

63   Petkoff, interview, Sept. 4, 1984.
64   Eleazar Díaz Rangel, "En el comunismo latinoamericano está germinando la renovación," *Deslinde* 25 (Jan. 22, 1971): 4.
65   Loscher, *Escrito con la izquierda*, pp. 172–73.

4   Ideology, Policy, and Style

1   For an interesting anthology on the role of the "intellectual worker," see Pat Walker, ed., *Between Labor and Capital* (Boston: South End Press, 1979), especially the lead chapters by Barbara and John Ehrenreich.
2   Anselmo Natale, *El moderno absurdo de los marxistas modernos* (mimeographed, n.d.); Antonio García Ponce, *Adecos, tucanes o marxistas? Una historia de la izquierda: 1959–1984* (Caracas: Editorial Domingo Fuentes, 1985), pp. 89–90.
3   *Bravo Pueblo*, March 25, 1971, p. 5.
4   Freddy Muñoz, *Posibilidades y peligros: proposiciones para la renovación y reconstrucción de MAS* (pamphlet, n.p., n.d.), pp. 43, 46–47.
5   Enrique A. Baloyra and John D. Martz, *Political Attitudes in Venezuela: Societal Cleavages and Political Opinion* (Austin: Univ. of Texas Press, 1979), p. 228.
6   "Relaciones con la Internacional Socialista definirá el MAS," *Foco* 1 (1986): 23.
7   Bayardo Sardi, "Versión no corregida, para uso exclusivo de los instructores del curso simultáneo nacional, sobre el MAS y su política" (mimeographed, Caracas, n.d.). This was a lecture delivered at a MAS internal conference.
8   Ramón Hernandez (interviewer), *Teodoro Petkoff: Viaje al fondo de si mismo* (Caracas: Editorial Fuentes, 1983), p. 234; Alfredo Peña (interviewer), *Conversaciones con José Vicente Rangel* (Caracas: Ateneo de Caracas, 1978), p. 69; Freddy Muñoz, "La proposición socialista de cambio," in *Diario de Caracas*, Feb. 28, 1983, p. 7.
9   Petkoff, "La falsa conducta revolucionaria," *Para la Acción* 1 (Nov. 1975): 2.
10   Freddy Muñoz, *Una alternativa socialista para Venezuela* (Caracas, n.p., n.d.), p. 12.
11   Carl Boggs, "Gramsci and Eurocommunism," *Radical America* (May–June 1980): 7–23; Steve Ellner, "Venezucommunism: Learning the Lesson of Chile?" *Commonweal* 107, no. 3 (Feb. 15, 1980): 70.
12   Adam Przeworski, "Social Democracy as a Historical Phenomenon," *New Left Review* 122 (July–Aug. 1980): 52–53; Enrique Ochoa Antich, *Para ser poder: Apuntes críticos para la renovación del MAS* (mimeographed; document written for MAS's sixth national convention in 1985), p. 14.
13   Santiago Carrillo and Dolores Ibarruri, *La propuesta comunista* (Barcelona: Editorial Laira, 1977), p. 175.
14   Carlos Raúl Hernández, *Democracia y mitología revolucionaria: Proceso del poder en Venezuela* (Caracas: Editorial La Enseñanza Viva, 1978), pp. 137–156.
15   Ibid., pp. 56–60.
16   Loscher (interviewer), *Escrito con la izquierda: Entrevistas* (Caracas: Libros Tepuy, 1977), p. 303.
17   Teodoro Petkoff, *Socialismo para Venezuela?* 3rd. ed. (Caracas: Editorial Fuentes, 1972), pp. 136, 139, 159.
18   Pompeyo Márquez, "Del dogmatismo al marxismo crítico," *Libre* 3 (March–May 1972): 33–34.
19   Loscher, *Escrito con la izquierda*, p. 234.

20 Haya de la Torre, *El antiimperialismo y el APRA*, 3rd ed. (Caracas: Ediciones Centauro 76, 1976), pp. 145–49.

21 Muñoz, *Más allá de las palabras: proposiciones para la renovación y reconstrucción del MAS* (pamphlet, n.p., n.d.), p. 48.

22 Carlos Arturo Pardo, "Lugar de los trabajadores asalariados en la sociedad venezolana," *Para la Acción* 3–4 (June 1977): 30.

23 Joanne Barhan, "The Italian Communists: Anatomy of a Party," *Radical America* 12, no. 5 (Sept.–Oct. 1978): 26–48.

24 Przeworski, "Social Democracy as a Historical Phenomenon" pp. 39–44.

25 For a well-known defense of the view that sees the middle class in Latin America as conservative and elitist, see Rodolfo Stavenhagen, "Seven Erroneous Theses about Latin America," in Irving Lous Horowitz et al., eds., *Latin American Radicalism* (New York: Vintage Books, 1969), pp. 112–13.

26 Teodoro Petkoff, interview with the author, Caracas, Sept. 5, 1984.

27 Francisco Mieres, "En qué país vivmos?" *Deslinde* 17 (April 1–15, 1970): 7.

28 Hector Silva Michelena, "Prólogo," in Hugo Cabello, *Ideología y neocolonialismo* (Caracas: UCV, 1969), p. 10.

29 Hector Silva Michelena, "Prólogo," in Andre Gunder Frank, *Lumpenburguesía: Lumpendesarrollo: dependencia clase y política en Latinoamerica* (Caracas: Editorial Nueva Izquierda, 1970), pp. 7–8.

30 Comisión Nacional de Programa (MAS), *Juventud* (brochure for the 1983 national elections), p. 18.

31 Pompeyo Márquez, "Las perspectivas de la pequeña y mediana industria en Venezuela" (lecture delivered on June 5, 1982 in Puerto La Cruz).

32 *Convención No. 1: Organo del MAS para la discusión* (Jan. 15, 1980), p. 2.

33 The orthodox stand dates back to Lenin's opposition to the "Workers Opposition," which in the early 1920s attempted to democratize and decentralize the mechanisms of decision making in the Soviet economy. The negative position of orthodox communism was reinforced as a result of the clash between the Soviet Union and Yugoslavia, with its model of workers' management, after 1948. The PCI, which was less hostile to Tito than the PCF, was more willing to accept the viability of the Yugoslavian experiment. Thomas Greene, "The Communist Parties of Italy and France: A Study in Comparative Communism," in *World Politics* 23, no. 1 (Oct. 1968): 4.

34 Teodoro Petkoff, "La autogestión: Gobierno del pueblo, por el pueblo y para el pueblo" (mimeographed; speech delivered to MAS's Comisión Nacional de Propaganda), p. 6.

35 Ibid.

36 This concept, promoted by the faction in COPEI led by Luis Herrera Campíns, was based on the modification of traditional forms of property relations. See Abdón Vivas Terán, "Prólogo," in *Sociedad comunitaria y participación* (Caracas: Editorial Ateneo de Caracas, 1979).

37 *Bravo Pueblo*, March 25, 1971, p. 1.

38 *Salud y socialismo* (Caracas, July–Aug. 1972), p. 6.

39 Neil McInnes, "From Comintern to Polycentrism," in Paolo Filo della Torre et al., eds., *Euro-Communism: Myth or Reality* (Middlesex, England: Penguin, 1979), p. 62; John D. Martz and Enrique A. Baloyra, *Electoral Mobilization and Public Opinion: The Venezuelan Campaign of 1973* (Chapel Hill: Univ. of North Carolina Press, 1976), pp. 157–58.

40 "Petkoff, candidato de la izquierda" (interview with Petkoff), *Resumen* 402 (July 19, 1981): 8.

41 *Punto del Domingo*, March 31, 1974, p. 3.

42 Petkoff, *Proceso a la izquierda* (Barcelona: Editorial Planeta, 1976), pp. 192–93.

43 K. N. Brutents, *National Liberation Revolutions Today*, vol. 1 (Moscow: Progress Publishers, 1977), p. 9.

44 V. Gavrilin, *La nacionalización socialista: Vía del progreso* (Moscow: Novosti, 1975), pp. 44–48.

45 Proceso Político, *CAP. 5 años: Un juicio crítico* (Caracas: Ateneo de Caracas, 1978). This thesis was undoubtedly influenced by the concept of "development of underdevelopment" first put forward by André Gunder Frank in *Capitalism and Underdevelopment in Latin America* (New York: Monthly Review Press, 1967).

46 Przeworski, "Social Democracy as a Historical Phenomenon", p. 53.

47 Eleazar Díaz Rangel, *Como se dividió el P.C.V.* (Caracas: Editorial Domingo Fuentes, 1971), p. 108.

48 *Bravo Pueblo*, June 1–15, 1971, p. 14.

49 Pompeyo Márquez, *Socialismo: Democratización y descolonización en el Caribe* (pamphlet; speech delivered by Márquez at the Center of Latin American Studies, University of Pittsburgh, Oct. 1981).

50 Petkoff, *Proceso a la izquierda*, p. 129.

51 Teodoro Petkoff, *El socialismo venezolano y la democracia* (Caracas: n.p., 1978), p. 16.

52 Bayardo Sardi, *Versión no corregida*, pp. 30–31.

53 Germán Lairet, "Un año de gobierno, un año de frustraciones," in José Vicente Rangel et al., *El año chucuto* (Caracas: Colección Parlamento y Socialismo, 1975), p. 129.

54 *El Nacional*, April 3, 1975, p. D-12; Carlos Rodríguez, interview with the author, Sept. 5, 1984, Caracas. According to one confidential source, Luers was criticized by more conservative State Department officials for going overboard in his public association with Petkoff and other MASistas.

55 *Fracción Parlamentaria del MAS* 2 (April 1984): 5.

56 "Foro: Moisés Moleiro," *El Nacional*, Aug. 29, 1983, p. C-1.

57 Carlos Raúl Hernández and Jean Maninat, *Cuba-Nicaragua: Expectativas y frustraciones* (Caracas: Adame-Producciones Editoriales, 1984), pp. 96, 111.

58 *El Nacional*, Dec. 1, 1984, p. D-14.

59 Pompeyo Márquez, "La frontera colombia-venezolana y el petróleo," *Deslinde* 26 (Feb. 1970?): 8.

60 Pompeyo Márquez, *En peligro la integridad territorial de Venezuela* (Caracas: Industrias Sorocaima, 1979); *Punto en Domingo* 522 (Sept. 22, 1974): 8–9.

61 Loscher, *Escrito con la izquierda*, pp. 186, 188.

62 The concept of the military as the fundamental prop of the capitalist system, which had to be destroyed rather than taken over, was laid out by Lenin in *The Proletarian Revolution and the Renegade Kautsky:* "Not a single great revolution has ever taken place or ever can take place, without the 'disorganization' of the army. For the army is the most ossified instrument for supporting the old regime, the most hardened bulwark of bourgeois discipline, buttressing up the rule of capital."

63 Jorge Abelardo Ramos, *El marxismo de indias* (Barcelona: Editorial Planeta, 1973), pp. 183–203.

64 Victor Volski, "Etapa actual de la lucha revolucionaria de liberación," *América Latina* 1 (1977): 5–23; Brutents, *National Liberation*, p. 248.

65　Helena Plaza, *El 23 de enero de 1958 y el proceso de consolidación de la democracia representativa en Venezuela* (Caracas: G&T Editores, 1978), p. 171.

66　Loscher, *Escrito con la izquierda*, pp. 242–43.

67　*El Nacional*, Nov. 14, 1985, p. 11.

68　MAS, *La Convención (Organo del MAS para la discusión)*, vol. 2 (text of "Declaración 80," Jan. 15, 1980), p. 6.

69　José Vicente Rangel, *Seguridad, defensa y democracia: Un tema para civiles y militares* (Caracas: Ediciones Centauro 80, 1980), pp. 133–34.

70　Teodoro Petkoff, "Venezuela en el mundo: Seguridad nacional desde la perspectiva del cambio social," in Aníbal Romero, ed., *Seguridad, defensa y democracia en Venezuela* (Caracas: Editorial de la Universidad Simón Bolívar, 1980), p. 136.

71　Ibid., p. 136.

72　Cesar O. Solórzano, *El socialismo y la democracia* (Caracas: Editorial Testimonios, n.d.), pp. 71–72; Alejandro Moreno, ed., *Antología del pensamiento revolucionario venezolano* (Caracas: Ediciones Centauro 83, 1983), p. 353.

73　*El Nacional*, Dec. 23, 1977, p. D-22.

74　Luis Esteban Rey, "Los militares y las responsibilidades claves" and "Militares, socialismo y petróleo," in José Vicente Rangel et al., *Militares y política (Una polémica inconclusa)* (Caracas: Ediciones Centauro 76, 1976), pp. 57, 114.

75　Pompeyo Márquez, *Santos Yorme o Pompeyo Márquez: Combatiente sin tregua* (Caracas: Ediciones Centauro 82, 1982), p. 241; Gene E. Bigler, "The Armed Forces and Patterns of Civil-Military Relations," in John D. Martz and David J. Myers, eds., *Venezuela: The Democratic Experience* (New York: Praeger, 1977), p. 128.

76　Steve Ellner, "Diverse Influences on the Venezuelan Left," *Journal of Interamerican Studies and World Affairs* 23, no. 4 (Nov. 1981): 487.

77　Teorodo Petkoff, "Los Tribunales de Salvaguarda deben conocer del caso," *Punto Socialista* 18 (Nov.–Dec. 1984): 7–8.

78　Rafael José Cortés of the PCV wrote: "When Dr. [José Vicente] Rangel makes these pronouncements [in favor of the honorability of the armed forces] he is falling into the trap of infantilism. . . . The very history of the Venezuelan armed forces indicates that it has always acted under the pressure of very powerful forces both from reactionary as well as from progressive quarters, and that the role of the class struggle and yanqui imperialism [within the institution] cannot be underestimated." See Cortés, *En defensa del socialismo (respuesta a las "conversaciones")* (Caracas: Gráfica Río Orinoco, 1979), pp. 152–53. See also *El Nacional*, Feb. 23, 1983, p. D-2; *Tribuna Popular*, June 24, 1971, p. 6; "El 'tabú' militar," *Almargen* 44 (June 1982), p. 17.

79　"Cuando las FF. AA. estrenan 108 nuevos ascensos" *Resumen* 453 (July 11, 1982): 7.

80　Augustín Blanco Muñoz, *La lucha armada: Hablan 5 jefes* (Caracas: UCV, 1980), p. 207.

81　Petkoff, *Socialismo para Venezuela?*, p. 129.

82　MAS, *La Convención*, p. 6.

83　Paul W. Drake, "Conclusion: Requiem for Populism?" in Michael L. Conniff, ed., *Latin American Populism in Comparative Perspective* (Albuquerque: Univ. of New Mexico Press, 1982), p. 243.

84　See, for instance, the works by two historians on APRA: Fredrick B. Pike, "Visions of Rebirth: The Spiritualist Facet of Peru's Haya de la Torre," *Hispanic American Historical Review* 63, no. 3 (Aug. 1983): 479–516; "Peru's

Haya de la Torre and Archetypal Regeneration Mythology," *Inter-American Economic Affairs* 34, no. 2 (Autumn 1980): 25–65; Steve Stein, *Populism in Peru: The Emergence of the Masses, and the Politics of Social Control* (Madison: Univ. of Wisconsin, 1980).

85 John D. Wirth, "Foreword," in Conniff, ed., *Latin American Populism*, p. xii. The term *living museum* was first employed by Charles Anderson.

86 Caballero, "El fin del comienzo?" in Federico Alvarez et al., *La izquierda venezolana y las elecciones de 73* (Caracas: Síntesis Dosmil, 1974), p. 117.

87 MAS, *Asamblea Nacional: Movimiento al Socialismo* (newspaper format, 1974?), pp. 1–2.

88 Pompeyo Márquez, *El socialismo es la patria* (pamphlet; speech delivered at meeting of MAS's National Directorate, April 1977), p. 9.

89 Leszek Kolakowski, *Main Currents in Marxism: Its Rise, Growth, and Dissolution*, trans. P. S. Falla, 3 vols. (New York, 1979); Robert C. Tucker, *Philosophy and Myth in Karl Marx* (Cambridge, England, 1965).

90 Rangel, "Unir al pueblo en torno al socialismo," in *José Vicente es unión del pueblo* (speeches at a MAS electoral gathering in Caracas, July 20, 1977; published by MAS).

91 *El Nacional*, July 5, 1978, p. D-1.

92 Bayardo Sardi, *Versión no corregida*, p. 22.

93 This strategy coincided with the concept of the political party put forward by Gramsci, whose works the MASistas began to take great interest in following the 1973 elections. According to Gramsci, the political party should root out dogmatism in its ranks and be receptive to popular ideas and attitudes and in constant communication with the masses. This view contrasted with Lenin's thesis in *What Is to Be Done*, which maintained that the party's mission was to introduce ideology to the working class, which, left to its own, would only concern itself with bread-and-butter issues.

94 *Punto*, Dec. 14, 1973, pp. 1, 8.

95 Freddy Muñoz, "Pasado, presente y futuro del MAS," *Reflexiones* 9 (June 1977): 37.

96 This phrase was frequently employed in campaign literature.

97 MAS, *La Convención*, p. 9.

98 Ibid., p. 7.

99 *Diario de Caracas*, Nov. 15, 1983, p. 26.

100 *Teodoro: MAS* (printed electoral material for the 1983 campaign).

101 Steve Ellner, "Advice and Dissent," *Progressive* 47, no. 6 (June 1983): 18.

102 Tania Ruíz (member of MAS's communications department), interview with the author, Sept. 6, 1984, Caracas.

103 Freddy Muñoz, interview with the author, March 2, 1983, Caracas.

104 Petkoff, "Alternativa hegemónica en Venezuela," in Julio Labastida Martín del Campo, ed., *Hegemonía y alternativas políticas en América Latina* (Mexico: Siglo Veintiuno Editores, 1985), p. 314.

105 *El Nacional*, Sept. 5, 1986, p. D-1.

5 MAS and Unity of the Left

1 Steve Ellner, *Los partidos políticos y su disputa por el control del movimiento sindical en Venezuela, 1936–1948* (Caracas: Universidad Católica Andrés Bello, 1980), pp. 141–44.

2   Steve Ellner, "Political Party Dynamics and the Outbreak of Guerrilla Warfare in Venezuela," *Inter-American Economic Affairs* 34, no. 2 (Autumn 1980): 12–20.

3   Steve Ellner, "The Venezuelan Left in the Era of the Popular Front, 1936–45," *Journal of Latin American Studies* 11, no. 1 (May 1979): 178.

4   For a particularly interesting collection of documents on the PRP(C) dedicated to that organization's main ideologue, Salvador de la Plaza, see *Antecedentes del revisionismo en Venezuela* (Caracas: Fondo Editorial Salvador de la Plaza, 1973); see also Steve Ellner, "Factionalism in the Venezuelan Communist Movement, 1937–1948," *Science & Society* 45, no. 1 (Spring 1981): 62–65.

5   Sheldon Liss, *Marxist Thought in Latin America* (Berkeley: Univ. of California Press, 1984), p. 94.

6   Freddy Muñoz, "Verdades y problemas sobre la unidad de la izquierda," *Para la acción* 3–4 (June 1977): 5; "Nueva Fuerza?" *Joven Guardia* 7 (May 1970): 39.

7   Teodoro Petkoff, *Socialismo para Venezuela?* 3rd ed. (Caracas: Editorial Fuentes, 1972), pp. 50, 131; Freddy Muñoz, *Revolución sin dogma* (Caracas: Ediciones Alcinoo, 1970), p. 84.

8   Lucas Leal, *De los orígenes y la historia de una fuerza para el socialismo en Venezuela* (Caracas: MAS, 1983), pp. 14–15.

9   José Vicente Rangel, *Tiempo de verdades* (Caracas: Editorial Avilarte, 1973), pp. 18, 30.

10 The concept of the "movement of movements" at first represented a *left position* and was reminiscent of the ultra-leftist "united front from below" policy followed by Communists during the Comintern's "third" period between 1928 and 1935. During these years Communists denounced the moderate left parties as "social fascists" and tried to capture their rank and file while eschewing interparty agreements. Needless to say, the attitude of the MASistas toward their political rivals was not nearly as aggressive. Nevertheless, MAS's strategy coincided with the "united front from below" approach in its emphasis on the left's long-term objectives and its extremely critical attitude toward parties to its right.

11 Pompeyo Márquez, *Hacia una nueva mayoría* (Caracas: Equipo Editor, 1979), p. 88.

6   The Elections of 1973

1   *El Nacional*, Aug. 9, 1969, p. C-8.

2   Ovidio González (MEP national deputy), interview with the author, Barcelona, Feb. 13, 1983.

3   Luis Bayardo Sardi (MAS national senator), interview with the author, Caracas, March 13, 1982.

4   Agustín Blanco Muñoz, *La lucha armada: Hablan 5 jefes* (Caracas: UCV, 1980), p. 274.

5   *Deslinde* 28 (Feb. 17, 1971): 1.

6   Manuel Caballero, "1973: el fin del comienzo?" in Federico Alvarez et al., *La izquierda venezolana y las elecciones del 73 (Un análisis político y polémico)* (Caracas: Síntesis Dosmil, 1974), p. 117.

7   John D. Martz and Enrique A. Baloyra, *Electoral Mobilization and Public Opinion: The Venezuelan Campaign of 1973* (Chapel Hill: Univ. of North Carolina Press, 1976), pp. 157–58.

8   Federico Alvarez, "Socialismo para cuando?" in Alvarez et al., *La izquierda venezolana*, p. 62.

9 Lucas Leal, *De los orígenes y la historia de una fuerza para el socialismo en Venezuela* (Caracas: MAS, 1983), p. 17.

10 Rangel's congressional speeches denouncing the assassination were published under the title *Expediente negro: El caso de Lovera* (Caracas: Ediciones La Muralla, 1967).

11 *El Nacional*, Nov. 8, 1973, p. D-1.

12 José Vicente Rangel, *Tiempo de verdades* (Caracas: Editorial Avilarte, 1973), p. 70.

13 Alvarez et al., *La izquierda venezolana*, p. 62.

14 Teodoro Petkoff, *Proceso a la izquierda* (Barcelona: Editorial Planeta, 1976), pp. 34, 39, 52–53.

7 The Elections of 1978–1979

1 Freddy Muñoz, *Más allá de las palabras* (n.p., n.d.), pp. 52–53.

2 MAS, *Asamblea Nacional: Movimiento al Socialismo* (newspaper format, 1974?), pp. 1–2.

3 Michael L. Conniff, "Introduction: Toward a Comparative Definition of Populism," in Conniff, ed., *Latin American Populism in Comparative Perspective* (Albuquerque: Univ. of New Mexico Press, 1982), pp. 3–30. The chapter by Jorge Basurto entitled "The Late Populism of Luis Echeverría" in the same volume makes a case for the ongoing presence of populism in Latin America.

4 This position was upheld by the Vanguardia Comunista, which split off from the PCV in 1974, "Proceso Político," and "El Pueblo Avanza" (EPA). See EPA, *Aquí hace falta una . . . oposición revolucionaria* (Caracas: Editorial Porvenir Socialista, 1979), pp. 79–95.

5 Proceso Político, *CAP: cinco años* (Caracas: Editorial Ateneo de Caracas, 1978), pp. 82–83; Eloy Lanza, *El sub-imperialismo venezolano* (Caracas: Editorial Confederación de Escritores Latinoamericanos, 1980).

6 *El Nacional*, July 26, 1974, p. D-12.

7 Teodoro Petkoff, *Proceso a la izquierda* (Barcelona: Editorial Planeta, 1976), pp. 192–93.

8 Ibid., p. 189; *Punto*, Dec. 13, 1973, p. 15.

9 Pompeyo Márquez, *Hacia una nueva mayoría* (Caracas: Equipo Editor, 1979), p. 139; Muñoz and Alonso Palacios, "Consideraciones políticas en turno a un año de gobierno de Carlos Andrés Pérez," *Otro gobierno que fracasa: un análisis del MAS para los venezolanos* (Caracas: G&T Editores, 1977), p. 257.

10 *Punto*, April 5, 1978, p. 13; Teodoro Petkoff, *Socialismo para Venezuela?*, 3rd ed. (Caracas: Editorial Fuentes, 1972), p. 153.

11 Enrique A. Baloyra and John D. Martz, *Political Attitudes in Venezuela: Societal Cleavages and Political Opinion* (Austin: Univ. of Texas Press, 1979), pp. 117–51.

12 *El Nacional*, April 5, 1975, p. D-9.

13 Freddy Muñoz, interview, April 6, 1984, Puerto La Cruz; Tirso Pinto, interview, Barcelona, Oct. 19, 1983.

14 Ramón Hernández (interviewer), *Teodoro Petkoff: Viaje al fondo de si mismo* (Caracas: Editorial Fuentes, 1983), p. 212.

15 Petkoff, *Razones para una decisión política* (Caracas: Impreso Tipografía Sorocaima, 1976), p. 7.

16 Andrés Stambouli, "La campaña electoral de 1978: análisis de las estrategias de comunicación masiva," *Politeia* 9 (1980): 111.

17 Freddy Muñoz, untitled document on MAS internal primaries, Gustavo Ramírez Archive, Puerto La Cruz, Caracas, July 1976.

18 Luis Bayardo Sardi, "La cuestión electoral, la izquierda y . . . ," *Para la acción* 3–4 (June 1977): 7.

19 Proceso Político, *CAP. 5 años: Un juicio crítico* (Caracas: Editorial Ateneo de Caracas, 1978), p. 249; Iván Loscher (interviewer), *Todas son izquierda* (Caracas: Libros Tepuy, 1978), p. 122.

20 This ambiguity was pointed out by two renowned pro-MAS sociologists who criticized MAS for failing to "adequately explain the reasons for opposing the idea of unity." See José Agustín Silva Michelena and Heinz Rudolf Sonntag, *El proceso electoral de 1978: su perspectiva histórica estructural* (Caracas: Editorial Ateneo de Caracas, 1979), p. 177; *El Nacional,* Dec. 26, 1977, p. A-4; Freddy Muñoz, "Verdades y problemas sobre la unidad de la izquierda," *Para la acción* 3–4 (June 1977): 6.

21 *Punto,* July 24–31, 1978, p. 3.

22 Pedro José Martínez I., "La unidad de la izquierda en Venezuela: Su evolución hasta las elecciones nacionales de 1978 y 1979," *Politeia* 9 (1980): 386; José Vicente Rangel, "La izquierda: la situación de las conversaciones," *Semana* 499 (Feb. 19, 1978): 45.

23 *Auténtico* 73 (Oct. 30, 1978): 23.

24 Joaquín Marta Sosa, *Venezuela: elecciones y transformación social* (Caracas: Editorial Centauro 84, 1984), pp. 221–22.

25 The returns for each electoral district for the 1973 and 1978 elections are published in Appendix B of Howard R. Penniman, ed., *Venezuela at the Polls: The National Elections of 1978* (Washington, D.C.: American Enterprise Institute, 1980).

26 Luis Bayardo Sardi, interview with the author, Caracas, March 13, 1982.

27 Martínez, "La unidad de la izquierda."

28 Freddy Muñoz, "Significado general de las elecciones," *Reflexiones* 18 (Feb.–March 1979): 26; Muñoz, *Más allá de las palabras,* p. 22.

29 Pompeyo Márquez, "El MAS: los resultados electorales" *Formación política* 3 (June 1979): 23.

8 The Elections of 1983–1984

1 David J. Myers, "Venezuela's MAS," *Problems of Communism* 29, no. 5 (Sept.–Oct. 1980); Steve Ellner, "Venezuelan Surprises," *New York Times,* Aug. 25, 1981, p. A-19.

2 Myers, "Venezuela's MAS," p. 25.

3 Cole Blasier, *The Hovering Giant: U.S. Responses to Revolutionary Change in Latin America* (Pittsburgh: Univ. of Pittsburgh, 1976), p. 242.

4 Luigi R. Einaudi, "U.S. Latin American Policy in the 1970s: New Forms of Control?" in Julio Cotler and Richard R. Fagen, eds., *Latin America and the United States: The Changing Political Realities* (Stanford: Stanford Univ. Press), pp. 243–55.

5 Victor Hugo D'Paola, "Construir un partido donde cada uno tenga una tarea," *Cartel* 3 (Nov. 1981): 11.

6 *Resumen* 343 (June 1, 1980): 12–13; Tirso Pinto, interview with the author, Oct. 19, 1983, Barcelona.

7 Bayardo Sardi, interview with the author, Caracas, March 13, 1982.

8 Tirso Pinto, interview with the author, Barcelona, Oct. 19, 1983.

9   *Diario de Caracas*, Jan. 22, 1983, p. 7.
10 Cesar Solórzano (MAS national leader), interview with the author, Sept. 9, 1984, Caracas.
11 Freddy Muñoz, *Desafíos y tentaciones: Una política para el poder* (Servicio Gráfico Editorial, n.d.), p. 84.
12 *El programa del cambio: Más democracia para Venezuela*, p. 11. See also Teodoro Petkoff, "Democracia y socialismo," in *Sobre la democracia* (Caracas: Editorial Ateneo de Caracas, 1979), pp. 39–64; Teodoro Petkoff, *Más democracia: Propuestas para la Reforma del Estado Venezolano* (n.p., 1982?).
13 Maracano Coello, "El socialismo asusta?" *Inforemas* 19 (Feb. 1, 1983): 6.
14 Enrique A. Baloyra and John D. Martz, *Political Attitudes in Venezuela* (Austin: Univ. of Texas Press, 1979), p. 228.
15 Luis Bayardo Sardi, "Orientaciones básicas para la campaña electoral," *Inforemas* 19 (Feb. 1, 1983): 20.
16 Luis Bayardo Sardi, "Los tres aspectos claves de nuestra campaña," in *En campaña: Boletín informativo del comando de campaña* (May 1983), p. 6.
17 *Tribuna Popular*, Dec. 10–16, 1982, p. 3.
18 *El Nacional*, Dec. 8, 1983, p. D-1.
19 Channel Five (Caracas) news brief, Dec. 17, 1983.
20 *El Nacional*, April 30, 1984, p. C-1; *El Nacional*, May 3, 1984, p. A-4; Teodoro Petkoff [essay without title], in *1984: A donde va Venezuela?* (Madrid: Editorial Planeta, 1984), pp. 525–27.
21 Channel Five (Caracas) news brief, Dec. 9, 1983.
22 Baloyra and Martz, *Political Attitudes in Venezuela;* David J. Myers, "Urban Voting, Structural Cleavages and the Party System Evolution: The Case of Venezuela," *Comparative Politics* 8 (Oct. 1975); Baloyra, "Public Attitudes toward the Democratic Regime," in Martz and Myers, *Venezuela: The Democratic Experience* (New York: Praeger, 1977); Baloyra, "Public Opinion and Support for the Regime: 1973–83," *Venezuela: The Democratic Experience*, rev. ed. (New York: Praeger, 1986); Robert O'Connor, "The Electorate," in Howard R. Penniman, ed., *Venezuela at the Polls* (Washington, D.C.: American Enterprise Institute, 1980), pp. 56–90; Arístides Torres, "Crisis o consolidación de los partidos en Venezuela" (unpublished paper, 1979?); Kenneth M. Coleman and Charles L. Davis, "Industrial Class vs. Nation: Psychological Identification among Latin American Industrial Workers" (1982, unpublished).
23 Baloyra, "Public Attitudes," pp. 49–50.
24 Estudios y Organización Eugenio Escuela, "Estudio de Opinión Pública" (unpublished survey carried out Sept. 23–26, 1982, in Caracas, from Teodoro Petkoff's personal archive, Caracas), questions 2.7, 2.8, 2.12.
25 "Las encuestas vistas con lupa," *Zeta* 226 (July 23, 1978): 6–7.
26 Survey team headed by Alejandro Morillo (unpublished survey carried out March 1986, from Petkoff archive), question 0011.
27 O'Connor, "The Electorate," p. 73.
28 Survey team headed by Morillo, question 0012.
29 Baloyra, "Public Opinion and Support," p. 63.
30 Fundación Solidaridad (unpublished survey carried out in Nov. 1983, from Petkoff archive), question 1-1.
31 Torres, "Crisis o consolidación," pp. 19, 23.
32 Baloyra and Martz, *Political Attitudes in Venezuela*, p. 173; O'Connor, "The Electorate," p. 87.
33 Baloyra, "Public Attitudes," p. 61.

246

34 Baloyra, "Public Opinion and Support," pp. 56–57.
35 Ibid., p. 60.
36 The orthodox Communists have been uncomfortable with this approach. In Peru, for instance, they rejected the issuance of membership cards in the name of the United Left, an electoral alliance that ran candidates in national and local elections in the 1980s.
37 Steve Ellner, "Inter-Party Agreements and Rivalry in Venezuela: A Comparative Perspective," *Studies in Comparative International Development* 19, no. 4 (Winter 1984–85): 38–66.
38 *El Nacional,* June 7, 1974, p. D-19; Aug. 29, 1974, p. D-10.

9 MAS's Participation in Organized Labor and University Politics

1   Steve Ellner, *Los partidos políticos y su disputa por el control del movimiento sindical en Venezuela, 1936–1948* (Caracas: Univ. Católica Andrés Bello, 1980), p. 165.
2   Rodolfo Quintero, *Hacia el renacimiento obrero en Venezuela* (Caracas: UCV, 1980), pp. 83–84.
3   Eloy Torres, *Un vuelvan caras hacia la clase obrera* (mimeographed, archive of Arturo Tremont, Caracas), pp. 5, 10.
4   Eloy Torres, "Informe sindical al XVI Pleno del Comité Central," *Tribuna Popular* ("Suplemento Sindical"), Sept. 17–23, 1970, p. 5.
5   Ibid.
6   Ibid., p. 4; Eloy Torres, interview with the author, Caracas, Sept. 4, 1984.
7   *Deslinde* 16 (Feb. 15–28, 1970): 7.
8   Arturo Tremont, interview with the author, Caracas, Sept. 3, 1984.
9   Torres, "Informe sindical," p. 5.
10 Jesús Urbieta, interview with the author, Caracas, Sept. 4, 1984.
11 Torres, "Informe sindical," p. 20; Torres, *La clase obrera y nuestra tarea* (mimeographed, archive of Arturo Tremont, Caracas, 1970?), p. 6.
12 *Almargen* 3 (March 15–31, 1971): 15.
13 *Acero* [periodical of the metal workers union affiliate of the CUTV-Clasista], Nov. 1972, p. 8.
14 Carlos Arturo Pardo, "10 años de actividad sindical del MAS" (archive of Arturo Tremont, Caracas, 1982?), p. 1.
15 Arturo Tremont, interview with the author, Sept. 3, 1984, Caracas.
16 Teodoro Petkoff, "En Matanzas: Obreros vs. sindicalerismo," *Reventón* 5 (July 3, 1971): 33–35; Alfredo Maneiro, Lucas Matheus, and Homero Arellano, *Notas negativas* (Caracas: Ediciones Venezuela 83, 1971), p. 98.
17 Petkoff, "En Matanzas," pp. 33–35; Radamés Larrazábal, *Estrategia de poder* (Caracas: Editorial Ateneo de Caracas, 1979), p. 94.
18 "De nueva sobre la acertada combinación de lucha y organización," *Formación Militante* (publication of the Liga Socialista) 6 (n.d.).
19 Urbieta, interview with the author, Caracas, Sept. 4, 1984; Carlos Arturo Pardo, "Qué pasó en SIDOR?" *Reflexiones* 10 (July 1977): 25–30.
20 Dirección Sindical Nacional, *Posición de la Dirección Sindical Nacional del MAS* (mimeographed, Caracas, Oct. 6, 1980), p. 5.
21 Freddy Muñoz, *Posibilidades y peligros de una gran alternativa* (pamphlet, n.p., n.d.), p. 63.
22 *Informe del frente nacional* (mimeographed, archive of Arturo Tremont, Caracas, June 1975), pp. 1–2.

23 Ellner, *Los partidos políticos*, pp. 131–35; Héctor Lucena, *El movimiento obrero petrolero: Proceso de formación y desarrollo* (Caracas: Ediciones Centauro 82, 1982), p. 354.
24 *Tribuna Popular*, Oct. 22–28, 1970, p. 5.
25 Jesús Paz Galarraga, interview with the author, Caracas, Nov. 26, 1986.
26 *El Nacional*, Jan. 22, 1984; Urbieta, interview with the author, Caracas, Sept. 8, 1984.
27 "Por qué no asistimos a la marcha?" *La hoja para el debate* 5 (Oct. 30, 1984); Eloy Torres, "La C.T.V. debe poner en consonancia las declaraciones con la acción," *Punto Socialista* 18 (Nov.–Dec. 1984): 10.
28 MAS, *Temas para la discusión: contenidos para la convención regional de Caracas* (mimeographed, June 1985), p. S-7.
29 Damian Prat, "Por la reafirmación de una política revolucionaria en el movimiento sindical," *Reflexiones* 9 (June 1977): 28.
30 Muñoz, *Posibilidades y peligros*, pp. 63–64; Muñoz, "En nuestra conducta ha disminuido el aliento combativo," *Reflexiones* 8 (1977?): 10.
31 Carlos Arturo Pardo, "10 años de actividad sindical del MAS," p. 6; Pardo, interview with the author, May 3, 1976, Caracas.
32 Petkoff, interview with the author, Sept. 5, 1985, Caracas.
33 Tremont, interview with the author, Sept. 1, 1985, Caracas.
34 D'Paula, interview with the author, Sept. 1, 1984, Caracas.
35 *El Nacional*, Dec. 6, 1984, p. D-5.
36 Matancero, *Cuadernos de la letra R: Desde la Venezuela que trabaja y lucha hablan: Los Matanceros* (Caracas: Ediciones del Agua Mansa, 1979), p. 16.
37 Maneiro et al., *Notas negativas*, pp. 102–103.
38 Andrés Pariche, "En Guayana: además de mineral," *Esfuerzo* (Aug.–Sept. 1981): 8, 38.
39 *El Nacional*, Oct. 16, 1981, p. D-7.
40 José Ignacio Arrieta, "Por qué intervinieron a SUTISS?" *Resumen* 427 (Jan. 10, 1982): 4–6; "El conflicto es fundamental," *Resumen* 432 (Feb. 14, 1982): 8–9.
41 Los Matanceros, *Cuadernos de la Letra R*, p. 5.
42 Carlos Arturo Pardo, "Informe de la secretaría sindical nacional del M.A.S. sobre el proceso electoral de ATISS" (mimeographed, Caracas, Nov. 29, 1974).
43 Pardo, "Qué pasó en SIDOR?" p. 30.
44 "Surge el proletariado: la lucha de los trabajadores textiles," *Proceso Político* 7 (April 1978): 35.
45 Santiago Arconada et al. [Proceso Político], "Conversando con: Judith Valencia" (transcript of forum at the second conference of Taller Movimiento Obrero Latinoamericano, Caracas, Oct.–Nov. 1980).
46 *Tribuna Popular*, Aug. 5–11, 1977, p. 5; July 25–31, 1980, p. 2; Sept. 12–18, 1980, p. 11.
47 Pardo, "Frente de los Trabajadores de la Dirección Sindical Nacional," *Carta Socialista* 1 (Sept. 1977): [n.p.]. See also Dirección Política y Dirección Sindical Nacional del MAS, *Sobre conflicto textilero: El heroico movimiento textilero no debe terminar en derrota* (Sept. 1980).
48 *Almargen* 1 (Feb. 1–15, 1971): 8–9; *Tribuna Popular*, July 8, 1971, p. 4.
49 Enrique Ochoa, "Juventud del MAS: Una evaluación imprescindible," *Reflexiones* 9 (June 1977): 33; *Diario de Caracas*, May 9, 1983, p. 7.
50 Moisés Moleiro, *La izquierda y su proceso* (Caracas: Ediciones Centauro 77, 1977), p. 167.

51 Muñoz, *Posibilidades y peligros*, pp. 9, 66; *Carta Socialista* 5 (Dec. 1977): 5.

52 Ellner, "Education Policy," in John D. Martz and David J. Myers, eds., *Venezuela: The Democratic Experience*, rev. ed. (New York: Praeger, 1986), p. 311.

53 Ramón Hernández, *Teodoro Petkoff: viaje al fondo de si mismo* (Caracas: Editorial Fuentes, 1983), p. 107.

54 Ibid., p. 105.

55 Carlos Raúl Hernández, interview with the author, Caracas, March 10, 1984.

56 Juventud Socialista-MIR, *Tesis del II Congreso* [documents of convention, Dec. 1981] (Caracas: Rojo y Negro Fondo Editorial), p. 31.

57 Ochoa, "Juventud del MAS," p. 34.

58 After leaving MAS, Heydra wrote a book-length history of the Venezuelan left, with a special emphasis on MAS, entitled *La izquierda: una autocrítica perpetua (50 años de encuentros y desencuentros del marxismo en Venezuela)* (Caracas: UCV, 1981).

59 Rafaelito Guerra (national youth leader of MAS), interview with the author, Aug. 14, 1985, Caracas.

60 Gonzalo González, interview with the author, Aug. 14, 1985, Caracas.

61 "Las elecciones estudiantiles en la UCV," *Punto* 24 (July 1985): 20. A similar slate of "independents," who were in fact members of leftist parties, also triumphed in student elections at the University of the Oriente in Puerto La Cruz.

10 Party Organization and Structure

1 Bayardo Sardi, Alonso Palacios, Franklin Guzmán et al., "El encuentro con la Venezuela del cambio: Por un MAS de puertas ABIERTAS" (document presented at MAS's 1985 convention), p. A-4.

2 MAS, "Tesis sobre la construcción del MAS," in *Asamblea Nacional: Movimiento al Socialismo* (published document, n.p., n.d.), p. 7.

3 Rollie Poppino, *International Communism in Latin America* (London: Free Press of Glencoe, 1964), p. 119.

4 Juan Pereira, interview with the author, Nov. 21, 1984, Puerto La Cruz.

5 Victor Hugo D'Paola, interview with the author, Sept. 1, 1984, Caracas.

6 MAS, *Estatutos del MAS* (Caracas: Productora Fotográfica Martín, 1982), p. 10.

7 Ibid., p. 62.

8 Ibid., pp. 6–8; "Los nuevos estatutos: Renovación democrática o reparto de posiciones?" in *5 convención: Órgano para la discusión del MAS* 3 (1980?), pp. 10–11.

9 Bayardo Sardi et al., "El encuentro," p. A-5.

10 Héctor José Sculpi, "La reforma de los estatutos del MAS," *Reflexiones* 9 (June 1977): 31–32. The distinction that was made between *militant* and *partisan* broke with a Communist tradition dating back to the division in the Russian Social Democratic Worker's Party in 1902. The split was set off by Lenin's rejection of Julius Martov's proposal to establish levels of responsibility for party members in order to facilitate the creation of a broad-based party.

11 Freddy Muñoz, *Más allá de las palabras: Proposiciones para la renovación y reconstrucción del MAS* (n.p.: n.d.), p. 49.

12 Muñoz, interview with the author, April 6, 1984, Puerto La Cruz.

13 *El Nacional*, May 7, 1978, p. D-1.

14 This phrase was first popularized in Betancourt's *Venezuela: Política y petróleo* (Mexico: Fondo de Cultura Económica, 1956).

15 Victor Hugo D'Paola, interview with the author, Sept. 1, 1984, Caracas; Manuel Caballero (national MAS leader), interview with the author, March 19, 1982, Caracas.

16 MAS, *Estatutos*, pp. 50–52.

17 The information for this discussion on Anzoátegui was derived from interviews in Barcelona and Puerto La Cruz with the following MAS regional leaders: Alexis Ortiz (Nov. 12, 1982); Juan Pereira (Oct. 12, 1982); Luis García (Sept. 22, 1982); Juan Rodríguez (Oct. 30, 1983); Alvaro Galindo (Dec. 3, 1982); Pablo Casals (Feb. 1, 1984); Jesús Silva (Oct. 3, 1983). MAS, *Un programa para Anzoátegui: 20 puntos para el cambio* (material for the 1983 national elections, n.p., n.d.).

18 Argelia Laya, interview with the author, Jan. 10, 1985, Caracas; Mayita Acosta, interview with the author, Jan. 8, 1985, Caracas. For more information on Laya, see Laya, *Nuestra Causa* (Caracas: Equipo Editor, 1979).

19 Mayita Acosta, "Una política del MAS hacia la mujer," *Punto Socialista* 18 (Nov.–Dec. 1984): 11; Milagros Villafane, "Femininas, pero no Feministas," *La hoja para el Debate* 5 (Oct. 30, 1984): [n.p.].

20 As quoted in Richard Parker, "Debate Over the Aristocracy of Labor" (unpublished manuscript), p. 26; Lenin, "The Jena Congress of the German Social Democratic Party," in *On Trade Unions* (Moscow: Progress Publishers, 1976), p. 139.

21 *Reorientar, reconstruir, renovar el proyecto del MAS: Separata de Espacio Abierto* (document presented by Freddy Muñoz at MAS 1985 convention, n.p., n.d.), p. 25.

22 *Nuestra tesis política* (mimeographed document drawn up by Bayardo Sardi, Caracas, July 1984); Carlos Rodríguez (MAS's city councilman in the Federal District), interview with the author, Sept. 5, 1984, Caracas.

23 Comité Directivo de la Nueva Democracia, *Documentos de la Nueva Democracia: Publicación para la renovación del MAS* (Caracas: Editorial Metrópolis, 1985?); Muñoz, interview with the author, April 6, 1984, Puerto La Cruz.

24 Petkoff, interview with the author, Sept. 4, 1984, Caracas.

25 MAS, *Estatutos*, p. 9.

26 *Reorientar, reconstruir, renovar*, p. 53.

27 *Proyecto de reforma de los estatutos: VI convención nacional* (Caracas, 1985), p. 18.

28 Juan Pereira, interview with the author, Aug. 4, 1985, Barcelona.

29 David J. Myers, "The Venezuelan Party System: Regime Maintenance under Stress," in John D. Martz and David J. Myers, eds., *Venezuela: The Democratic Experience*, rev. ed. (New York: Praeger, 1986), pp. 131–34.

30 *El Nacional*, June 22, 1985, p. A-4; July 5, 1985, p. D-17; July 27, 1985, p. A-4.

31 Perry Anderson, *Arguments within English Marxism* (London: NLB and Verso Editions, 1980), p. 113.

32 Jordi Borja, "Prólogo," in Maurice Duverger, *Carta abierta a los socialistas* (Barcelona: Ediciones Martínez Roca, 1976), p. 21.

11 Internal Currents of Opinion and Factionalism

1 Ted Grant, in *James P. Cannon, As We Knew Him: By Thirty-Three Comrades, Friends, and Relatives* (New York: Pathfinder Press, 1976), p. 95.

2 Teodoro Petkoff, *Socialismo para Venezuela?* 3rd ed. (Caracas: Editorial Fuentes, 1972), p. 88.

3   Lucas Leal, *De los orígenes y la historia de una fuerza para el socialismo en Venezuela* (Caracas: MAS, 1983), p. 21.
4   Petkoff, "Los nuevos problemas del MAS," *Reflecciones* 7 (n.d.): 32–35.
5   *Auténtico* 58 (July 17, 1978): 26.
6   *Auténtico* 67 (Sept. 18, 1978): 25.
7   *El Nacional*, July 9, 1978, p. D-4.
8   Petkoff, "Los nuevos problemas," pp. 32–35.
9   *El Nacional*, Oct. 9, 1977, p. D-20; Oct. 7, 1977, p. D-21.
10 *El Nacional*, Aug. 3, 1976, p. D-7; Oct. 10, 1977, p. D-9.
11 *El Nacional*, March 16, 1976, p. D-8.
12 Pompeyo Márquez, *Socialismo: Nuevas situaciones reclaman nuevas elaboraciones* (n.c.: Versión Taquigráfica, 1981?), p. 21.
13 Alfredo Peña (interviewer), "Foro: Pompeyo Márquez . . . ," *El Nacional*, July 11, 1983, p. C-1.
14 Diego Bautista Urbaneja, *Documento No. 1* (mimeographed), p. 25; Luis Bayardo Sardi, *Señales de una política para el MAS* (pamphlet; text of a speech delivered by Bayardo in Caracas in July 1983), (n.p.).
15 *Diario de Caracas*, Dec. 11, 1983, p. 9; Carlos Raúl Hernández, interview with the author, Sept. 8, 1984, Caracas.
16 In rejecting absolute models and formulas, the *tucanes* were in basic agreement with those Marxists (such as the members of the "Frankfurt School") who are most concerned with the early writings of Marx in which the dialectic is viewed as a tool to analyze changing social conditions. A contrary tendency in Marxism is represented by the French Communist Louis Althuser, who claims that Marxism is a science and not just a methodology. Those who adhere to this position, rather than stress change and diversity, emphasize the immutable laws of history.
17 Bayardo Sardi, interview with the author, March 13, 1982, Caracas: Bayardo Sardi, "Definamos al MAS como una fuerza de reivindicación social" (speech delivered in Caracas, May 11, 1985), p. 10.
18 Comisión Nacional de Formación Política de MAS, *Boletín Formación Política* 5, "Orientaciones básicas para la actividad del MAS en el presente período" (document issued by a committee headed by Anselmo Natale), p. 40.
19 Urbaneja, *Documento*, pp. 1–2; Alonso Palacios, "El conflicto de la política revolucionaria: La distancia entre la voluntad y los logros" (unpublished paper to be used as part of dissertation, London School of Economics), p. 91.
20 Alexis Ortiz, interview with the author, Nov. 12, 1982, Puerto La Cruz.
21 Freddy Muñoz, interview with the author, April 6, 1984, Puerto La Cruz; Carlos Tablante [MAS national deputy], interview with the author, Sept. 6, 1984, Caracas.
22 Freddy Muñoz, *Desafíos y tentaciones: Una política para el poder* (Caracas: Servicio Gráfico, n.d.), pp. 25–27.
23 Freddy Muñoz, *El reto es la esperanza: Palabras prounciadas en el acto de proclamación* (Caracas: [published by "*Espacio Abierto*"], 1985).
24 Freddy Muñoz, "En nuestra conducta ha dismunuido el aliento combativo," *Reflexiones* 8 (April 1977): 10; Muñoz, *Una política para el poder*, pp. 20–24.
25 Arturo Tremont, "Una fuerza que sí se ve," *Espacio Abierto* 2 (Nov. 1984): 13–14.
26 *Los delegados al IX Congreso de la . . . C.T.V., que apoyamos la candidatura de Freddy Muñoz a secretaria general . . .* (Caracas, June 20, 1985), p. 7.

27 Freddy Muñoz, *Más allá de las palabras: Proposiciones para la renovación y recon-strucción del MAS* (n.p., n.d.), p. 43.
28 Quimi Alsina, "Un S.O.S. para la inscripción," in *La hoja para el debate* 4 (Oct. 15, 1984).
29 Freddy Muñoz, *SIR: Sistema nacional de inscripción y recenso* (brochure, n.p., n.d.), pp. 7–11; Muñoz, *Más allá de las palabras*, p. 53.
30 Ronald H. Chilcote, *The Brazilian Communist Party: Conflict and Integration, 1922–1972* (New York: Oxford Univ. Press, 1974), p. 138.
31 Juan Pereira, interview with the author, Nov. 12, 1984, Barcelona.
32 "Tercera Vía," *Programa para una esperanza revolucionaria* (Caracas: 1979?).
33 Américo Martín, interview with the author, Feb. 9, 1983, Barcelona.
34 *El Nacional*, May 13, 1980, p. D-2.
35 *El Nacional*, July 13, 1983, p. 10; "Impasse: Tirso Pinto-MAS: nueva fuerza socialdemócrata de relevo?" *Noticrítica*, March 1983, pp. 2–4.
36 *El Nacional*, Aug. 9, 1983, p. D-14.
37 Bayardo Sardi et al., "El encuentro con la Venezuela del cambio" (mimeographed; document for MAS's sixth national convention, 1985?).
38 Nueva Democracia, *Documentos de la Nueva Democracia: Publicación para la renovación del MAS* (Caracas: Editorial Metrópolis, 1984?), p. 5.
39 *Juvencio Pulgar a la secretaría general* (newspaper format; internal MAS publication, 1985); Juvencio Pulgar, *Declaración política de la VI Convención del MAS (Proyecto)* (June 1985); *Diario de Caracas*, Oct. 22, 1984, p. 12.
40 Fuerza Emergente (the name of Thielen's faction), *Reafirmación socialista, renovación democrática: documento para la discusión de la VI Convención Nacional* (newspaper format; internal MAS publication, 1985); Thielen, "Una estimulante experiencia movilizadora," *Punto Socialista* 12 (May 1984): 5–6.

Bibliography

Newspapers and Magazines

Almargen (director: Simón Sáez Mérida). 1979–82.
Auténtico. 1978–79.
Bravo Pueblo (newspaper published by MAS). 1971.
Carta Socialista (MAS publication). 1977.
Cartel (MAS publication). 1981.
Deslinde. 1969–71.
Deslinde Ideológico. 1970.
Diario de Caracas. 1983–85.
Documéntos Políticos (published by the PCV; editor: Manuel Caballero). 1967–68.
El Nacional. 1969–85.
Espacio Abierto (magazine published by *halcón* tendency of MAS). 1984–85.
Formación Política (published by Comisión Nacional de Formación Política of MAS). 1979.
Ideas Juveniles (published by *tucán* tendency of MAS). 1983.
Inforemas (published by MAS). 1983.
Joven Guardia (Communist Youth publication). 1970.
La Hoja para el Debate (magazine published by *tucán* tendency of MAS; director: Franklin Guzmán). 1984–85.
Papeles Universitarios (directors: Pastor Heydra and Andrés Rojas). 1977.
Para la Acción (magazine published by MAS). 1976.
Punto (newspaper published by MAS). 1974–77.
Punto Socialista (magazine published by MAS). 1984–85.
Quinta Convención: Órgano para la discusión del MAS. 1980?
Reflexiones (magazine published by MAS). 1976–79.
Resumen. 1981–84.
Semana. 1976–80.
Seminario [MAS weekly]. 1983–84.
Sic. 1978–85.
Tribuna Popular (PCV newspaper). 1969–85.
Yearbook on International Communist Affairs. 1968–75.

Books, Articles, Pamphlets, and Documents

Acosta Favelo, María. *Día de la Mujer* (pamphlet; speech delivered by Acosta). Caracas: Concejo Municipal del Distrito Federal, 1984.

Aguilar, Pedro Pablo, Orlando Albornoz, Federico Alvarez, et al. *1984: A donde va Venezuela?* Madrid: Editorial Planeta, 1985.

Alexander, Robert Jackson. *The Communist Party of Venezuela.* Stanford: Hoover Institution Press, 1969.

Alvarez, Federico, Manuel Caballero, Américo Martín, et al. *La izquierda venezolana y las elecciones del 73 (Un análisis político y polémico).* Caracas: Síntesis Dosmil, 1974.

Alvarez, Luis. *Proposiciones para una nueva estructura organizativa del MAS* (mimeographed). April 1985.

———, Elizabeth Acosta, José M. Cadenas, et al. *Proyecto de reforma de los estatutos: VI Convención Nacional.* Caracas, 1985.

Bayardo Sardi, Luis. "Definamos al MAS como una fuerza de reivindicación social" (speech delivered at the Hotel Tamanaco in Caracas, May 11, 1985).

———. "La cuestión electoral, la izquierda y . . . ." *Para la nación* 3–4 (June 1977).

———. *Nuestra tesis política* (mimeographed document drawn up by Bayardo Sardi). Caracas, July 1984.

———. *Señales de una política para el MAS* (pamphlet; text of a speech delivered in Caracas in July 1983).

———. "Versión no corregida, para uso de los instructores del curso simultáneo nacional, sobre el MAS y su política" (mimeographed). Caracas, n.d.

Bayardo Sardi, Luis, Alonso Palacios, Franklin Guzmán, et al. "El encuentro con la Venezuela del cambio: Por un MAS de puertas ABIERTAS" (mimeographed; document for MAS's sixth national convention, 1985?).

Berlinguer, Enrico. *Gobierno de unidad democrática y compromiso histórico: Discursos, 1969–1976.* Madrid: Editorial Ayuso, 1977.

Blackmer, Donald. *Unity in Diversity: Italian Communism and the Communist World.* Cambridge, Mass.: MIT Press, 1968.

Blanco Muñoz, Agustín. *La lucha armada: Hablan 5 jefes.* Caracas: UCV, 1980.

———. *La lucha armada: Hablan 6 comandantes.* Caracas: UCV, 1981.

Blank, David Eugene. "Venezuela." Richard F. Starr, ed., *1981 Yearbook on International Communist Affairs.* Stanford: Hoover Institution Press, 1982.

Brutents, K. N. *National Liberation Revolutions Today.* 2 vols. Moscow: Progress Publishers, 1977.

Caballero, Manuel. *El desarrollo desigual del socialismo y otros ensayos polémicos.* Caracas: Editorial Domingo Fuentes, 1970.

Carrillo, Santiago. *"Eurocomunismo" y estado.* Barcelona: Editorial Crítica, 1977.

Chilcote, Ronald H. *The Brazilian Communist Party: Conflict and Integration, 1922–1972.* New York: Oxford Univ. Press, 1974.

Cortés, Rafael José. *El MAS: Desbandada hacia la derecha.* Caracas: Ediciones Centauro 79, 1979.

———. *En defensa del socialismo (respuesta a las "conversaciones").* Caracas: Gráfica Río Orinoco, 1979.

Debate sobre debate. Caracas: Editorial Primero de Mayo, 1975.

Díaz Rangel, Eleazar. *Como se dividió el P.C.V.* Caracas: Editorial Domingo Fuentes, 1971.

Dirección Sindical Nacional (MAS). *Esquema para la discusión* (mimeographed). Caracas: Feb. 27, 1982.

Duno, Pedro. *Sobre aparatos, desviaciones y dogmas.* Caracas: Editorial Nueva Izquierda, 1969.

Duverger, Maurice. *Carta abierta a los socialistas.* Barcelona: Ediciones Martínez Roca, 1976.

El programa del Cambio: Teodoro. Más democracia para Venezuela. (n.p., 1983?).

El reto es la esperanza (speeches delivered in the proclamation of the candidacy of Freddy Muñoz as secretary general of MAS, Feb. 9, 1985).

Ellner, Steve. "Diverse Influences on the Venezuelan Left." *Journal of Interamerican Studies and World Affairs* 23, no. 4 (Nov. 1981).

———. "Factionalism in the Venezuelan Communist Movement, 1937–1948." *Science & Society* 45, no. 1 (Spring 1981).

———. "Inter-Party Agreement and Rivalry in Venezuela: A Comparative Perspective." *Studies in Comparative International Development* 19, no. 4 (Winter 1984–85).

———. *Los partidos políticos y su disputa por el control del movimiento sindical en Venezuela, 1936–1948.* Caracas: Univ. Católica Andrés Bello, 1980.

———. "Political Party Dynamics and the Outbreak of Guerrilla Warfare in Venezuela." *Inter-American Economic Affairs* 34, no. 2 (Autumn 1980).

———. "The Venezuela Left in the Era of the Popular Front, 1936–1945." *Journal of Latin American Studies* 11, no. 1 (May 1979).

———. Venezucommunism: Learning the Lesson of Chile?" *Commonweal* 107, no. 3 (Feb. 15, 1980).

———. "Venezuelan Surprises." *New York Times,* Aug. 25, 1981, p. A-19.

Estatutos del MAS. (n.p., 1982).

Fioravanti, Eduardo. *Ni eurocomunismo ni Estado.* Barcelona: Editorial Península, 1978.

Fuerza Emergente. *Reafirmación socialista, renovación democrática: Documento para la discusión de la VI Convención Nacional.* 1985 (internal MAS publication).

García Ponce, Antonio. *Adecos, tucanes o marxistas? Una historia de la izquierda, 1959–1984.* Caracas: Editorial Domingo Fuentes, 1985.

García Ponce, Guillermo. *El país: La izquierda y las elecciones de 1978.* Caracas: Miguel Angel García e Hijos, 1977.

Greene, Thomas. "The Communist Parties of Italy and France: A Study in Comparative Communism." *World Politics* 21, no. 1 (Oct. 1968).

Herman, Donald L., ed. *The Communist Tide in Latin America: A Selected Treatment.* Austin: Univ. of Texas, 1973.

Hernández, Carlos Raúl. *Democracia y mitología revolucionaria: Proceso del poder en Venezuela.* Caracas: Editorial La Enseñanza Viva, 1978.

———, and Jean Maninat. *Cuba-Nicaragua: Expectativas y frustraciones.* Caracas: Adame-Producciones Editoriales, 1984.

Hernández, Ramón (interviewer). *Teodoro Petkoff: Viaje al fondo de si mismo.* Caracas: Editorial Fuentes, 1983.

Heydra, Pastor. *La izquierda: Una autocrítica perpetua (50 años de encuentros y desencuentros del marxismo en Venezuela).* Caracas: UCV, 1981.

Hinton, Harold C. *Communist China in World Politics.* Boston: Houghton Mifflin, 1966.

José Vicente es unión del Pueblo (speeches delivered at a MAS rally on July 20, 1977).

Lairet, Germán. "La crisis de la democracia," in *El Mundo: Documentos.* Medellín, Colombia: April 15, 1982.

Larrazábal, Radamés. *Socialismo bobo o socialismo para Venezuela?* Caracas: Ediciones Cantaclaro, 1970.

Laya, Argelia. *La condición de la mujer: Un asunto de interés nacional.* n.p., n.d.
———. *Nuestra causa.* Caracas: Equipo Editor, 1979.
Leal, Lucas. *De los orígenes y la historia de una fuerza para el socialismo en Venezuela.* Caracas: Comisión Nacional de Formación Política del MAS, 1983.
Leonhard, Wolfgang. *Eurocomunism: Challenge for East and West.* New York: Holt, Rinehart and Winston, 1978.
Liss, Sheldon B. *Marxist Thought in Latin America.* Berkeley: Univ. of California Press, 1984.
López Raimundo and A. Gutiérrez Díaz. *El PSUC y el eurocomunismo.* Barcelona: Grijalbo, 1981.
"Los delegados al IX Congreso de la Confederación de Trabajadores de Venezuela C.T.V., que apoyamos la condidatura de Freddy Muñoz a secretaría general . . ." (mimeographed). Caracas, June 20, 1985.
Loscher, Iván [interviewer]. *Escrito con la izquierda: Entrevistas.* Caracas: Libros Tepuy, 1977.
———. *Todas son izquierda.* Caracas, Tepuy, 1978.
McInnes, Neil. *Euro-Communism.* Washington, D.C.: Center for Strategic and International Studies, 1976.
Maneiro, Alfredo, Lucas Matheus, and Homero Arellano. *Notas negativas.* Caracas: Ediciones Venezuela 83, 1971.
Márquez, Pompeyo. "Del dogmatismo al marxismo crítico." *Libre* 3 (March–May 1972).
———. *En peligro la integridad territorial de Venezuela.* Caracas: Industrias Sorocaima, 1979?.
———. *Hacia una nueva mayoría.* Caracas: Equipo Editor, 1979.
———. *La respuesta de la oposición socialista.* Caracas: Ediciones "Punto," 1978.
———. *Que discuten los Comunistas.* Caracas: Ediciones "Deslinde," 1970.
———. *Santos Yorme o Pompeyo Márquez: Combatiente sin tregua.* Caracas: Ediciones Centauro 82, 1982.
———. *Socialismo: Democratización y descolonización en el caribe: La posición venezolana en la zona* (pamphlet; speech delivered by Márquez at the University of Pittsburgh on Oct. 5–6, 1981). n.p., n.d.
———. *Socialismo en tiempo presente.* Caracas: Avilarte, 1973.
Marta Sosa, Joaquín. *Venezuela: Elecciones y transformación social.* Caracas: Editorial Centauro 84, 1984.
Martínez, Pedro José. "La unidad de la izquierda . . . ." *Politeia.* 1980.
Martz, John D. "The Minor Parties." Howard R. Penniman, ed., *Venezuela at the Polls: The National Elections of 1978.* Washington, D.C.: American Enterprise Institute, 1980.
———, and Enrique A. Baloyra. *Electoral Mobilization and Public Opinion: The Venezuelan Campaign of 1973.* Chapel Hill: Univ. of North Carolina Press, 1976.
Matanceros. *Cuadernos de la letra R: Desde la Venezuela que trabaja y lucha hablan: Los Matanceros.* Caracas: Ediciones del Agua Mansa, 1979.
Moleiro, Moisés. *La izquierda superada.* Caracas: Ateneo de Caracas, 1983.
———. *La izquierda y su proceso.* Caracas: Ediciones Centauro 77, 1977.
Mujal-León, Eusebio. "Cataluña, Carrillo, and Eurocommunism." *Problems of Communism* 30, no. 2 (March–April 1981).
———. "The PCE in Spanish Politics." *Problems of Communism* 27, no. 4 (July–Aug. 1978).
Muñoz, Freddy. *Desafíos y tentaciones: Una política para el poder.* Caracas: Servicio Gráfico, n.d.

———. *Más allá de las palabras: Proposiciones para la renovación y reconstrucción del MAS*. n.p., n.d.

———. *Nuestra proposición de cambio para Venezuela* (mimeographed document written for MAS's VI Convention of 1985).

———. *Posibilidades y peligros de una gran alternativa* (pamphlet). n.p., n.d.

———. *Reorientar, reconstruir, renovar el proyecto del MAS: Separata de Espacio Abierto* (document presented at MAS's 1985 convention). n.p., n.d.

———. *Revolución sin dogma*. Caracas: Ediciones Alcinoo, 1970.

———. *SIR: Sistema nacional de inscripción y recenso*. n.p., n.d.

———. *Una alternativa socialista para Venezuela* (mimeographed copy of speech delivered at symposium entitled "Del socialismo existente al nuevo socialismo" in Caracas in May 1981). Caracas: n.p., n.d.

Myers, David J. "Venezuela's MAS." *Problems of Communism* 29, no. 5 (Sept.–Oct. 1980).

Napolitano, Giorgio. *La alternativa eurocomunista* (interview by Eric J. Hobsbawm). Barcelona: Editorial Blume, 1977.

Natale, Anselmo. *El moderno absurdo de los marxistas modernos* (mimeographed). n.p., n.d.

Nueva Democracia. *Documentos de la Nueva Democracia: Publicación para la renovación del MAS* (pamphlet). Caracas: Editorial Metrópolis, 1984?

Ochoa Antich, Enrique. *Para ser poder: Apuntes críticos para la renovación del MAS* (mimeographed; document written for MAS's sixth national convention in 1985).

Olavarría, Jorge. "Petkoff, candidato de la izquierda." *Resumen* 402 (July 19, 1981).

Otro gobierno que fracasa: Un análisis del MAS para los venezolanos. Caracas: G&T Editores, 1977.

Pardo, Carlos Arturo. "Un Conjunto de experiencias importantes." *Sindicato de Trabajadores Textiles de la Empresa Texfin: Los obreros textiles demostraron la unidad* (newspaper format). Maracay, Nov. 1977.

Peña, Alfredo (interviewer). "Al MAS no le conviene un golpe militar" (interview of Teodoro Petkoff). *Corrupción y golpe de estado*. Caracas: Editorial Ateneo de Caracas, 1980?

——— (interviewer). *Conversaciones con José Vicente Rangel*. Caracas: Editorial Ateneo de Caracas, 1978.

——— (interviewer). *Conversaciones con Luis Beltrán Prieto*. Caracas: Editorial Ateneo de Caracas, 1978.

Petkoff, Teodoro. *Checoeslovaquia: El socialismo como problema*. 3rd ed. Caracas: Sorocaima, 1981.

———. "Democracia y socialismo." *Sobre la democracia*. Caracas: Editorial Ateneo de Caracas, 1979.

———. *El socialismo venezolano y la democracia*. Caracas: n.p., 1978.

———. "Hacia un nuevo socialismo." *Nueva Sociedad* 56–57 (Nov.–Dec. 1981).

———. "La autogestión: Gobierno del pueblo, por el pueblo y para el pueblo" (mimeographed; speech delivered to MAS's Comisión Nacional de Propaganda). n.p., n.d.

———. *La corrupción administrativa*. Caracas: Equipo Editor, 1978.

———. "La división del Partido Comunista de Venezuela." *Libre* 1 (Sept.–Nov. 1971).

———. "Los nuevos problemas del MAS." *Reflecciones* 7 (1977?)

———. *Más democracia: Propuestas para la Reforma del Estado Venezolano* (selected speeches). n.p., 1982?

———. *Proceso a la izquierda*. Barcelona: Editorial Planeta, 1976.

258

———. *Razones para una decisión política.* Caracas: Tipografía Sorocaima, 1976.
———. *Socialismo para Venezuela?* 3rd ed. Caracas: Editorial Fuentes, 1972.
———. "Venezuela en el mundo: Seguridad nacional desde la perspectiva del cambio social." Aníbal Romero, ed., *Seguridad, defensa y democracia en Venezuela.* Caracas: Editorial de la Univ. Simón Bolívar, 1980.
———. *Una juventud para la Venezuela necesaria* (pamphlet; speech delivered to the City Council of the Federal District). Caracas: Concejo Municipal del Distrito Federal, 1983.
Proceso Político. *CAP. 5 años: Un juicio crítico.* Caracas: Editorial Ateneo de Caracas, 1978.
Pulgar, Juvencio. *Declaración política de la VI Convención del MAS (Proyecto)* (mimeographed document written for MAS's VI Convention). n.p. June 1985.
Przeworski, Adam. "Social Democracy as a Historical Phenomenon." *New Left Review* 122 (July–Aug. 1980).
Rangel, José Vicente. *Seguridad, defensa y democracia: Un tema para civiles y militares.* Caracas: Ediciones Centauro 80, 1980.
———. *Tiempo de verdades.* Caracas: Editorial Avilarte, 1973.
Rangel, José Vicente, Luis Esteban Rey, Pompeyo Márquez, et al. *Militares y política (Una polémica inconclusa).* Caracas: Ediciones Centauro, 1976.
Rangel, José Vicente, Teodoro Petkoff, and Germán Lairet. *El año chucuto.* Caracas: Colección Parlamento y Socialismo, 1975.
Rodríguez, Ileana, and William L. Rowe, eds. *New Left Ideology.* Minneapolis: Marxist Educational Press, 1977.
Sales, Vidal. *Santiago Carrillo:biografía.* Barcelona: A.T.E., 1977.
Santiago and El Tabano [pseudonyms]. *Teodoro Petkoff: Dos épocas del oportunismo de derecha.* Caracas: Ediciones Hombre Nuevo, 1972.
Solórzano, Cesar O. *El socialismo y la democracia.* Caracas: Editorial Testimonios, n.d.
———. "Evolución crítica del pensamiento del MAS" (typewritten, unpublished). 1983.
———. *Una opinión desde el M.A.S.: El socialismo y la democracia.* Caracas: Editorial Testimonios, 1981.
Stambouli, Andrés. "La campaña electoral de 1978: Análisis de las estrategias de comunicación masiva." *Politeia* 9 (1980).
Temas para la discusión: Contenidos para la Convención Regional de Caracas (mimeographed). n.p., June 1985.
"Tercera Vía." *Programa para una esperanza revolucionaria.* Caracas, 1979?
Timmermann, Heinz. "The Eurocommunists and the West." *Problems of Communism,* May–June 1979.
Togliatti, Palmiro. *Comunistas, socialistas, católicos.* Barcelona: Editorial Laia, 1978.
Torres, Eloy. *Cuarenta años de la Confederación de Trabajadores de Venezuela . . .* (mimeographed). n.p., May 1976.
———. "El IX Pleno del CC del PCV y la cuestión sindical y campesina." *Documentos políticos* 10 (April 1968).
———. *La clase obrera y nuestra tarea* (mimeographed). n.p., 1970?
Urbaneja, Diego Bautista. *Documento No. 1* (mimeographed). n.d.
Valdivieso, Magdalena. *El trabajo hacia la mujer* (pamphlet on MAS's policy toward women). n.p., July 1983.
Valli, Bernardo. *Los Eurocomunistas: Historia, polémica y documentos.* Barcelona: Duplex, 1977.

Index

About the Author

Steve Ellner is Professor, Department of
Economics and Administration, Universidad de
Oriente, Puerto La Cruz, Venezuela. Previous
publications include *Los partidos políticos y su
disputa por el control del movimiento sindical en
Venezuela, 1936–1948,* as well as many articles
on political parties and organized labor in
Venezuela since 1936.

Library of Congress Cataloging-in-Publication
Data
Ellner, Steve
Venezuela's *Movimiento al Socialismo:* From
guerrilla defeat to innovative politics / by Steve
Ellner.
   p. cm.
  Bibliography: p.
  Includes index.
  ISBN 0-8223-0808-8
  1. Movimiento al Socialismo (Venezuela) 2.
Political parties—Venezuela. 3. Socialist
parties—Venezuela. 4. Socialist parties—Latin
America. I. Title.
JL3898.M55E44 1988
324.287'075—dc19   87-30456 CIP

The *tucinos* also viewed MAS's evolution away from Marxist dogma as incomplete. Although MAS had abandoned the Marxist and communist labels in quick succession, the party's position on Marxism was still under discussion. The orthodox *soisistas*, though willing to accept non-Marxists in the party and to cease calling itself a Marxist organization, insisted that its leadership should be committed to Marxism. The *tucinos*, on the other hand, opposed this requirement and discarded the validity of Marxism as a doctrine while maintaining that its chief value lay in its use as an instrument of social analysis. The *tucinos*, unlike their two rival factions, questioned two pillars of Marxist dogma: the primacy of the working class in the struggle for socialism, and the revolutionary path to socialism.

The *tucinos* saw themselves as a vanguard within MAS that favored extending the radical reforms and policy changes the party had already undertaken. More than their rival factions, the *tucinos* put a premium on introspection and self-criticism, and felt that renovation should be an ongoing process in the party. They complained that MAS had lost its original innovative spirit, whose two major achievements had been the New Mode of Being Socialist thesis and the movement of movements strategy.

By the late 1990s the New Mode document became a source of internal party debate. Freddy Muñoz and other orthodox *soisistas* felt that the party had gone too far in the implementation of the thesis. The *tucinos*, for their part, maintained just the opposite: namely, that MAS had not yet fully "assimilated" the concept. The *tucino* critique was expressed by a commission headed by national deputy Anselmo Natale, which stated that "the New Mode of Being Socialist has to be implemented on a higher level than ever before in order to promote a more accurate perception of our identity and policies."

The *tucinos*' ardent defense of the movement of movements and their minimization of the role of the political party were indicative of the importance they assigned to the "vanguard." The *soisistas* defended the primacy of the vanguard both in the society as a whole (in the form of the movement of movements) and within the party (in the form of their own faction). In the *tucino* version of the movement of movements, the movement displaces the party as the motor force—or the vanguard—in the revolutionary process. The *tucinos*' opposition to proposals to strengthen party discipline and to limit the radius of action of the individual factions was also evidence of the importance they attached to the vanguard within the party.

The movement of movements was originally conceived of as autonomous organizations that united students, trade unionists, and commu-

Figure 11-1.   Distribution of Votes for Principal Factions at the Time of National Elections of 19[??]

bers of other groups regardless of their party affiliation. In practice,
however, they became closely associated and linked with parties of the
left. The parties called on them to devote themselves by making greater
efforts to reach out to tendencies rather than solve the conceptual...
together. The basic strategy implied that measures at the organizational level would be first in line to deal with Adorno or Horkheimer
and thus disassociate themselves from the rest of the left. According
to the second, such appearances would have been desirable as long as
the different parties were not being controlled or manipulated in any
way by their respective parties. The parties deplored four-party merit
this non-devastating, who had never fully committed itself to the
fulfillment of movements, and that, in the words of Urbinati, the
concept was "neither well thought-out nor diligently practiced."[?]
"It acquired our end, although the constituencies considered part of
the movement of movements were independent of one another, most
of them were controlled by ... and were not allowed to deviate
any way to them.

The most grouping represented a fusion of members of the
faster in and new factions of the party [see figure 11-1]. Patriots
Sardi and Adeoline Natale had been leading academics, but others,
such as Michele Lancia and those who had been accused of being
"social climbers" (Lionel Lindau, and Urbino) had belonged to the
party. This realignment reflected the two sources of internal debate
[citation]. The former combined the economical views on innovation and
democracy with the party, convinced in large numbers
of party leaders who identified with or belonged to other parties.[?]

control at the organization's base.[29] This difference is characteristic of heterodox and orthodox currents in other leftist parties throughout the world: the former generally promotes recruitment campaigns and an open-admissions policy in contrast to the latter, which favors defining criteria for accepting new members.

MAS's Three Factions: A Comparative Overview

Political scientists generally recognize the different roles and ideological preferences of distinct prototypes of Communist and Socialist party members. Two such categories are especially fitting for leading MASistas: the *intellectual* and the *organizational person*. The intellectual (or ideologue), in the words of the author of one study on the Brazilian Communist Party, "resents the status quo, desires social change, and is an articulate spokesman of Marxist and Leninist philosophies."[30] Such a person is especially concerned with promoting democracy and thus favors pluralistic policies and a loose and open party structure. The organizational person is concerned mostly with party affairs and views the popular movement mainly as a vehicle for strengthening the party.

These categories are useful for describing the *tuanos* and *licuos*, respectively. The intellectualness of the *tuanos* was demonstrated by their tendency to dwell on the type of socialist utopia that MAS was trying to achieve. The speculative nature of such thinking is telling of the concerns of intellectuals, who are generally highly motivated by utopian visions. Like leftwing intellectuals elsewhere, the *tuanos* favored renovation and displayed a special interest in searching for new formulas to strengthen internal democracy. As may have been expected from leftist intellectuals who lack a vocation for power, the *tuanos* were inept at building an organizational base within the party. Though attracting top party leaders and intellectuals, the *tuanos* failed to establish an important presence in more than a handful of states. They were not even able to control the party's two sections in Caracas (the Federal District and the state of Miranda), even though a large number of important MAS leaders were from the nation's capital. The loss of influence at the highest leadership level following the 1983 national elections induced a large number of *licuos* to leave the party. These defections, however, were piecemeal and were not accompanied by a move to regroup in a new party. Had the *tuanos* had greater organizational interests and skills, they would have thought in terms of forming a splinter group rather than withdrawing from party politics altogether.

The leadership traits of the *licuos* contrasted sharply with those